GREAT LAKES SHIPWRECKS
AND SURVIVALS

GREAT LAKES

written by

pictures by

published by

Shipwrecks & Survivals

WILLIAM RATIGAN

Reynold H. Weidenaar

STR. EDMUND FITZGERALD edition

WM. B. EERDMANS PUBLISHING COMPANY
GRAND RAPIDS, MICHIGAN

Illustrations © 1960 William B. Eerdmans Publishing Co.
255 Jefferson Ave. S.E., Grand Rapids, Michigan 49503
Text © 1960 William Ratigan
Revised text © 1977 William Ratigan
First edition 1960
Revised edition 1977
Printed in the United States of America

00 99   17 16

Library of Congress catalog card number, 60-10088

ISBN 0-8028-7010-4

For my son Shannon
and my Pelton and Ranger grandchildren
loyal crewmates all

"O wha is this has don this deid,
  This ill deid don to me,
To send me out this time o' the yeir,
  To sail upon the se!

"Mak hast, mak haste, my mirry men all,
  Our guid schip sails the morne":
"O say na sae, my master deir,
  For I feir a deadlie storme.

"Late, late yestreen I saw the new moone,
  Wi the auld moone in her arme,
And I feir, I feir, my deir master,
  That we will cum to harme."

*   *   *

O lang, lang may the ladies stand,
  Wi thar gold kems in their hair,
Waiting for thair ain deir lords,
  For they'll se thame na mair.

(from *Sir Patrick Spens*, old Scots ballad)

ACKNOWLEDGMENTS

I want to pay my respects in print to Walter Havighurst, Fred Landon, and Harlan Hatcher, loyal chroniclers of the Lakes; John Brandt Mansfield, editor and compiler of the monumental *History of the Great Lakes,* storehouse of source materials (1899); the editors of *Inland Seas,* Quarterly Bulletin of the Great Lakes Historical Society; Capt. Marryat, whose *Mr. Midshipman Easy* is Britain's Huckleberry Finn; and the author (name unremembered) who thrilled my boyhood with a book called *Heroic Deeds of American Sailors.*

Many seafaring men who never dreamed of writing a book but who were born storytellers have contributed one way or another to this volume. The best of the lot was my own father, who always recalled his brief years as a sailor with fresh enthusiasm. On holiday outings he introduced me to the clanging mysteries of the engine room, and he could sing out the name of an oncoming freighter long before my young eyes could spell the letters. Without his inspiration, and without the indelible impression left upon me by my mother's love for boat trips (she never missed a chance, despite the work involved, to pack up her four boys and a bulging picnic basket for an excursion to Bob-lo or Tashmoo or Put-in-Bay), this book would never have been written. In view of title and contents it seems appropriate to add that, while I was working on the manuscript, she sent a faded clipping from Ripley's *Believe It or Not,* to the effect that Effie Laing (her maiden name) had been burned as a witch in the year 1689 for raising a storm that destroyed a lighthouse off the coast of Scotland, thereby causing a number of shipwrecks.

W. R.

CONTENTS

LIST OF ILLUSTRATIONS

FRONT ENDSHEET: *Charcoal and wash.* The sinking of the limestone carrier *Carl D. Bradley* in Lake Michigan.

FACING PAGE 50: *Oil.* A Lake freighter against the sun in a stormy sky.

FACING PAGE 114: *Water color.* Decks awash on a Great Lake ore carrier.

FACING PAGE 194: *Photograph.* Survivors rescued from the wrecked ore carrier *Mataafa* following a storm on Lake Superior. The forward end of the broken ship lies in the background, just off Duluth. Courtesy, U.S. Steel.

CENTER SPREAD: Artist's map of the five Great Lakes showing several points of interest in the history of ship-wrecks and survivals.

FACING PAGE 195: *Etching.* An engineering tug at the Grand Haven, Michigan, quay.

FACING PAGE 254: *Charcoal.* Mackinac Bridge and Great Lakes tanker passing underneath.

FACING PAGE 304: *Mezzotint.* Beach scene after one of the Lake storms.

PAGE 314: The *Edmund Fitzgerald.*

BOOK ONE

LOST IN LAKE MICHIGAN

Of death these jolly lads
Never once did dream;
Brave hearts sailed under canvas
And brave hearts sailed in steam.

Lost in Lake Michigan
They failed to reach the shore;
The gallant ships and crews
Will sail the Lakes no more!

(Fresh-water chantey, 1892)

The original version of the chantey on the preceding page told of the loss of the large new steel freighter *W. H. Gilcher,* with all hands, 21, on the stormy night of October 28, 1892, most probably in a collision with the schooner *Ostrich,* also lost with all hands, 7, on the same date. Wreckage from the two vessels washed ashore not a hundred feet apart on High Island in Lake Michigan's Beaver archipelago, where wreckage from the *Carl D. Bradley* was found after the spring breakup in 1959.

1. Full Many a Midnight Ship

Neither the Americans who dwell along the seaboards nor those who hail from the inland reaches of plains and mountains can understand the vastness of the Great Lakes. Here, where the high walls of water stretch in lonesome grandeur to the horizon, only seeing is believing.

Perhaps the best impression of the size of the Great Lakes may be given in the following typical reactions. Newcomers from the Atlantic or the Pacific coasts, unconsciously paying their respects to these wide bodies of water generally unbroken by landmarks, call whichever Lake they visit "the ocean." Similarly, when people from the inland-sea area take their families on a visit to California or Florida, the children, at first sight of an ocean, cry out: "Look, there's the Lake!"

The greatest of all American seafaring stories, *Moby Dick*, offers due homage to the Great Lakes. Ishmael, spinning a yarn at the Golden Inn to a group of South Americans, sets the scene:

"Now, gentlemen, in their interflowing aggregate, these grand fresh-water seas of ours — Erie, and Ontario, and Huron, and Superior, and Michigan — possess an ocean-like expansiveness. They contain round archipelagoes of romantic isles. They have heard the fleet thunderings of naval victories. They are swept by Borean and dismasting waves as direful as any that lash the salted wave. They know what shipwrecks are; for, out of sight of land, however inland, they have drowned many a midnight ship with all its shrieking crew."

2. Stage-Setting for Sudden Death

There are fifteen hundred rolling miles of water from the top of Lake Superior to the toe of Lake Ontario. When the Jesuit explorers first came upon Lake Huron and Lake Michigan, they knelt down and tasted the waters, marveling that such mighty inland oceans were fresh instead of salt. When Champlain's canoe burst out upon a single bay in Lake Huron, Georgian Bay, he was so impressed with this "fragment" of the great lake that he named it the fresh-water sea.

In modern times, Champlain's canoe has yielded to ore and grain carriers longer than football fields. During the season of navigation, an average of more than ninety long ships a day pass through the Soo Canal, a busier waterway than the Panama and Suez canals put together. Every twelve minutes a big Great Lakes freighter passes Windmill Point between Lake Erie and Lake St. Clair on the Detroit River.

These steamboats are equipped with the most modern navigational aids — radio, radar, and depthometers; they are supplied with advance information by the finest weather-warning system in the world; and yet they do not always reach port.

These great ships sail Great Lakes that can swallow them in one black moment without a trace. Storms exploding across hundreds of miles of open water pile up mountainous seas that strike swifter, and more often, than the deadliest waves on any ocean. Before the ship has a chance to recover from the last blow, the next is upon her. The Lakes captain has no sea room in which to maneuver; unlike his salt-water counterpart he must stay on course throughout the storm; he must weather the teeth of the gale.

It is an old joke, and a true one, on the Great Lakes that salt-water sailors often become seasick on what they have been known to call, disparagingly, our inland *ponds,* before closer acquaintance turns them green in the face and forces a respectful bow over the rail. The waves on the Lakes have a different motion; they are much sharper than ocean waves; they jump and tumble rather than roll and swell.

The waves of the Lakes strike quicker in comparison to the more lethargic ocean waves because they are less dense. When a ship bound down from fresh water sails out of Lake Ontario into the St. Lawrence River, she will raise herself two or three inches at the Plimsoll line as soon as she begins to hit the more buoyant salt water.

Just as there are differences between storms on the oceans and storms on the Lakes, so are there differences in the way each Lake acts up in a blow. Most veteran mates and captains and engineers whom I have known, like yellow-green Lake Erie least of all, in fair weather or foul. Even a line squall on treacherous Erie seems to scoop this shallowest of the Great Lakes from its muddy bottom and hurl it at the sky.

Despite its violent temper and rock-bound coasts, mariners would prefer to navigate Lake Superior in a storm rather than any of the other four Lakes, because of the sea room this greatest body of fresh water affords.

To Lake Michigan — the only one of the Great Lakes without an international boundary — sailing masters pay the utmost respect, not only because of this Lake's long history of sudden disaster, but because of the prevailing winds that can sweep its length to roll up backbreaking seas, the scarcity of natural harbors or even man-made places of refuge, and the crowning fact that it is the trickiest of the Lakes to keep a course on, due to currents caused by a flow around the Straits of Mackinac when the wind shifts.

3. Letters of Doom

With the Straits of Mackinac for a stem, cucumber-shaped Lake Michigan hangs on the map between Wisconsin and Michigan, touching Indiana and Illinois at the bottom. The ships that ply this three-hundred-mile length of waterway perform international chores and run national errands: they carry Canadian wheat to Milwaukee and the granaries of the Midwest; they haul the ore from the iron ranges of Lake Superior to the steel mills of Gary and South Chicago; they deliver cement from Petoskey and Rogers City to supply construction needs in the sprawling cities of Middle America.

In performance of their various duties, the long bulk carriers pass through more degrees of latitude than there are along the entire New England coast. When they sail past Michigan City in the southern reaches of the Lake, they are in the latitude of New Bedford and the southern coast of Cape Cod; when they sail up the Lake around the Straits of Mackinac at St. Ignace, they are closer to the North Pole than Montreal or the bulk of New Brunswick.

To get their jobs done, these steamboats go out in the spring as soon as the Coast Guard icebreakers — the *Mackinaw,* the *Sundew,* the *Hollyhock* — can open passage for them; and they stay out late in the season, challenging the pitiless month of great storms, November. To meet the needs of the nation, they often stay out on the Lake beyond the time of regular insurance, beyond the time of navigational prudence. Once in a while, striving to make one last trip before winter locks up the Lakes, they make one last trip indeed — the last trip forever.

Toward mid-November of 1958 the limestone carrier *Carl D. Bradley* put out from Rogers City, Michigan, and headed up Lake Huron to round the Straits of Mackinac into Lake Michigan. She was bound for Buffington, Indiana, on her forty-sixth trip of the year and had already cov-

16

ered more than 27,000 miles in all kinds of weather during the 1958 season of navigation.

The huge steamboat's owners, the Bradley Transportation Line, a division of the U. S. Steel Corporation, had scheduled this as her last trip of the year — a schedule on which fate itself was to stamp grim approval.

Only three of the thirty-five men aboard the *Bradley* were outstaters; the remainder came from Northern Michigan harbors, with twenty-six of them calling the freighter's port, Rogers City, their home, too. The departure featured the heart-warming farewells familiar in waterfront towns along the Lakes. Families waved to sons and brothers; an engaged girl blew a kiss to the boy she had promised to marry as soon as he returned; mothers held youngsters high in their arms for a last glimpse of their seafaring daddies. One regular crew member remained ashore to attend a funeral. There had been a death in his family, and, as events turned out, that death was to save his life.

The *Bradley* steamed from sight up Lake Huron, sailing into history books yet unwritten. She already had records to her credit. Built at Lorain, Ohio, in 1927, she was launched with the proud distinction of being the longest over-all-length ship on the Great Lakes, longer than two football fields spliced together in Paul Bunyan style — 640 feet of riveted steel plates formed into a hull that was judged unsinkable, the safest vessel afloat on the inland seas.

Another record had been set by the *Bradley* during the summer of 1929 when she carried the largest single cargo ever transported on the Great Lakes up to that time — 18,114 tons of limestone, put aboard at Calcite, Michigan, and dumped at Gary, Indiana — a haul of crushed stone that would require three complete freight trains each fitted out with a string of one hundred railroad cars to move overland.

Now, in November of 1958, although there were a few Lake carriers nudging seven hundred feet in length, the

Bradley still held a place among the giants of her kind. She could even look down her long patrician nose at all but a finger-count number of ocean-going liners.

On the eve of celebrating her thirtieth birthday, the *Bradley* was in the prime of life as Lake freighters go. Her skipper, Captain Roland Bryan, 52, of Loudonville, New York, brought the old girl cautiously around the Straits of Mackinac into the rock-studded northern reaches of Lake Michigan. He gave respectful clearance to dangerous Boulder Reef and, with the Beaver Islands off the port bow and the Wisconsin coast to starboard, he took the wide middle of the road down the Lake toward Milwaukee and Chicago and the Indiana shore.

Captain Bryan had gone sailoring at the age of fourteen. Put in command of the *Bradley* in 1954, he had previously served seventeen years as mate and seven years as a captain in the transportation line's fleet. A veteran who lived by the unwritten law of the Lakes — *constant vigilance is the price of staying afloat* — he worried about his ship, on duty and off.

About two weeks before starting this final trip, the *Bradley* had struck bottom at Cedarville, Michigan, and ruptured a plate. The damage had been repaired and the owners had decided that the ship would have a new $800,000 cargo hold installed at the end of the '58 season.

The bachelor captain of the *Bradley* looked forward to these new installations. Meanwhile, he had written a letter to Mrs. Florence Herd, a widow from Port Huron, saying in part:

"This boat is getting pretty ripe for too much weather. I'll be glad when they get her fixed up."

In another letter, this one to his best friend, Ken Faweet of Port Huron, Captain Bryan also betrayed concern:

"The hull is not good . . . have to nurse her along . . . . 'Take it easy' were my instructions . . . . The hull was badly damaged at Cedarville. . . ."

If the freighter had completed her final trip, these letters would be considered to express the natural anxieties of a captain who wanted to put his forty-sixth, and last, run of the year behind him so that his ship could be fitted out during the winter layover for a fresh start next season. But in the light of what happened, Captain Bryan's letters must be regarded as foreshadowings of the doom to come.

Until that doom arrived, the Bradley Transportation Line had never lost a ship. By a weird stroke of irony, earlier in 1958, the fleet of which the *Bradley* was a part had been given the ranking of the safest in the world by the National Safety Council.

4. Headed for the Bottom

The *Bradley* made the foot of Lake Michigan without incident, discharged her cargo of limestone at Buffington, Indiana, and turned for home at 6:30 p.m., Monday, November 17. Safe refuge for the bulk carrier and a friends-and-family winter ashore for her crew lay only thirty hours or so up the Lake.

Rule of thumb on the upper Great Lakes is that it takes three days for a storm to blow itself in and then another three days to blow itself out. The wind and waves had been building strength for a couple of days when the *Bradley* pulled out, and the weather got dirtier overnight.

However, there seemed no reason for any real concern aboard the big boat as she plowed up the map in a following sea whipped to whitecaps by a southwest wind. The *Bradley* had been inspected by the Coast Guard in January and April, and found to be seaworthy. The inspection did show weakened and missing rivets in the interior wall of a ballast tank, but these had been replaced with bolts.

True, there was scuttlebutt, voiced by a deck watchman and the first assistant engineer, that several bulkheads were so badly rusted that a man could see from one compartment into the next, that the ship had "rust pouring from her hold" on trips prior to this final run, that the ballast tanks leaked constantly, that the pumps had to be kept on full time to carry off water in the cargo tunnel, that there was as much as a foot of water in the tunnel at times.

Courts would have to weigh such testimony. Meanwhile, the *Bradley* proceeded up Lake Michigan in a mounting storm, certified as seaworthy not only by the Coast Guard but also by Lloyds Register of Shipping Inspection Service. The owners who had ordered her out were honorable and responsible men. The captain and his chief officers who took her out were dedicated to their calling. They would have taken no part in any dubious or foolhardy venture.

There are no fly-by-night, fast-dollar men giving orders and making decisions aboard Great Lakes carriers. On every trip those in authority, on the bridge and in the engine room, lay it on the line; they stake their reputations, their long-earned careers, their very lives; they have everything to lose.

But any man may make an honest mistake in judgment, and every ship may have an Achilles' heel, and there is always the element of chance, and human nature is still no match for Mother Nature on a rampage. The Irish poet Thomas Moore, who himself sailed the St. Lawrence Seaway and wrote one of its greatest songs, put all these thoughts into a picture when he said: "If there is one thing which impresses me more than another regarding that puny object, *man,* it is a ship under full sail, bearing with her trustful and hopeful hearts."

On Tuesday gale warnings were posted on Lake Michigan and many small ships went to the nearest coastal haven. But the *Bradley,* as most of the bigger freighters usually do, kept moving along, expecting to ride out the storm as she had done for thirty years.

No extraordinary measures were taken aboard but all reasonable caution was exercised. The *Bradley* was coming up the Lake empty, and seamen know that a loaded ship can take more sea. An empty vessel rides high and takes a worse beating. Therefore, to counteract her lack of cargo, the freighter was carrying about 9,000 tons of water ballast, about half of her pay-load tonnage capacity, thus discounting any possibility that she might break up because of traveling too light.

Toward late afternoon the *Bradley* began to swing into the long arc toward the top of Lake Michigan. She was in the regular ship channel out in the mid-center of the Lake, which stretches at this point about ninety miles from the Wisconsin to the Michigan shore. The chart showed 350 feet of water below.

The wind had increased to sixty-five miles an hour and the waves, rolled up by this southwest wind across three hundred miles of open water, were by now mountainous. In regular sequence these breakers went twenty feet high, with the proverbial seventh wave cresting at perhaps thirty feet.

Approaching the general vicinity of the Beaver Island archipelago, the *Bradley* was proceeding comfortably. There were no bad creaks or groans to indicate that the ship was under undue stress. In seaman's language, she was working well in the seas, meaning that the big boat was twisting and humping like a giant serpent in the water. The long carriers are built to be flexible, the same as a skyscraper is built to bend rather than break in a severe wind.

Down below, of course, this violent exercise was causing a certain number of the *Bradley's* rivets to shear off, the rivets that held her steel hull plates together. The more modern steamboats have their plates welded, but after older boats come through a bad storm there are always rivetheads to be picked up down in the hold. Many engineers can verify that after a storm these rivets can be picked up by the bucketful, and anyone who has been alongside a freighter in motion during a blow has shared the uncanny experience of being fired at by rivets. They break off from the steel hull plates and shoot out like bullets from a gun, whistling overhead in an eerie display of marksmanship.

The same thing was happening aboard the *Bradley*. Rivets were popping, but the phenomenon was so common that, even if the men noticed, they thought nothing of it. The whole crew was in high spirits, unaware of any imminent danger, looking forward to arriving home in a few more hours. There was not even a case of seasickness. They brought good appetites to their last supper: hamburgers, french fries, cold tomatoes, sponge cake and peaches.

At 5:15 p.m., with the *Bradley's* starboard bow off the Beavers and Boulder Reef, Captain Roland Bryan radioed the Bradley Transportation Line at Rogers City a routine message, saying that he expected to bring his ship into port by 2 a.m.

If Providence had spared the freighter another hour on the water, she would have rounded the Beavers and, bending in toward the Straits of Mackinac, she would have been in the lee of the islands, in quieter seas and out of danger. She missed finding a safe haven for her crew by sixty minutes.

Even when the skipper sent his confident wireless of expected arrival home, the *Bradley* was on the brink of starting her plunge to the bottom of Lake Michigan. She had sixteen minutes to live after it became clear that her death spasms had already begun.

5. Broken in Half

At 5:30 p.m., the serpentine length of the bulk carrier seemed to be riding the twenty-foot waves as well as ever. But at 5:31 p.m., First Mate Elmer Fleming and Captain Bryan, both on watch in the pilot house, heard an unusual thud. They spun around and looked down the six-hundred-foot deck toward the stern. The stormy day was darkling into sunset but the deck lights were glowing and, at the end of this string of lights, the two officers saw the aft section of the boat sag. They realized the *Bradley* was in mortal trouble.

Captain Bryan stopped the engines and rang the general alarm. Twenty seconds later there was a second thud and the boat humped upward slightly as the aft section continued its sag. The skipper ordered his first mate to send out distress signals. Fleming grabbed the radio phone and shouted:

"Mayday! Mayday! Mayday!"

A code signal of danger, the word *mayday* constituted a most fitting call for help on the Great Lakes, a cry of distress indicating the early influence of the French explorers and voyageurs. How many had cried out as they felt their ships going down? Cried out — not into radio phones but into unanswering blackness — *M'aidez! M'aidez!* Help me! Help me! It was an echo across more than three hundred years of shipwreck history on the inland seas, from LaSalle's ill-fated *Griffin* to the doomed *Bradley*:

"*M'aidez! Help me! Mayday!*"

At first there were a number of ham radio operators at their home sets and workaday wireless men aboard vessels going about their business on the connecting waters of the Great Lakes who failed to get the significance of the message and continued sending out their routine calls, drowning out the Mayday appeal with static and inconsequential dispatches. But to them the operator of the

23

Marine Radio Station at Port Washington, Wisconsin, very much alive to the perilous situation halfway across the Lake from his post, cut in with the stern warning:

"This is an emergency! This is an emergency! Clear the channel!"

For a moment there was a deathlike silence on channel 51. Then Coast Guard signalmen at posts all around the Great Lakes and radio operators on ships plying the Ohio and far down the Mississippi froze to attention as the words of First Mate Fleming crackled through space:

"Mayday! Mayday! Mayday! This is the *Carl D. Bradley*. Our position is approximately twelve miles southwest of Gull Island. We are in serious trouble."

In the background, horrified short-wave radio operators monitoring channel 51 could hear another voice, presumably that of Captain Bryan, shouting:

"Run, grab life jackets! Get your life jackets!"

The first mate's voice rang out again as there was another thud, the third, aboard the boat, and the long freighter humped once more as the aft section sagged still farther:

"Mayday! This is the *Carl D. Bradley,* about twelve miles southwest of Gull Island. The ship is breaking up in heavy seas. We're breaking up. We're going to sink. We're going down!"

While Fleming continued to shout his Mayday appeal into the radio phone, Captain Bryan reached for the *Bradley's* whistle and gave seven short blasts and one long one — the abandon-ship signal.

There was a fourth thud and the *Bradley* humped and sagged for the last time, then suddenly seemed to split in half. The officers in the pilothouse stared in awe at the widening gap between the fore and aft sections. Fleming stopped talking into the radio phone. There was no use any longer. The breakup had severed the power cables. Channel 51 went dead as the first mate's voice broke off:

"Mayday! Mayday! May . . .!"

Radio contact with the sinking vessel was lost at 5:45

p.m., Tuesday, November 18, 1958. Both sections of the back-broken ship were going under fast. The forward end lurched and started to roll over. Men went awash in the wild seas. When the stern plunged below there was an explosion as the freighter's hot boilers were engulfed by ice-cold water.

Seconds later the greatest ship ever to be lost on the Great Lakes had vanished, as if the 640-foot length of man's proudest seagoing workmanship and machinery had never existed, as if a giant's hand had sponged the *Carl D. Bradley* right off the slate-colored blackboard of Lake Michigan. Captain Roland O. Bryan went down with his ship.

When she sank in separate halves to the bottom, the *Bradley* left the majority of her shipwrecked crew still alive on the surface. Most of the thirty-five men aboard had managed to put on life jackets, but they were struggling to keep their heads up above merciless seas. The setting was a nightmare, haunted by the spectral glow of the water lights on the ring buoys and by the cries of crew members lost in this Lake Michigan wilderness, calling to one another, separated by towering walls of waves.

The only boat near the scene was the 250-foot German freighter, *Christian Sartori,* commanded by Captain Muller, onetime German U-boat officer. In broken English he radioed that he would head at once for the spot where the *Bradley* had disappeared, only four miles distant. Ordinarily the *Sartori* would have covered this distance in little more than fifteen minutes, but the rescue attempt through the storm, bucking mountainous seas, took two hours.

Crewmen on the *Sartori* spotted red flares on the horizon shortly after the *Bradley* sank and, when Captain Muller reached the scene of the breakup, he radioed:

"The flares probably were from survivors. They must have used up their flares quickly because they saw us nearby, but the storm made it impossible for us to reach them in time."

Although the German skipper drove his boat through

the storm at a speed that put it in grave peril, he found on arrival only what appeared to be a raincoat and a tank that apparently had been torn from the *Bradley's* interior by an explosion.

Captain Muller kept his ship in the area many hours, hoping against hope, searching with his own lights and under the flares dropped by a Coast Guard amphibian plane; but his radio report stated curtly:

"I believe all hands are lost. No lifeboats are visible."

6. Night Watch and Sea Hunt

All day long the storm had battered the Northern Michigan mainland. At Charlevoix, nearest Coast Guard port to the scene of the *Bradley* break-up, the waves were exploding like bombs against the piers of the Lake Michigan channel entrance, hurling spray almost to the top of the lighthouse tower and clear across the foghorn installation. Huge combers went spilling over the breakwater. Out on the Lake the waves had lost their whitecaps; they were whipped into flying mist. One of the red gale flags hoisted above the Coast Guard station along the breakwater had been ripped into tatters by the wind. An occasional gust of snow rattled the windows of the houses as if they had been hit by buckshot.

From the Charlevoix Coast Guard station, on days when unusual atmospheric conditions prevail, the Beaver Islands may be sighted straight out across the water, visible to the naked eye as a broken line of black cloud sitting just above the horizon. To the spot twelve miles southwest of Gull Island in the Beaver archipelago, the last reported position of the *Bradley* as given in First Mate Fleming's *Mayday* call, it is forty-seven miles from Charlevoix Harbor.

On the day the *Bradley* went down, there were no islands

visible from the station. Even the jagged line of high waves along the horizon often seen during an ordinary blow and called "Christmas trees" by Lakemen, had been hammered out of sight by the full gale. The mounting waves and the lowering clouds presented such a confusion of violence that it was hard to tell where water ended and sky began.

A thirty-six-foot lifeboat, manned by three men, put out from the Coast Guard station into the wilderness of Lake Michigan. It was frightening to watch. The boat seemed to stand on end to climb each wave, tumbled into the trough to be swallowed from sight, then staggered up to climb again. No one of the little group of spectators had any premonition that a major disaster had occurred and no idea that these Coast Guard men in their pygmy craft were braving seas where a giant had been torn in two.

The lifeboat, unable to make headway beyond four miles, was recalled and, at about 6:30 p.m., the United States Coast Guard cutter *Sundew*, a 180-foot combination of buoy tender and icebreaker, plowed out the channel into the teeth of the howling gale. Later it was learned that Lieutenant Commander Harold Muth, after issuing an emergency recall for members on shore leave, had set out with what amounted to a skeleton crew into the storm that already had proven itself a killer.

The *Sundew* and her sister ship, the *Hollyhock,* out of Sturgeon Bay, Wisconsin, rolling fifty degrees in the raging storm, reached the general area of the *Bradley* breakup just before eleven o'clock, and joined the *Sartori* in criss-crossing the surface, their searchlights sweeping the scene while parachute flares from an Albatros out of the Traverse City Coast Guard air base also fought the darkness.

There was hardly any conversation in the Coast Guard station at Charlevoix as the men waited out the hours toward dawn. Over the short-wave receiver they heard the various reports, in the broken English of the German skipper and the measured tones of the Coast Guard commanders. Out on Lansing Shoals winds were recorded of sixty-two to sixty-four miles an hour. Captain Muller of the *Sartori* put in a few words distorted by static and his thick accent:

"In six years of sailing the Great Lakes, I have never seen such rough waters."

Coast Guard Chief Etienne, a little man who had seen a lot of tall water himself, stared out of the black roaring Lake and nodded somberly. "Lots of boys out there tonight being hammered into men."

Among the Coast Guard uniforms, storm jackets, and working blue jeans, there was a tall young man in civilian clothes who seemed out of place among those keeping vigil. Someone asked:

"What's your interest in this?"

"My big brother Marty's out there. He's a stoker on the *Bradley*. I was supposed to pick him up at two o'clock this morning over at Rogers City, but when I got the news I drove over to Charlevoix. This is the place to meet him now. He'll be coming in here."

Reporters crowded around the cheerful-faced young man who had no doubts about his big brother being rescued. He mentioned, with a broad smile, the glad news that Marty would be getting married in a few days to his sweetheart in Cheboygan. The two of them had been planning and looking ahead to the wedding throughout the whole season of navigation. They had wanted to wait until Marty had made his last trip.

Up in the Coast Guard observation tower, lookouts stared across the scream and thunder of Lake Michigan, lighted now and then in these darkest hours before dawn by parachute flares dropped from the aircraft as aids to the searching vessels. Men spoke in hushed voices of the *Sundew* and the *Hollyhock*. These were names to fit a summer garden, not an all-night gale on Lake Michigan in mid-November. Join the two Coast Guard vessels together, add the German *Sartori,* and the three boats hunting those mountainous seas for survivors could not equal the length of the *Carl D. Bradley*. But they were giving proof tonight that they more than equaled any ship afloat in gallantry and seamanship.

What about the shipwrecked crew of the *Bradley*? Could anything live, unprotected, out there in that berserk water? It seemed incredible that men might be clinging to life out there, tossed and tumbled in the crashing blackness, struggling in thirty-six-degree water with the air temperature fallen to the twenties, feeling the ice form in their hair, fighting sleep and nightmare thoughts, praying for strength to keep their heads above the suffocating seas, steeling themselves with the will to live for just one hour, and then another, until dawn.

Cars started to line the beach, and more arrived by the minute. They were the cars of the wives and families of the men and boys aboard the *Sundew,* the cars of wives and families from Posen, Onaway, St. Ignace, Cheboygan, Rogers City, the ports and inland towns of Northern Michigan from which the crewmen of the *Bradley* had hailed. Headlights were turned on, hopefully, fearfully, shining out from the gale-whipped beach across the tumult of water, as if to help in the search.

The tall young man in civilian clothes said bravely: "If anybody can make it, my big brother will." Then he added quickly. "Don't worry, they'll *all* make it!"

In his words he expressed the courageous spirit of the men who went out to the rescue and of the families who waited ashore. But his big brother never made it, and neither did thirty-two others. When the *Bradley* went down, fifty-five youngsters were left bereaved. Rogers City, population 3,873, became overnight the port on the Great Lakes with the greatest percentage per capita of fatherless children.

At dawn, November 19, a Coast Guard helicopter from the Traverse City station sighted an empty lifeboat. Then, moments later, the helicopter spotted an eight-by-ten-foot orange-colored life raft mounted on oil drums. There were two men aboard.

Lieutenant Commander Muth drove the *Sundew* to the scene and at 9:07 a.m. flashed a terse message: "Picked up two survivors on raft, seventy-one degrees, 5.25 miles from Gull Island."

During the day seventeen bodies in all were recovered and brought into Charlevoix, where a temporary morgue had been set up at the waterfront-town's City Hall so next of kin could make identification. Another body, picked up by the lake freighter *Transontario*, was taken to Milwaukee.

At 4:20 p.m. Lieutenant Commander Muth brought the *Sundew* into her home port while press-men and network television crews directed cameras from the roof of the Beaver Island ferryboat warehouse as the only survivors, their faces raw from exposure and their bodies wrapped in blankets, were carried across the gangplank on stretchers. The skipper spoke into the TV microphone which was held out to him by a reporter.

"They had a little help," he said, referring to the survivors. "Someone looked after them."

7. Story of Two Survivors

Within sight and sound of the dying Lake Michigan storm that had broken their ship in two, First Mate Fleming, 42, and Frank Mays, 26-year-old deck watchman, told the incredible story of how they had clung, half-frozen, to a life raft for fourteen and a half nightmare hours until rescued by the Coast Guard's gallant *Sundew*. Furious waves were still smashing at the beach only fifty yards from the safety of their hospital cots, and gusts of snow kept spitting at the windows as if they had been blown off the top of the whitecapped waters.

These two steamboat men (and there is no higher title of honor on the Lakes) left a great deal of heartbreak and heroism unspoken in their account of the ordeal, because courage is taken for granted on the Great Lakes and there lives no sailor who has not looked with steady eyes at death.

As the *Bradley* went down, the young crew member Mays and the older officer Fleming were thrown into the water when the forward end plunged under. By happy accident they came to the surface near the ship's only life raft, and they crawled onto it just in time to see the stern of the *Bradley* rise, propeller high out of water, and then slide to the Lake bottom.

Sometime later Fleming and Mays helped pull Gary Strzelecki, 21-year-old deck watchman, and Dennis Meredith, 25, a deck hand, onto the wildly pitching raft. They all had the bitter experience of watching other shipmates being swept past them by the raging seas. They had seen frantic attempts to launch the starboard lifeboat at the moment of disaster but the tilting vessel prevented anyone from getting aboard.

On the life raft the four men huddled together for warmth. In the early hours of the night, First Mate Fleming took command and fired off the flares that were part of the raft's survival gear. He saved the last flare until such time as one of the rescue vessels, *Sartori, Hollyhock,* or *Sundew,* might pass near them in the darkness. When the moment came, and a big ship seemed to be right on top of the raft, the flare would not fire. Fleming worked at it with his teeth, trying to get it operating, but the lashing waves had ruined this final hope.

The faces of the survivors were raw and red, their hands were puffed from the death grip they had kept on the railing of the raft, their bodies were black and blue from the pounding they had taken on the eight-by-ten stretch of boards tossed around atop the oil drums by mountainous seas. Time after time the four men were hurled off their refuge as the raft flipped completely over, and they had to find their way back through the darkness, fighting the black, thunderous waves, to pull themselves aboard again.

After one of these wild flips, deck hand Meredith failed to return. In the darkest hour before dawn, young Strzelecki, temporarily out of his mind with the strain of exhaustion, shock, and exposure, lost his will to survive and, despite desperate efforts by Fleming and Mays, slipped from the raft. His cheerful and brave spirit during the long roaring night had sparked the others, his confident voice announcing the lights of a rescue vessel or an airplane and warning his shipmates to get set for a big coming wave.

Mays and Fleming swallowed a lot of water during their ordeal, but young Mays, father of three small children, spoke of a worse terror. "There never was any doubt in my mind that someone would find us if we could last through the night," he said. "I prayed every minute of the time. I got pretty scared when I found there was ice forming in my hair and there was ice encrusted on my jacket, but I felt that, if we were still on the raft by morning, someone would surely find us."

At daylight, twenty miles from where the *Bradley* had gone down fourteen hours before, the two survivors saw land, High Island, in the Beavers, and they knew the Coast Guard would be around to pick them up.

"You can always count on those boys," Fleming said, "but we're steamboat men, we know how long it takes. You aren't driving a car around the block out there."

After they were picked up by the *Sundew,* both men asked to be kept aboard while the search continued, rather than be flown to a mainland hospital by helicopter. They wanted to be out there on Lake Michigan with their thirty-three lost shipmates as long as possible.

The older man was a Presbyterian, the younger a Catholic. The former revealed a very thoughtful attitude about their being saved. "I couldn't tell you any special prayer

I said on the raft," he told. "The mysteries of religion are beyond me. You've got to believe, and that is it. When they say our two wives' prayers were answered, what about the other thirty-three? Those other fellows in the water prayed just as hard as we, and their wives prayed all night, same as ours. Why my prayers and Frank's were answered is something we'll never understand. It's like my wife had to tell our son when the report came in that the *Bradley* was sunk. She said, 'Your father might not come back, Douglas, but you've got to remember we're not waiting alone.'"

8. Last Words

One of the poignant sidelines to the interview story was the fact that the gallant young deck watchman, who had buoyed up their spirits all night long only to drop from the raft shortly before dawn, was picked up in his bright orange life jacket and taken aboard the freighter *Transontario* shortly after Mays and Fleming were rescued. The ship's radio messaged that the boy's body still retained "a breath of life," and in one of the many quiet acts of heroism that accompanied the *Bradley* disaster and its aftermath, the nearest doctor to the scene, 79-year-old Dr. Frank E. Lubon, lifted himself aboard a helicopter on Beaver Island. It would have been highly dangerous for a professional stunt man to attempt the transfer from plane to ship in the high wind and with the freighter rocked by heavy seas, but the octogenarian physician was hovering above the *Transontario's* rolling deck in the helicopter and preparing to be lowered on a sling, when word flashed that the boy was dead.

On the very day of the long interview with the two survivors, mass funeral services, attended by Catholics and Protestants alike, were held at Rogers City for the recovered bodies of *Bradley* victims. Bishop Womicki of Saginaw uttered a thought already engraved on the hearts of his listeners:

"While reaching for the stars and moon, we have not yet mastered our elements of air, water, and fire."

He spoke the words amidst the sound of the wind-whipped waters of Lake Huron, beating against the docks of Rogers City.

No hymns had been sung aboard the survival raft, but there were hymns sung ashore during the day-long rites, among them the one most familiar to seafaring men, "Jesus, Saviour, Pilot Me." That hymn was sung and prayers were said at inland Posen and Onaway, at water-front St. Ignace and Cheboygan as well as Rogers City, and at grief-stricken places remote from these Northern Michigan towns, at Lakewood, Ohio, Loudonville, New York, Clairton, Pennsylvania.

Special prayers were offered in Detroit's Old Mariners Church, where it is the long-established custom to pray regularly for the safety of sailors on the Lakes and for the souls of sailors who died in the performance of duty.

While these prayers went up, no work was done on any of Michigan Limestone's fleet of ships except those already on the Lakes. Ships between ports dropped anchor at noon for memorial services, before continuing their duties in the tradition that the *Bradley* had maintained until her violent disappearance.

With fifteen bodies yet unrecovered, there were still those in Rogers City who, like Mrs. Alex Selke (whose eighteen-year-old son had signed aboard the *Bradley* as a porter to save up money for college), refused to accept the all-too-evident truth:

"We still have hope that James will turn up safe. He could have landed on one of those islands out in Lake Michigan. I understand there are a lot of them out there."

And there were those who took their grief away, like the family of the thirty-year-old first assistant engineer, John

34

Bauers. They left a note behind, written on the back of a blank check, which said:

"Please do not leave any milk or papers until further notice. Thank you."

In due course, during the winter, the fifteen missing men were declared legally dead. The family of Martin Enos, Jr. held empty casket funeral services for the young oiler-stoker who had planned to come back home and marry his Cheboygan sweetheart at the close of navigation.

Coast Guard hearings and other investigations were held. Charges of negligence were countered by Company arguments that the *Bradley* might have crashed into an uncharted reef or foreign obstruction, a mystery rock, a "pinnacle of doom." The transportation line's offer of an out-of-court blanket settlement of $660,000 to the survivors of the thirty-three lost men was met with upwards of ten million dollars in lawsuits.

Search operations, started as soon as the spring breakup cleared the ice from the Beavers and Boulder Reef, resulted in quick discovery of the submerged hulk. An underwater scanning device located the wreck lying with its broken back six miles off Boulder Reef at a depth of 365 feet, far too deep for any practical diving operations, hat or skin. It was ironic to realize that, even if salvage had been possible, the two thousand tons of scrap metal at the bottom of the Lake would have brought no more than eighty thousand dollars at the mill, only one-tenth of the amount the Company had intended to spend on a new cargo hold for the *Bradley* during her winter lay-up.

After weeks of careful underwater sweeping of the general shipwreck area, the 150-foot sea tug *Williams*, manned by the U. S. Corps of Engineers, ruled out the remotest possibility of any uncharted reef or sudden-death pinnacle. The mystery of the breakup remained unsolved as investigations droned on and lawsuits piled up and undersea TV cameras tried to clarify the picture, but this much already was known and could never be remedied by the findings

35

in any court of appeal: the greatest shipwreck in modern
annals of the Great Lakes had happened in one thunderbolt
moment off storm-washed Gull Island and Boulder Reef
in the Beavers; the largest ship ever to go down in Great
Lakes history had plummeted to the bottom in the northern
reaches of the third largest body of fresh water in North
America; and thirty-three men, with all their hopes and
dreams, were lost in Lake Michigan.

9. Flying Dutchmen on Lake Michigan

The Great Lakes have their
full quota of Flying Dutchmen or ghost-ship stories, mirages
evoked by the sand dunes, forested headlands, and unusual
cloud formations on the inland seas. Mysterious disappearances of vessels have not been uncommon since the
first historic Flying Dutchman of fresh water sailed away
without trace, "sailed through a crack in the Lake," almost
three hundred years ago.

LASALLE'S *GRIFFIN*

Sixty feet long, forty-five tons burden, launched in 1679,
the leviathan of the Lakes in its time, LaSalle's *Griffin*,
first commercial vessel in the New World, leads the parade
of phantom schooners and steamboats that have vanished
never to be seen again, fated to sail until doomsday, ghost
ships sighted now and then in the atmospheric haze and
spectral mist that quickens every Lakeman's imagination.

The tiny *Griffin*, in August of 1679, came through a
storm off Thunder Bay in Lake Huron. Crew and passengers went down on their knees in prayer. The pilot,
a salt-water veteran, was the only exception, and he spent
all his breath in calling LaSalle dirty names for having

"brought him thither to make him perish in a nasty lake, and lose the glory he had acquired by his long and happy navigations on the ocean."

But the pilot and crew still had a month to live. The *Griffin* rode out the storm on Lake Huron and rounded the Straits of Mackinac into Lake Michigan. At Green Bay she took on a cargo of furs and set sail from Washington Island, September 18, 1679, with a light and favorable west wind, bound for Niagara. She was never seen again. Not so much as a splinter ever washed up on a Lake Michigan beach to give a clue to her fate.

LaSalle lived to reach the mouth of the Mississippi and claim Louisiana Territory for his French king only because he had chosen to travel by canoe and portage through the Death Door entrance to Green Bay. He watched from land while the *Griffin* sailed away toward a death door unmarked on any chart.

WHEAT BOUND FOR THE BOTTOM

During the first week of December, 1875, almost two hundred years after the *Griffin* sailed through a crack in the Lake, the *Cornealia E. Windiate,* a staunch three-master named after the builder's wife, lay at the dock in Milwaukee while her hold was slowly filled with twenty thousand bushels of Wisconsin wheat.

There were some dock-side pessimists who inquired what business any vessel had to set sail for Buffalo so late in the season. The owners and Captain Mackay wondered if it was wise too, but they took a calculated risk because others were doing the same — and because profits from such a late haul were tempting.

Built only two years before at Manitowoc, the *Cornealia E. Windiate* was a good performer in bad weather. Considered as seaworthy as any schooner in the grain trade at her tonnage of 332, she had secured an A-2 rating. On December 8, deep laden with the golden cargo of wheat, she cleared Milwaukee bound for Buffalo, a proud sight with her three towering masts and spanking canvas.

Forty-eight hours later a killer storm ripped across the Lake with insane December fury. A week passed. The *Cornealia E. Windiate* went unreported at the Straits of Mackinac or at the Straits of Detroit, or anywhere. She disappeared with all hands, forever.

CHRISTMAS TREES FOR DAVY JONES

The most poignant of all the Flying Dutchman stories is that of the "Christmas Tree Ship," the three-masted schooner *Rouse Simmons,* captained by Herman Schunemann, a popular dealer in holiday evergreens at the Clark Street dock at Chicago.

A great storm had just swept across the top of Lake Michigan and another big one was brewing when the *Simmons* headed out of Manistique on the three-hundred-mile haul to Chicago. The wind screamed louder with every gust and ice had begun to form on her rigging, but the gallant schooner started down below because Santa Claus could not wait.

There were tantalizing glimpses of the *Simmons* as she fought her way through the gale. The tug *Burger* and the brig *Dutch Boy* sighted her as she plowed into the great expanse of open and rolling Lake, her deck piled high with spruce and balsam which were to be decorated with lights and ornaments for happy holidays.

That was on November 25, 1913. The next day, with a full hurricane blowing and the temperature far below freezing, the *Simmons* was sighted off Sturgeon Bay, Wisconsin, by a Coast Guard lookout. The "Christmas Tree Ship" was flying distress signals but she could not be reached because of the distance and the mountainous waves in between.

All efforts to send help to the stricken craft met with failure. Right after being sighted, she sailed back into the storm. A heavy snow cut visibility to zero.

Farther down the Lake, another jagged break in the

weather gave members of a courageous lifeboat crew the last tantalizing glimpse of the *Simmons,* her hull coated with ice, her sails in tatters. Then the storm closed around her for the final death struggle.

After the gale blew itself out, a corked.bottle was picked up along the Wisconsin shore line near Sheboygan:

"Friday. Everybody good-bye. I guess we are all through. Sea washed over our deck load Thursday. During the night the small boat was washed over. Ingvald and Steve fell overboard Thursday. God help us. Herman Schunemann."

There was a footnote to the story. Next spring, commercial fishermen, wondering what made their nets haul so heavily, brought load after load of balsam and spruce to the surface, the farewell cargo of the "Christmas Tree Ship" that was consigned to Davy Jones instead of Santa Claus.

UNHAPPY HOLIDAYS

Even a reader, only vaguely acquainted with the Lakes, must by now understand that the families of men who sail the inland seas never plan a Thanksgiving celebration until the day arrives and the sailor is safely home. Nor do they look ahead to a merry Christmas or shout "Happy New Year" prematurely.

Although not a Flying Dutchman, the story of the one-time pleasure craft *Marold* fits here because of its ill-omened obituary date, New Year's Day, 1927. Once owned by the pioneer automobile builder Winton and having done a tour of duty as a World War I submarine chaser, the *Marold* had been put on the Charlevoix-Beaver Island ferry run. A long and handsome steamer, she carried nine cars.

Almost two months before the *Marold* was blown off the map, leaving no survivors, the tanker *J. Oswald Boyd,* low laden with 900,000 gallons of gasoline, had gone aground on Simmons Reef, a few miles northwest of Beaver Island. Rescue tugs saved the crew but were unable to pull the tanker free or salvage the cargo because of the shoals. Small-boat owners from Beaver Island enjoyed a picnic of gasoline that was finders-keepers until salvage rights were purchased, but they were careful to shut off their motors as they approached, because there was an oil slick on the water all around the grounded tanker.

Finally the salvage rights were purchased by the Beaver Island Transit Company. The first steamer that contracted to do the job backed out because her captain feared that the green ice, then forming on the Lake, and always sharp as windowpanes in contrast to the later rubbery ice, might cut the bottom of his boat.

So the *Marold* got her chance. She made one trip, pumping out twenty thousand gallons, with trucks from all over Michigan standing by to share in the windfall of fresh-water treasure. Eager to get more while the getting was good, her eighty-three-year-old captain pulled out of Charlevoix bright and early New Year's morning.

About sundown, mainlanders forty miles away from Simmons Reef saw unusual bursts of smoke out on the horizon toward the Beavers. The tanker *J. Oswald Boyd* had exploded while the *Marold* was busy pumping out her gasoline. Perhaps a nail in a crew member's boot set off a spark on a deck heavy with chain-reaction fumes. At any rate, the dead had to be identified by dental fillings. The hull of the *Marold* was never found.

This story has come down from various sources, but the unforgettable version came from the only "survivor" of the tragedy, a gentleman well known in Northern Michigan, Mr. F. E. Cartier. Slated to be a passenger aboard the *Marold,* he overslept a quarter of an hour on New Year's morning. Rubbing the dreams out of his eyes and hustling into his clothes, he made a run for the dock, but he was too late. He missed the boat. The *Marold* was hull down on the big Lake, gone beyond recall.

Mr. Cartier died in the spring of 1959. Contrary to the copyright maxim of early-to-bed-and-early-to-rise, the fifteen minutes he overslept on January 1, 1937, allowed him more than that many years of added life, and, to make it a bargain all the way around, they were years well spent in good deeds and public works.

TRAGEDY CAN HAVE GLAMOR

Disasters, the same as people, take on personalities. The number of victims or the size of the shipwrecked vessel, as in the record-breaking case of the *Carl D. Bradley,* will insure a prominent place in history books, but otherwise even the most tragic events must submit to the court of popular opinion, which labels them as dull, routine, and soon forgotten, or as colorful, glamorous, memorable facts.

For example, compare the tragic fate of the car ferry *Pere Marquette* 18 with that of the car ferry *Milwaukee.* Number 18 moved out of Ludington, Michigan, bound across the Lake for Milwaukee, Wisconsin, on September 8, 1910. She carried twenty-nine loaded railroad freight cars and there were sixty-two persons aboard, counting crew, passengers, and two stowaways.

Number 18 had sailed shortly before midnight and was out in the middle of the Lake at about three in the morning when an excited oiler hurried into the engine room and reported:

"A lot of water back aft, Chief, more'n I ever saw before!"

Captain Kilty ordered all pumps started but the water kept climbing. An old hand at car-ferrying, he gave further orders that sent nine railroad cars rolling out the stern into Lake Michigan. At five o'clock he realized that nothing could save his ship, and he gave the ultimate order to his wireless operator who flashed the word:

"Car ferry 18 sinking. . . . Help."

A sister ship, the *Pere Marquette* 17, picked up the signal, altered course, and at dawn her lights could be seen as she sped to the rescue. But Number 18 plunged four hundred feet to the bottom before help could arrive. Captain Kilty went down with his ship; so did every other

41

officer. The *Pere Marquette* 17 picked up thirty-seven survivors.

That makes an interesting story but it must hold its own in car-ferry annals against that of the *Milwaukee* which left its Wisconsin dock on October 22, 1929, and was never seen again. Low in the water with twenty-seven freight-packed boxcars and with an estimated total of fifty-two persons aboard, she just sailed away, sailed through a crack in the Lake.

There is a haunting appeal about any Flying Dutchman. Concerning the *Pere Marquette* 18, we *know*; concerning the car ferry *Milwaukee,* we *wonder.* Its dead man's message makes us wonder all the more. A battered can was washed up on the Lake Michigan shore. The note inside, signed by the car ferry's purser, said:

"Ship is taking water fast. We have turned and headed for Milwaukee. Pumps are all working, but sea-gate is bent and won't keep water out. Flickers [crew's quarters] are flooded. Seas are tremendous. Things look bad. Crew roll about the same as last pay day."

So, like many another Flying Dutchman before her, the *Milwaukee* sailed away. But where? Why? When? How? What finally happened, for sure?

Tell us, schooner *Black Hawk,* how did you vanish with all hands on Lake Michigan, in November, 1847?

Tell us, steamer *Omar Pasha,* where on the chart have you been buried since November, 1855?

Tell us, schooner *Thomas Hume,* why did you disappear with all hands in the foggy month of May, 1891?

What happened to you on October 26, 1898, steamer *L. R. Doty?*

We know there were winds of 80 to 125 miles an hour kicking up waves higher than houses on Lake Michigan when two steamers sailed away on that date of awesome memory on the Great Lakes, November 11, 1940. But how could you, *Anna C. Minch* and *William B. Davock,* be swept into oblivion without leaving a trace?

The Flying Dutchmen, lost with all hands, bear the charmed lives. The ghost ships sail forever because we cannot pin them to the chart and mark them off as wrecks. They are well manned because they sent back no survivors to bear witness to their deeds, and therefore they must also be judged by one proud statement made ashore:

"Thermopylae had its messenger of woe. The Alamo had none."

10. Good-Bye Lady Elgin

In 1855 the Soo Canal opened for traffic, clearing the way between Lake Superior and the lower Lakes. Captain Jack Wilson, who had hauled much of the equipment and many of the Canal gangs to complete the big ditch, was given the honor of taking the first boat through, the side-wheel steamer *Illinois,* with a German band playing on what Lakemen call the back porch to celebrate the historic occasion that marked Captain Jack's proudest hour. There was nobody in the Sault to find ill omens in the music or to prophesy that another German band would be playing when Captain Jack sailed into his darkest hour.

Nothing but good things seemed ahead for the steamboat master. In 1856 he again led the way through the Canal and in 1857, promoted to the command of the large new side-wheel steamer *Lady Elgin,* he cleared the ice through the Straits of Mackinac on May 1 ahead of every other craft on the Lakes. In 1859 he kept up the habit of being first by opening the season of navigation through the Soo Canal on May 3, again with the *Lady Elgin.*

In 1860, the names of Captain Jack Wilson and the *Lady Elgin* were not listed as breaking first passage around the Straits of Mackinac or blazing trail through the Canal into

Lake Superior, but their names were listed, along with the names of some three hundred crew members and passengers, as lost in one of the worst collisions in marine history.

There are strange side lights to the *Lady Elgin* story, and it has proven impossible for most storytellers to recite the unvarnished facts without dragging in the political battle between Stephen A. Douglas, "the Little Giant," and Abe Lincoln, the prairie lawyer, among other romantic aspects and aftermaths of the tragedy. But the grim details speak better than any dragged-in-by-the-heels trimmings.

Suffice it to say that politics were rather warm during the summer of 1860, and the Irish, who always have felt that the City Hall and the State House were built especially to offer them both amusement and a livelihood, came out with a series of conventions and picnic rallies. On Friday morning, September 7, a party of these Hibernian patriots, known as the Independent Union Guards and numbering about three hundred along with their wives and sweethearts, hired the fanciest excursion boat out of Milwaukee and spent a gala day on the Lake. They went down to Chicago where they swapped blarney until the *Lady Elgin* blew for the return trip. Then they trooped aboard full of high spirits, looking forward to a moonlight cruise on the way home.

But a moderately high wind swept across Lake Michigan as the *Lady Elgin,* with a bone between her teeth, cut into the one hundred miles of black water to Milwaukee. A sharp thunderstorm came up about midnight and heavy seas began to roll.

The excursionists were having too much fun to dream of any danger. Convivial as bugs in a rug, they had invited the fifty regular passengers who came aboard at Chicago en route to Mackinac to join their merrymaking and dancing. The German band was ready to call it quits but the Irish still had perpetual motion in their shoes. Then, out of the night, with a sharp bow and a heavy load of Muskegon pine, came the schooner *Augusta* carrying no running lights and a skipper who waited until the last fatal moment to change his course, although a lookout had sighted the lights of the *Lady Elgin* twenty minutes before the two boats came together.

Captain D. M. Malott brought the schooner *Augusta* into Chicago early Saturday morning and reported that shortly after midnight he had suffered damage in colliding with a large steamer, name unknown, and extent of damage to the other vessel undetermined. The crash had shifted the cargo of lumber in his own vessel. She had lost her headgear and was leaking badly. More than that Captain Malott could not say.

All through the night the lightning flashes on Lake Michigan lit up the scene of disaster on which the *Augusta* had turned her fantail. It was close to 2:30 Saturday morning, about ten miles off the Winnetka, Illinois, shore line and sixteen miles north of Chicago, when the *Augusta* rammed into the *Lady Elgin* at the midship's gangway on the port side, tearing off the wheel, and cutting through the guards into the cabin and hull.

The active seas separated the two vessels instantly, and the *Augusta* drifted by in the darkness. Most of her sails were in working order but she was no white-winged angel of mercy.

Dancing came to a halt in the forward cabin of the *Lady Elgin*. Couples went sliding across a floor that suddenly had become a steep siding when the side-wheel steamer lurched at the blow.

Captain Jack Wilson ordered that a lifeboat be lowered and he instructed the men to row around the vessel and discover the extent of the injury. The boat dropped astern and never regained the *Lady Elgin*. Captain Jack headed west at full speed, hoping to reach shore and beach the side-wheeler before deep water could swallow her. But she rapidly began to fill and list.

Instead of screams, a deathlike silence prevailed aboard

the doomed craft, an unearthly silence after all the noise and merrymaking, a strange silence that distinguishes this disaster from all others on the Lakes.

Freight rolled and banged as the *Lady Elgin* began to settle and reel. Her engines fell through the bottom. Captain Wilson and his heroic crew handed out life preservers to passengers. As the vessel took the final plunge — the "deep six" of sailor lingo — a huge sea struck her upper works, smashing them from the hull into several large floating pieces.

A survivor named Bellman described how Captain Wilson led the passengers to this wreckage: "On this extempore raft not less than three hundred persons were collected; the majority of them clung to their places until nearly daylight. The raft was mostly under water from the weight of its living burden, and very few who clung to it were above the waist in the turbulent sea. The captain was constantly on his feet, encouraging the crowd, the only man who dared stir from his recumbent position, which was necessary to keep a secure hold on the precarious raft. He carried a child, which he found in the arms of an exhausted and submerged woman, to an elevated portion of the raft, and left it in charge of another woman, when it was soon lost."

During the time while the raft kept together, there was scarcely a sound from man, woman, or child. They clung to their places in silent terror. Neither groans nor prayers were audible. Only the voice of Captain Jack Wilson cried encouragement and good cheer above the roar of wind and crash of waves. Captain Jack was too busy helping others ever to reach shore himself.

Through Bellman's eyes, and the jagged flashes of lightning, the scene is a haunted one, carried across not quite a hundred years. Even at this distance of time, what makes primeval hairs stand on end is the awful silence remarked upon by the survivors.

The constant action of the water finally broke up the

raft. Large groups of passengers floated off on detached pieces of wreckage. These in turn disintegrated until˙what had been a multitude on one wreck melted away into couples and solitary individuals facing death alone.

Bellman reached shore on his piece of wreckage, shared with two other survivors, in ten hours. He related that he and his companions were thrown off the raft every third minute on their mile-an-hour drift to the beach, where pounding surf claimed still more lives on the verge of safety.

Along this wind-swept, wave-lashed shore people from Winnetka, Evanston, Waukegan, and other nearby towns gathered in horrified groups to gaze helplessly while scores of shipwrecked men and women, sometimes with children in their arms, were smashed into the shoals and smothered. The appalling spectacle lasted so long that reporters from Chicago arrived to watch the death struggles of dozens of victims.

Two heroes emerged from the disaster: Captain Jack Wilson who gave his life that others might have a chance to live, and a young student from Northwestern University whose heart proved as dauntless as his swimming stroke was powerful. Fifteen times he plunged into the rough seas and fifteen drowning men and women he saved from the icy clutches of the Lake. When he collapsed from exhaustion and exposure, he dragged himself across the sand and built a driftwood fire to gain warmth and strength for another attempt at rescue.

Stiff and weak from battling the waves, and with the chill still in his bones, he sat huddled over this fire when he saw a man drifting toward shore, apparently holding another person in his grasp. The sight inspired him to one last effort. He plunged back into the wild surf for the sixteenth time. The final couple he saved turned out to be husband and wife.

His body looked as if it had been flogged and the young student, delirious from battling the elements, was unable to make another trip. Over and over he repeated the question that obsessed him after watching so many go to their deaths:

"Did I do my best? . . . Did I do my best?"

Northwestern University answered that question. Today on the campus there is a bronze tablet inscribed as a memorial to an undergraduate hero, Edward Spencer — a divinity student who never became a minister. But his soul-searching question was to inspire more sermons than he could have preached in his lifetime — and he lived to be eighty-one.

During the winter lay-over the owners of the schooner *Augusta* tried to take the curse off her reputation by painting her hull black and renaming her the *Colonel Cook*. On May 1, 1861, she moved under the tipple of a Milwaukee grain elevator to take aboard a cargo of wheat bound for Buffalo.

Word spread to the part of Milwaukee called Corktown, and the aroused Irish formed into a shillalah-brandishing mob determined to avenge the brave lads and pert colleens who had gone down with the *Lady Elgin*. They marched toward the water front, promising that the murderous schooner would never sail the Lakes again. They would burn her at the dock and "bad 'cess to her ashes!"

The owners heard about the mob's plans and wasted no time in giving the *Colonel Cook's* new captain his emergency orders:

"Pull out at once. Take her down to the Atlantic and sell her for the first decent offer. Don't bring her back to the Lakes."

The *Colonel Cook* slipped her moorings ahead of the Irish mob and sailed out the St. Lawrence Seaway to the ocean. Later she became a tramp schooner. For a long time the new captain could find no buyer for the bad-luck ship, and his ten-year-old daughter Emily, who sailed with him, had grown into a woman when he finally sold the old *Augusta* in the harbor of New York.

Emily later married a Great Lakes master and often made

trips with him when he commanded the large passenger steamboat *Minnesota.* One morning, in the harbor of Marquette, her husband saw a schooner tied up under the *Minnesota's* stern and he called out to his wife.

Emily stared at a "ragged waif of a ship, with the paint cracking off, and sadly needing overhauling." She did not need to look at the name on the bow, she could tell the *Augusta,* alias the *Colonel Cook,* by her lines, and by the place which showed where a jib boom once had been shattered in a long-ago collision. There she lay, quiet on the green water, silhouetted against the gray hills beyond — the sharp-bowed killer who had drilled a hole in the *Lady Elgin* that had let out 297 lives, by official count, in what still remains after one hundred years the second-worst disaster in loss of life in Great Lakes shipping history.

No headlines marked the end of the old *Augusta* when she was wrecked near Cleveland in 1894. The world seemed to want to be rid even of her memory. A malignant fate had caught up with Captain Malott and his crew much sooner. They changed ships after the collision, going into the schooner *Mahor,* and paid with their lives whatever debt the Lakes had coming when they all were lost in the wreck of the *Mahor* a few years later.

11. No Miracled Phoenix

In the religion of ancient Egypt, the Phoenix bird, so-called miraculous embodiment of the sun god, was fabled to be consumed by fire by its own act and then to rise, as good as new, from its own ashes.

There are no phoenix birds afloat on the Great Lakes, but there have been great fires and awesome burnings, with Lake Michigan claiming its share. Steamboats and

sailing vessels have been consumed by their own acts —
that is, by the carelessness of their crews or passengers —
and they have been consumed by acts of God, such as bolts
of lightning; but they always have hit the beach in charred
ruins or gone down to the bottom. They have never risen
of their own accord from waterlogged ashes.

BURNING OF THE *CHAMPLAIN*

Fisherman's Island, in Lake Michigan, is a small wooded
outcropping, only a stepping stone from the mainland. At
midnight, June 16, 1887, the passenger steamer *Champlain,*
bound from Norwood into Charlevoix, was approaching
the island on her final stretch home.

Somehow a fire broke out, in or near the engine room.
When the chief engineer tried to put out the flames, his
own clothing caught fire. By the time a general alarm
could be sounded, the engine room was a roaring furnace.
No one, however courageous, could enter the inferno.

Naturally, within sight of harbor, the *Champlain* had
been proceeding at full steam. Now her engines could not
be turned off and the very speed of her passage created a
wind that fanned the flames. Racing to her own destruction, she went ablaze from stem to stern in moments.

No lifeboats could be launched at the *Champlain's* speed,
and when she jarred onto a reef about a mile offshore, most
of the passengers leaped overboard to escape being turned
into human torches. Some drowned, some burned to death.
In all, twenty-two perished. Commercial fishermen in
Mackinaw boats, attracted to the scene by the red skies,
picked up floating survivors, many of them badly burned.
Among them was Minnie Bedford, a close relative of
Thomas Bedford who had put his name into many a history
book by shooting to death from ambush the Mormon mon-
arch of Lake Michigan, King Strang of Big Beaver Island.
This was exactly thirty years before to the day, on June 16,
1857, a red date on the Great Lakes indeed.

NEVER SPIT TO WINDWARD

One of the first rules a landlubber is supposed to be taught on the Lakes or at sea requires that everything be aimed overboard from the leeward side of the ship. The man who spits to windward is spitting in his own face, because the wind slaps back.

Violation of this elemental rule caused the tenth most terrible ship disaster, based on the number of lives lost, in Great Lakes annals.

An elegant side-wheel steamer named the *Seabird* had wintered at Manitowoc, Wisconsin, and was making her first run of the season down the Lake. She had made calls at Sheboygan and Milwaukee, and her nose was pointed for Chicago in the proverbial darkest hour before dawn, on April 9, 1868.

The passengers were all asleep, secure in their belief that they would be in the Big Town, the Windy City, within a few hours. Records of the number aboard, counting the crew, are as variable as those of most mid-nineteenth-century passenger sailings. There were at least seventy-five people on the *Seabird*, perhaps as many as 103, and of these only the odd three were destined to survive the careless act of a white-coated porter with a coal scuttle in his hand. The way he handled that coal scuttle, he might as well have sprayed the deck, the bridge, the engine room, the cabins, and the main salon with a Gatling gun.

In the biting cold of the pre-dawn April day, the porter, perhaps a little sleepy-eyed, went through his chores of tending the stove in the after cabin and shoveling hot ashes into the coal scuttle. Then he walked through the companionway, pushed open a door leading out on the promenade deck, and heaved the smouldering ashes into Lake Michigan.

He ducked back through the door so fast, to escape the outside chill and warm his hands over the stove, that he failed to realize that he had thrown red coals into the teeth of a strong northeast wind. The wind shot them back at the *Seabird* like musket balls and shrapnel heated for a cannonade. All it took was one glowing coal to land on the deck below where highly combustible freight had been stowed, namely, freshly varnished tubs packed with straw.

Apparently there were only two men awake in the aft section. They fought the flames and called for help, but by the time others could stagger out of their bunks to lend aid, the fire already had gained enough headway to doom the *Seabird*. The captain, recognizing this, changed course and headed at full steam for the Waukegan beach.

This altered course was the only chance for the *Seabird* to bring her passengers to safety, but it gave the northeast wind the full sweep of her length, from stern to stem. The fire started in the aft section. It was blown forward and spread as if by the puffs of a mighty bellows. Flames leaped skyward. An explosion destroyed or cut adrift the *Seabird's* four lifeboats.

Passengers and crew members, some with clothing ablaze, others nearly naked from their sleep, leaped screaming overboard. Most went down like rocks. In the icy waters of Lake Michigan in April the chances of survival for even the strongest constitution are measured in minutes rather than hours, no matter how good the swimmer, how buoyant the life jacket, or how secure the clung-to wreckage. Chances increased aboard a raft or lifeboat. But the very shock of jumping into waters just freed of ice by the spring breakup often drives the breath from the body or even brings on sudden heart failure.

Consequently, many of those who plunged from the *Seabird* into Lake Michigan never came up for air. The only survivor who rode out the waves had the good fortune to clamber onto a piece of wreckage that amounted to a raft. The wind carried him away from the burning sidewheeler and the waves drifted him ashore three miles north of Evanston, Illinois, about eight hours later. A rugged man and a stout swimmer, he told of being one of twenty or more persons who leaped into the water, a small number sinking almost at once while others swam about for a while, eventually losing strength or the will to survive.

Abandoning any attempt to reach the beach, the captain meanwhile lashed the helm hard-a-port and the *Seabird* continued to move in long, slow circles around her struggling victims in the ice-blue water as long as her engines kept operating.

The schooner *Cordelia,* off Waukegan, Illinois, sighted the holocaust from four to five miles away and set all sail to the rescue. She arrived to witness the insane circling of the blazing *Seabird,* but she could locate only one survivor in the floating wreckage and another clinging to the side of the heat-blistered boat. The *Cordelia* stood by, in a vain search of more survivors, until the once proud *Seabird* had burned down to the water's edge.

Then the schooner hoisted sail and went home to tell the story, putting behind her the black smoke of the sixth greatest funeral pyre in Great Lakes history.

AN ILL-OMENED NAME

By one of the bitter touches of irony that are common in the annals of disaster, the greatest loss of life by fire on Lake Michigan came aboard a passenger liner named the *Phoenix.* As in the case of the *Seabird* the recorded death lists give varied figures, but at least 190 died in the holocaust, and perhaps a total of 250.

Built in 1845, the *Phoenix* was one of the prides of the Lakes, with propulsion not by old-fashioned paddle wheels but by the newfangled propeller or screw. For two years she had been making the run between Buffalo and Chicago, "sailing the horseshoe," as Lake men termed it, or, "sailing the Michigan mitten."

The *Phoenix* sailed from Buffalo on November 11, 1847. This was another last scheduled trip of the season of navigation that turned out to be the steamboat's last trip forever. She carried a routine cargo of coffee, sugar, molasses,

53

and hardware. It was her passenger list that carried the special cargo: hopes and dreams.

Most of the passengers were immigrants from the Netherlands, and their voyage to the New World bore a striking resemblance to that of the Puritans from England two centuries before. A reform movement had taken place within the Dutch State Church and when the civil authorities clamped down on the reformers, a number of them organized an exodus to the midlands of America where, in addition to good cheap land, they could find religious freedom.

"The Society of Christians for the Holland Emigration to the United States" pointed the way to favorable locations along the west shore of Michigan and the east shore of Wisconsin, about three-quarters of the way down the Lake, as well as to places inland to Iowa. Such present-day midwestern towns as Holland, Zeeland, Vriesland, Borculo, Batavia, Waldo and New Holland were settled during this migration, which left its sturdy Dutch stamp of cleanliness, thriftiness, and love for tulips on larger centers such as Grand Rapids and others.

In the autumn of the year before the *Phoenix* sailed on her final voyage, the first party of freedom-loving Hollanders had made the trip from Rotterdam to New York, and thence around the Lakes to the east shore of Lake Michigan where they secured title to one thousand acres of government land.

The passengers aboard the *Phoenix* represented the second wave of this migration. They were going to join friends and relatives already settled in a free world, and nothing could daunt their high spirits, although bad weather and an accident tried.

Running through heavy seas to Fairport Harbor on Lake Erie, the *Phoenix* met her first foreshadowing of disaster. Captain G. B. Sweet, a highly respected sailing master, had a heavy fall on deck, injuring his knee so badly that he was confined to his cabin for the rest of the run, putting the steamer in charge of First Mate Watts, a Cleveland sailor.

Under sunnier skies the *Phoenix* called at Cleveland and Detroit, then threaded the St. Clair River into Lake Huron where Indian summer was having a last fling. Substantial Dutch burghers, mostly from the provinces of Gelderland and Overijsel, promenaded the deck with their buxom *vrouwen* on wooden shoes which made a pleasant klomping sound, wooden shoes destined for grim and desperate duty on Lake Michigan.

The children — blue-eyed, tow-headed Rikas and Annetjes and Gerritjes and Johanneses and Katrinas romping the decks with Dirks and Hanses and Hendriks and Jans — were mercifully spared any premonition that their playground would turn into a flaming springboard to watery death.

Behind their hands the crew repeated a rumor that might well have been true — the Geerlings family was reported to be carrying more than 100,000 guilders in their heavy chests — but the wildest scuttlebutt never consigned that Netherlands' fortune to Davy Jones' Locker.

As she rounded the seldom quiet Straits of Mackinac, the *Phoenix* ran into turbulent seas and dirty weather. Her engines had to work hot and heavy to make headway, and she put into the snug harbor of Manitowac, Wisconsin, to take on cordwood to replenish her bunker hatches and to wait out the storm.

By the time the fresh supply of fuel had been stowed aboard, the wind had blown itself out and the big Lake had quieted down. It was midnight, Sunday, November 21, 1847. The passenger steamer had now been ten days on the road that drew the shape of a horseshoe on the chart between Buffalo and Chicago.

There is an old sailor superstition about this horseshoe, a remark voiced after every shipwreck. The horseshoe has been nailed on the map of the Great Lakes region in the wrong position, prongs down, so that all the luck falls out.

Anxious to reach the Chicago prong of the horseshoe, the *Phoenix* pulled out of Manitowoc at midnight. Her running

55

lights flickered on the black expanse of open lake as she went wide open, with the firemen down below ramming six-foot lengths of cordwood into furnaces to give her red-hot, boiler-shaking, full steam ahead.

At four o'clock in the morning, fifteen miles north of Sheboygan and five miles off the dark Wisconsin shore line, a fireman discovered flames on the under side of the deck above a boiler. Smoke billowed from the engine room and seeped along the passageways. The general alarm clanged through the steamer. Three pumps were manned and several bucket brigades of half-dressed Hollanders were formed, but the fire raged, unchecked and spreading.

First Mate Watts, following standard procedure in such an emergency, ordered the wheelsman to steer for shore. The lights of Sheboygan were rising into sight on the starboard quarter. But there was no time to make it, not in a steamer which, by some terrible accident, had turned into a floating Fourth-of-July display gone out of control.

As the tragedy unfolded, there were deeds of heroism to match hardhearted decisions. The law of survival at sea is the law of the jungle — sometimes fangs appear unexpectedly in gentle faces.

First Mate Watts ordered the two lifeboats lowered. Invalid Captain Sweet was helped into one of them, and David Blish, a well-known Southport merchant, was offered a place.

Blish looked at the officers and crew of the *Phoenix* who had crowded into the lifeboats, leaving room only for a few Hollanders. He had four small children at home to live for, but he had made friends this trip with the immigrants, especially with the Dutch youngsters, and he could not bear to turn his back on them now.

"No, thanks," he said. "I prefer to take my chances with the rest."

The engineer of the *Phoenix,* who also preferred to take his chances with the rest, and survived by clinging to one of the steamboat's fenders until rescue arrived, brought

56

back stories about David Blish. He told how the merchant, when the fire was at its height, had taken a lost and terror-stricken little girl in his arms and protected her against the flames with his own body. He told how, at the end, the businessman from Southport had managed to put together a kind of small raft which he had launched and clung to, holding a child in each arm, until he slipped down in the cold water.

As the lifeboats pulled away toward shore, people leaped overboard to reach them. Hands reached out and were ruthlessly shoved away. A girl who fought until both hands had a firm grip was sent to her death by ordinarily decent people who pounded and pried at her fingers until they came loose and freed the overcrowded lifeboat of her extra weight.

One of the lifeboats lost an oar and had to be sculled on one side by a broom. When seas broke over the sides, the handful of Hollanders in either boat used their wooden shoes to bail for dear life.

But the vast majority of the Netherlanders were still on the *Phoenix* or struggling in the red-lit waters around. Left without hope of escape, they tried what they could, throwing chests, mattresses, hatch covers, wooden bulkheads, and cabin doors overboard to serve as makeshift rafts.

The ones who took their chances with the pitiless November waters had at least what is called a painless death, but there were others who, in vain efforts to escape the licking flames and suffocating smoke, climbed the shrouds, clinging in beehive masses to the ratlines, up to the very crosstrees, until the fire ate its way up the ropes and tumbled its victims down into the roaring inferno on deck.

There were scenes to break any heart. A mother went into a smoke-filled passageway to fetch a wrap for her child. She never came out again. At the very last, with the *Phoenix* a mass of flames and all hope gone, two young Wisconsin girls, sisters who were coming home from an

Eastern school, joined hands and jumped overboard together, immediately disappearing.

For quite a while cries and prayers were heard on the water as people clung to bits of wreckage; then only the noise of the fire and the slap of waves against the burning hulk could be heard by the engineer and the two other survivors clinging to the steamboat's rudder chains.

Only these three were found by the first rescue vessel to reach the scene from Sheboygan harbor. The lifeboats had carried another forty-three to safety. A total of forty-six were alive at dawn from a passenger list that may have been within a finger-count of three hundred at midnight.

The gutted hull of the *Phoenix* was towed into Sheboygan harbor where the steamer, named after the miraculous bird supposed to rise anew from its own ashes, sank in shallow water where part of her cargo was salvaged.

In Sheboygan, during the rest of that year, a number of fire-scarred foreign coins went into circulation, and four thousand miles away in Holland the church bells in many a town rang out to summon grief-stricken relatives to memorial services for the dead lost in Lake Michigan, the graveyard of so many hopes and dreams, from the voyageurs aboard the *Griffin* to the immigrants aboard the *Phoenix* to the workaday seamen on the *Carl D. Bradley.*

AND MRS. O'LEARY'S COW

The most dreaded cry on fresh or salt water continues to be, "Fire!" but in modern times Lake Michigan has escaped this shrill alarm, as far as great disaster is concerned. Her trial by fire encompassed the nineteenth century, and particularly the third quarter of that century, when steamboats and sailing vessels seemed to be blowing up and burning to the waterline all over the map of the Great Lakes.

Burnings, aship and ashore, go hand in hand with fresh starts, new towns, boom times, record sailings. Haste raises sparks and carelessness spreads them.

Today in north-woods and Lake-shore towns, the newspapers print combustibility indexes during the dangerous hot and dry season. No such warnings were issued during the latter half of the past century when sail and steam were in their heyday on the upper Lakes and logging crews were going full blast through Michigan, Wisconsin, Minnesota, and the province of Ontario. There must have been times when the combustibility index of the wilderness surrounding the Lakes made the woods one rustling bomb ready to explode at a sawmill spark, a careless hunter's fire, or a bolt of lightning.

Old-timers who sailed through those days remember the haze of forest-fire smoke on the Lakes as vividly as they recall the smothering Lake fogs of spring and late autumn. They have told of sails blackened by smoke and riddled with burnt holes by cinders hurled by the wind from far-inland pine trees turned into giants' torches.

Disaster on land meant danger on the Lakes. In the ied, acrid fog haze ships lost their bearings, went aground, rammed each other, caught fire, and burned like haystacks. For two generations the smoke of great forest disasters, raised by such inhuman conflagrations as the one that ravaged the Wisconsin pineries at Peshtigo, was a unique and dreaded peril on the Lakes.

The great Chicago fire and the wilderness blazes of that same year created havoc among Lake shipping. Dense smoke hovered over the upper Lakes like a pall, rendering navigation extremely hazardous the entire season. As an index, and eliminating countless mishaps, there were 1,167 shipwrecks on the Lakes during 1871. No major disasters marked the season on Lake Michigan, but when Mrs. O'Leary's cow kicked over the lantern to start the Chicago fire, docks and grain elevators were destroyed by flames that leaped across the harbor waters to devour a large new steamboat, three schooners, a bark, and a brigantine that could not pull away in time.

True, as we sum up the story, the city of Chicago rose from its ashes like the fabled Egyptian god, new and greater than ever, but the real *Seabird* and the *Phoenix* of the Great Lakes, in company with all the classic fire ships that have sailed fresh water to their doom, have risen only to be listed toward the top among the major disasters.

12. Sit Down, You're Rocking the Boat

Lakemen of today who were small boys in the second decade of this century can remember their mothers singing a sprightly tune that ended each verse with the refrain, "Sit down, you're rocking the boat!" Some of these men recall the song as perhaps having been one of the top hits of the day, and nothing more; others recall that in their boyhood they took the song in dead earnest. When they stepped into sailboats on the Detroit or St. Clair rivers, they were careful to take a seat and not jiggle around. When Mother packed up the family and a large picnic basket for an all-day outing on one of the excursion boats to Put-in-Bay on Lake Erie or for a moonlight cruise on Lake Huron, these youngsters had a little-boy frown for careless grownups who rushed to the rail to see one of the sights along the way. Didn't grownups know that even a great passenger liner could tip over if enough people crowded to the rail on one side? It made a boy feel like shouting at them, "Sit down, you're rocking the boat!"

Perhaps the expression had nothing to do with the *Eastland* disaster; perhaps it was only a song writer's picturesque way of capping his ballad with a catchy refrain that meant: "Don't get excited; mind your own business; take it easy; watch your step." But for some reason lost in the mist of boyhood memories, grownup Lakemen of today then accepted the words as a stern warning that could mean the difference between life and death aboard a boat, whether on a car ferry plowing the Detroit River, a fishing launch on the Flats, or a steamer on the open Lake.

The passenger liner *Eastland* capsized on one July morning of dread memory in 1915 at the foot of Lake Michigan as she was pulling away from her dock in the Chicago River and drowned 835 men, women, and children in the greatest of all disasters in the history of the Great Lakes.

The loss of life adds up to more than half the number that went down with the *Titanic* three years before the *Eastland* rolled on her side, but whereas the mind can accept the former tragedy, it labels the latter as unthinkable. There is, in the *Titanic* disaster, a certain inevitability of fate. After all, the White Star liner, the largest ship the world had ever known, was racing to set a new record for a transatlantic crossing and she was making her maiden effort in April, a dangerous season for icebergs on the north Atlantic run. A violent accident at midnight under the circumstances is not unimaginable, and no ship, whatever its size or however acclaimed as unsinkable, can be expected to survive a headlong collision with a floating mountain of ice.

But the imagination recoils at the spectacle of more than eight hundred helpless human beings drowning almost in the heart of a major city, barely a hand's reach from shore, on a pleasant summer day.

There were ugly rumors about the *Eastland* years before she capsized, but her record showed no basis for anyone pointing a dirty finger at the boat. Built at Port Huron, she went into the Lake Michigan excursion trade out of Chicago for several years and then transferred to Cleveland where she was hailed as the "Speed Queen of the Lakes." Daily excursions to Cedar Point and moonlight rides on Lake Erie were her specialties. She could cut through the waves at twenty-two miles an hour. Tall and white and trim, she looked like two slices of wedding cake back to back on the water. The steam calliope on her hurricane deck, playing the popular hits of the day, carried the tunes miles ashore to make an unforgettable impression on listeners who envied the carefree souls aboard the proud luxury liner.

But the ugly rumors, to the effect that the *Eastland* was unsafe for passenger travel, would not die. They became so persistent that the owners of the boat, the Eastland Navigation Company, placed the following half-page advertisement in the August 9, 1910, edition of the *Cleveland Plain Dealer*:

Five Thousand Dollars Reward

The steamer *Eastland* was built in 1903. She is built of steel and is of ocean-type construction. Her water compartments when filled carry eight hundred tons of ballast. She is 269 feet long, beam thirty-six feet, and draws fourteen feet of water. She has twin screws driven by two powerful triple expansion engines supplied with steam from four Scotch boilers.

The material she is built of, the type of her construction, together with the power in her hold, makes her the staunchest, fastest, and safest boat devoted to pleasure on the Great Lakes.

All this is well known to people acquainted with marine matters. But there are thousands of people who know absolutely nothing about boats, the rules and regulations for their running, and the inspection and licensing of the same by the United States Government. In the hope of influencing this class of people there have been put into circulation stories to the effect the steamer *Eastland* is not safe.

Unfortunately we do not know who the persons are that have caused to be put into circulation these scandalous stories. Their motives, however, are easily guessed. Therefore, in justice to ourselves and in fairness to the 400,000 people that have enjoyed themselves during the past four years in this palatial craft (and that without a single mishap), we offer the above reward to any person that will bring forth a navál engineer, a marine architect, a ship builder, or anyone qualified to pass judgment on the merits of a ship, who will say that the steamer *Eastland is* not a seaworthy ship or that she would not ride out any storm or weather any condition that can arise on either lake or ocean.

No one came forward to claim the reward. The implication seemed to be that a rival excursion line was at the bottom of the rumors. But the *Eastland's* business showed no ill effects. In the year 1913 she reportedly carried well over 200,000 passengers with a perfect safety record.

Under the operation of new owners, the St. Joseph-Chicago Steamship Company, the *Eastland* returned to her original Lake Michigan runs in 1914 and ended the season with flying colors as one of the most popular excursion boats ever to sail the big Lake. Except for rumor there never was a scratch against her record until the day in 1915 that made her name infamous.

The date was July 24, a Saturday, and the time was 7:20 in the morning. An estimated 2,500 passengers were aboard the *Eastland,* three hundred persons more than the *Titanic,* three times as large a ship, had carried on her ill-fated 1912 trip.

The Western Electric Company excursion to Michigan City, Indiana, was about to begin. Employees and their friends had gladly paid 75 cents a ticket to get out of Chicago for a breezy ride on the Lake. The outing offered free transportation for children, so there were quite a number of them along who might not ordinarily have been taken.

Out for fun and larks the crowd had trooped aboard in holiday garb to the music of the steam calliope. The ladies had feathers and artificial flowers and waxed fruit in their bonnets, the men wore their summer straws with the black bands, little boys strutted in sailor suits, and little girls had ribbons in their hair.

Lying starboard to the dock, the *Eastland* had a steam tug at her bow, ready to help her out the Chicago River into Lake Michigan. The gangplank was hauled in. The stern line was slacked off. Captain Pedersen stood on the bridge ready to give further orders and Chief Engineer J. M. Ericson stood by to see that they were carried out. They both survived the disaster to come in the next split second.

What happened no one ever could tell for sure. It goes

without saying that the *Eastland* was crowded far beyond capacity, and official investigators later found that she was unstable because her water-ballast tanks had not been filled properly. But what event led directly to the capsizing remains in doubt. It could be hazarded that, since everyone had crowded aboard, there was no one left on the Clark Street dock to wave good-bye to from the starboard side of the boat and so a majority of the passengers simply strolled over to the port side and looked out at the sights on the busy river.

Perhaps there was a sudden rush of passengers to the port side. There might have been something amusing or exciting to watch from that railing. Maybe friends and relatives called and pointed: "Look! Come over here! Look!"

There was no one to sing out: "Sit down, you're rocking the boat!"

At any rate, the *Eastland,* on the point of departure for a pleasure cruise, lost her balance and slowly toppled over on her port side into the Chicago River, where she lay in twenty-one feet of water with part of her starboard expanse fifteen feet above the surface.

As she went over, the scene must have resembled a film in slow motion. Death came at such a snail's pace that at first there was no alarm among the passengers. They noticed without comment the slant of the steamboat's decks. Then the list increased. Deck chairs and other unattached furniture came sliding from starboard to port. The icebox in the refreshment stand tore loose and rolled across the deck. A woman screamed. Others joined her in shrill terror as the listing *Eastland* turned so far on her side that passengers, unable to hold their footing, were slammed downhill against the port rails in struggling masses or jammed against the inner cabin walls. Hundreds were hurled into the river. Other hundreds were trapped in cabins below deck.

People struggled in the water like a commercial haul of fish in a surface net, fighting for air, moving across one another, submerging the weak. Again, as always in the showdown of survival, fangs showed unexpectedly in gentle faces, while the other side of the coin showed heroism stamped in equally surprising mould.

From that tangle of legs and arms and water-sogged skirts and floating summer straws, there were those lucky enough to catch onto the boxes, crates, deck furniture, and other wreckage that, along with her human freight, had been slammed out of the *Eastland*.

As rescue attempts got underway, bedlam reigned.

The quick thinking and prompt action of a famed Great Lakes captain saved hundreds of lives that would otherwise have been added to the death toll. Captain William T. Bright had just brought in the popular steamboat *Missouri* to the Northern Michigan Transportation Company dock immediately below the Michigan Boulevard bridge on the Chicago River.

Captain Bright took the news in full stride from his own steamer, hailed a taxi, and raced to the scene of the accident. He found the crowds so dense around the tragic vicinity that it was impossible to see what was taking place or to do anything to assist in disembarking the panic-stricken survivors. He fought his way to the second floor of one of the commission houses that used to line the river along what is now Wacker Drive.

From this point of vantage the Great Lakes skipper observed that the *Eastland* was on her beam-ends. From the starling of her bow to the stem, as she lay, it was dangerously steep and slippery. A score or more policemen and other rescue workers were attempting to assist passengers down the treacherous descent and to hoped-for safety on three harbor tugs that had pulled alongside.

But Captain Bright saw that almost all of those who tried this way of escape were sliding off into the mucky waters of the river, some unable to swim, others so injured by their fall that they were unable to strike out for themselves. Many were drowning on the spot and under the horrified eyes of the helpless onlookers.

What could a man on the second floor of a nearby building do when those at hand on the water were unable to carry out rescue operations? Captain Bright's blue eyes analyzed the scene. That second story on Wacker Drive became his pilothouse. He leaned out a window, cupped his fists into a megaphone, and sang out to the rescue party:

"Take the ashes out of the fire holds of those three tugs and scatter them on the *Eastland's* bow!"

When that work was underway, he grabbed a phone and put in an emergency call to Marshall Field & Company, a few blocks away:

"Rush fifty blankets to the *Eastland* dock!"

Once the ashes from the fire holds of the three tugs were scattered on the exposed starboard side of the *Eastland*, and once the blankets were spread along the steep bow, no more clinging survivors fell to death. Captain Bright, in the fresh-water tradition that splices land and lake so close together, had called out the right orders from his makeshift Wacker Drive pilothouse. In his distinguished career he went on up to command in turn two of the proudest liners that ever sailed the Upper Lakes, the *North* and *South American*.

For days after the tragedy, the death list of the *Eastland* disaster grew as missing persons were checked off as dead. Many bodies were removed through holes cut by acetylene torches into the side of the boat that still lay above the water. A few were not found until the *Eastland* had been righted and floated away.

The death ship that had drowned 835 people herself lived to sail again, never as a passenger liner, but as one of the finest Naval Reserve training ships in the United States. Millions, unfamiliar with the *Eastland's* tragic history, have seen the *U.S.S. Wilmette* moored to her Randolph Street dock in Chicago and admired the trim lines of the boat that rumor once called unsafe for passenger travel, rumor with the scarlet tongue so often wrong but once in a while so dead-right.

The lawsuits that followed the *Eastland* disaster have modern implications as may be judged by a news item that appeared in the August 7, 1935, edition of the *Cleveland Plain Dealer*:

Eastland CASE BOBS UP

U.S. Appeals Court Upholds Decision in 1915
Steamer Disaster

Chicago, Aug. 7. — (AP) — The United States Circuit Court of Appeals today upheld a Circuit Court ruling that the St. Joseph-Chicago Steamship Co., former owners of the steamer *Eastland,* which sank in the Chicago River July 24, 1915, is not liable for the 835 deaths in the disaster.

The Court held that the company was liable only to the extent of the salvage value of the vessel; that the boat was seaworthy; that the operators had taken proper precautions and that the responsibility was traced to an engineer who neglected to fill the ballast tanks properly.

It took twenty years for a final legal decision on the *Eastland* lawsuits, raising a question of how long the *Carl D. Bradley* lawsuits might drag on through the courts. The Bradley Transportation Company, Michigan Limestone Division of U.S. Steel, significantly had offered a blanket settlement almost at once, amounting to the salvage value of the freighter that had broken up and gone to the bottom. Unless unseaworthiness could be proved — a rather dubious experiment in 360 feet of water — or negligence of the operators could be maintained, or out-of-court settlements could be reached, it seemed likely that the notorious *Eastland* might play still another role in Great Lakes history, as a case in precedent to the *Bradley;* and this indeed proved to be the decision of the Courts in 1960.

13. Skinny Dips and Sunken Treasures

From the *Griffin's* disappearance in 1679 to the capsizing of the *Cedarville* in 1965, the record books show that Lake Michigan is not to be trifled with, even on a summer day. She lays claim both to the most historic shipwreck and to one of the two most recent major disasters. Her northern waters have swallowed the largest vessel ever lost on the Great Lakes proper (second largest on the St. Lawrence Seaway), and her southernmost harbor has taken the greatest single toll of lives in the history of fresh water.

A list of the thirteen worst shipping disasters in the annals of the Great Lakes finds an unfortunate seven of them written off to Lake Michigan and, with the list based on numbers of lives lost, she holds three of the four top places:

BLACK-BORDERED THIRTEEN

1st. On July 24, 1915, in Chicago Harbor at the foot of Lake Michigan, the *Eastland* capsized with a loss of 835 lives.

2nd. On September 8, 1860, the *Lady Elgin* went down after a collision on lower Lake Michigan, with 297 lives lost.

3rd. On June 27, 1850, the *G. P. Griffith* caught fire in Lake Erie with a loss of from 250 to 295 lives.

4th. On November 21, 1847, the *Phoenix* was swept by fire on upper Lake Michigan with 190 to 250 lives lost.

5th. On August 20, 1852, the *Atlantic* was the victim in a Lake Erie collision that cost from 150 to 250 lives.

6th. On August 9, 1841, the *Erie* caught fire on Lake Erie with a loss of from 100 to 175 lives.

7th. On August 9, 1865, the *Pewabic* was involved in a collision on Lake Huron that cost 125 lives.

8th. On September 15, 1882, the *Asia* foundered in Lake Huron with a loss of 123 lives.

9th. On September 17, 1949, the *Noronic,* in Toronto Harbor on Lake Ontario, was swept by fire that took 119 lives.

10th. On April 9, 1868, the *Seabird* caught fire on lower Lake Michigan with a loss of from 68 to 100 lives.

11th. On October 16, 1880, the *Alpena* foundered in lower Lake Michigan with a loss of 60 to 101 lives.

12th. On September 24, 1856, the *Niagara* burned in upper Lake Michigan at a cost of 65 lives.

13th. On October 22, 1929, the *Milwaukee* disappeared in the middle of Lake Michigan sailing away with from 46 to 52 lives.

The disaster list is an impressive testimonial to the unpredictable violence of Lake Michigan in comparison with her four great sisters, and a stern warning of the awful penalties she may exact even in her softest moods for any carelessness on her waters. The propeller *Toledo* could be given the thirteenth position instead of the car ferry *Milwaukee,* but Lake Michigan would still keep the place.

On the stormy night of October 22, 1856, the *Toledo* dropped anchor about half a mile off Port Washington, Wisconsin, hoping to ride out the blow in these more sheltered waters. But the wind and waves increased to the point where the captain tried to raise the doomed vessel's anchors and beach her as a last resort.

Fate took a hand and fouled the anchor chains. The *Toledo* opened at the seams and settled to the bottom. Three deck hands were saved. The remainder of the crew and all of the passengers, at least forty people and perhaps as many as fifty-five, were lost in Lake Michigan.

SUDDEN WEATHER

There is a saying on the Lakes: "If you don't like the weather, wait five minutes, it will change."

The truth of the saying is exemplified in the case of the

69

ill-starred ship that holds eleventh place in the all-time listing of major Great Lakes disasters, the steamer *Alpena*.
This 170-foot cargo and passenger boat started her last
haul on a beautiful and balmy day of Indian summer that
turned sharply into squaw winter at nightfall.

The date was October 15, 1880, the weather pleasant, the sun shining, the thermometer ranging between
sixty and seventy degrees. Light southerly winds prevailed
over Lake Michigan. The *Alpena* coasted along the east
shore paying a call at Muskegon and then putting in at
Grand Haven a little further down the Lake, where she
took on two carloads of apples and more passengers.

Counting new ticket holders, the steamer may have carried
a total of 101 persons when she cleared Grand Haven early
in the evening and cut across the Lake for Chicago, 108
miles away. Captain Nelson Napier, a veteran sailing master, noted a shift in wind and a fast tumble in barometric
pressure, sure indications of an oncoming storm, but he
took his chances on being off the Lake before the worst of
it hit.

The *Alpena* was sighted by other vessels several times
before midnight, proceeding on course and with no trouble,
although the seas had begun to kick up. At midnight a
violent southwesterly gale struck Lake Michigan with savage bursts of cyclonic fury. Temperatures dropped below
freezing. Snow squalls rattled Chicago windows. Sometime between midnight and dawn the *Alpena* must have
broken up and gone to the bottom in a storm that wrecked
or badly damaged ninety other vessels.

A lightkeeper on Pilot Island reported that the waters
of Lake Michigan were white for a week after the gale
blew itself out, his theory being that the churning waves
had smashed together so many of the limestone rocks on
the Lake bottom that enough of them had been pulverized
to coat the water with a white lime powder.

After three days of uncertainty and suspense concerning
the *Alpena's* fate, the last hope died when debris first drifted

to shore at Holland, Michigan. Later evidence became overwhelming. The storm had torn the *Alpena* apart so badly that bodies and wreckage were scattered along the beach for seventy miles — fire buckets with the name of the steamboat stencilled on them, a piano with the lid torn off, a fragment of stairway, cabin doors, life preservers, and apples bobbing in the surf and rolling up on the sand.

Even a scrawled note was found, tucked behind a piece of moulding in a portion of cabin washed ashore:

"This is terrible. The steamer is breaking up fast. I am aboard from Grand Haven to Chicago."

The signature might have been George Conner, or Connell. It was so water-soaked as to be barely legible. The mystery of the writer's identity and why he wanted the world to know that he was aboard remains as shrouded as the ultimate cause of the *Alpena's* storm-bound trip into oblivion.

THE REST IS SILENCE

The fact that Lake Michigan has had more major shipping disasters than all the other Great Lakes combined is pointed up by the passing mention of the steamboat *Niagara,* holder of twelfth place on the all-time list of fresh-water shipwrecks. In all the histories and the record books the following is the longest notice found:

Other complete losses of the season were: brig *Oxford* sunk by propeller *Cataract* in Lake Erie, and five lives lost; schooner *Kate Hayes* lost on Spectacle Reef, Lake Huron; steamer *Welland* burned at Port Dalhousie, Lake Ontario; steamer *Superior* lost on Lake Superior during a storm; brig *Sandusky* sunk in the Straits of Mackinac, and seven lives lost; schooner *Maria Hilliard* wrecked at Death's Door, Lake Michigan; steamer *Northerner* sunk by steamer *Forest Queen* in Lake Huron with twelve lives lost; steamer *Niagara* burned off Port Washington, Lake Michigan, and sixty-five lives lost.

In the year 1856 there were 597 disasters recorded on

the Great Lakes during the season of navigation. The *Niagara* simply had to be lumped with the rest.

THREE BROTHERS TO THE RESCUE

To match the major disasters, there have been great and heroic rescues on Lake Michigan. One of the greatest occurred on August 29, 1906, when the steamer *Illinois* went aground immediately south of the Charlevoix harbor entrance.

The Charlevoix Coast Guard group saved more than four hundred lives that day. All were brought ashore by breeches buoy and surfboat for the largest rescue in the station's seventy-year history.

One of the most thrilling, and also one of the most controversial, rescues in Lake annals took place during one of the worst storms ever to lash the inland seas, the Big Blow of November 10-11, 1940, already mentioned in this book and destined to be mentioned as long as sailors spin yarns about shipwrecks.

The 1940 storm already had sent two Lake Michigan freighters to join the Flying Dutchmen that will sail forever, when it picked up the Canadian steel freighter *Novadoc,* bound from Chicago to Fort William, Ontario, and broke her back off Pentwater, Michigan, where she lay aground at the mercy of pounding seas.

The local Coast Guard apparently had trouble in launching a lifeboat in time, but the little fish tug *Three Brothers* took off into the storm. At the wheel was a member of the Cross family, a commercial fishing clan renowned for seamanship from the fishing banks of the upper Lakes to the fisheries off lower California.

When Captain Clyde Cross headed the *Three Brothers* out over wind-lashed Lake Michigan, the waves were running so high that he could not see over their tops until they lifted the fish tug up to ride their crests before the next roller-coaster plunge. But the tiny *Three Brothers* reached the giant *Novadoc* and brought all of the crew back alive, except two, and they had washed overboard before rescue could arrive.

Hailed in the press of the nation as a hero deserving the Congressional Medal, Captain Cross found himself called other names by members of the local Coast Guard who sourly denounced him as a mere glory-seeker who had ignored the unwritten law of the sea by refusing to come to their aid when asked to help in launching their lifeboat.

The incident typifies the feeling between fishermen and Coast Guard men on the Lakes. There is a natural rivalry as between the branches of the armed forces. But let no outsider say a word of disrespect about one to the other, or do so at peril!

This particular member of the Cross clan simply saw that there was a job to do and he did it without delay. As a result, instead of her ordinary cargo of whitefish and Mackinaw trout, the *Three Brothers* rode the storm home with seventeen survivors from the shipwrecked *Novadoc*.

The gallant fish tug herself became a victim of Lake Michigan a few years later, but no lives were lost, and her bones rest secure in the knowledge that she rode out the Great Storm of 1940 with human cargo snatched from death.

DOWN THE DRAIN

According to estimates, there are $800,000,000 worth of salvageable shipwrecks on the floor of the Great Lakes. They await the new generation of undersea explorers, the skin divers, to locate them with the help of such electronic devices as sonar, echo sounders, triangulated radio beams from shore beacons, sea scanners, and underwater TV cameras.

Early in the second half of the nineteenth century there already were so many shipwrecks with valuable cargoes lying on the bottom of Lake Michigan that a fantastic scheme for draining the Lake completely dry to facilitate salvage operations was proposed. Presumably a system of coffer dams would have been installed at the Straits of Mackinac, halting the flow there, and then the waters of the third Great Lake would have poured out through the Chicago drainage canal into the Mississippi to mingle with the salt water at the Gulf of Mexico.

"Nothing to it," said one of the promoters. "Same principle as a bathtub. Just pull the plug!"

Wiser heads prevailed and the depths of Lake Michigan remained inscrutable, biding the skin-diving era. Quite recently skin divers and their salvage attempts have acquired the nickname of "skinny dips," a term formerly applied to beach parties featuring moonlight swims in birthday suits. The up-to-date skinny dip has any variety of thermal and pressurized clothing instead of the bare essentials with which the sport began, and the enthusiasts seem destined to locate and pry open a good many secrets and strong vaults of the deep.

Lake Michigan has its full share of romantic wrecks and golden cargoes to offer: *St. Nicholas, Reindeer, Phantom, Grand Turk, Gold Hunter, Restless, Morning Star, Flying Mist, Rising Sun, Star Light, Flying Cloud, Jenny Lind, Hercules, Bully Kate, Lac la Belle, Two Fannies, Amazon, Equinox, Orphan Boy, Minnehaha, Ironsides, Souvenir,* and countless others with plainer names but perhaps fancier spoils to offer brave hearts and skinny dips.

Fortunes in copper ingots, prize lumber, beverages, cheese, *name anything,* have lain in wait across almost three centuries. If legend holds true, the most fabulous sunken treasure on the Great Lakes is still begging discovery off Poverty Island, near Escanaba, at the top of Lake Michigan, where a nameless vessel "sailed away" with five million dollars in her strongbox.

MAD AS A LAKER

Above all the stories told about Lake Michigan — and the truest would frighten the wildest thing in fiction — there is a prosaic notice in the shipping news of 1872 that tells more about the Lake and about the Lakers who have sailed into legend than anything we might run across:

> *Foundered in Mid-Lake* — The loss of the schooner *George F. Whitney*, in September, was a peculiar one. She must have foundered in mid-lake, as not one of the crew of eight men were ever heard of, nor has the manner of her loss ever been known. Captain Carpenter was in command. A strange fatality seems to have hung over the *Whitney* for more than a year. She had been wrecked on Sugar Island, on a trip from Buffalo to Chicago in 1871; was released in the spring of 1872, and reconstructed, and on her first trip she was wrecked again at Vermilion. During the next voyage she was lost with all on board. It was said that while lying at dock at Chicago, Captain Carpenter displayed all his flags at halfmast, the American ensign with union down. Upon inquiry why he did this, the captain explained that it was merely an invitation for the tugs to transfer him up the river.

On top of all the other hazards connected with sailing the Lake, there were mad captains at the helm on occasion, as lunatic as the storms on which they sailed away.

Perhaps they had to be a little mad, even to dream of navigating Lake Michigan, those early-day Lakers.

Even in modern times, skippers have literally gone mad at sea, and sane captains have wondered in the wake of catastrophe what caused them to do what they did or to neglect doing what they should have done, what made them act as they would not ordinarily act, what set them on a collision course with relentless happenings. Perhaps the following will go down in the annals as a case in point.

UNEASY TRUCE

Between the foundering of the *Carl D. Bradley* off Gull Island in November, 1958, and the next major shipwreck on the Great Lakes, there elapsed an uneasy truce of six seasons of navigation for the United States fleet. The Annual Report of the Lake Carriers Association pointed with pride to the announcement in its 1964 Bluebook:

"With unusual satisfaction, it can be reported that for the sixth consecutive year no United States commercial lake vessel was lost in operation during the 1964 season. It is believed that this achievement is unmatched in any other major facet of the maritime trades."

The report went on to mention with regret that the maximum-size bulk carrier *Leecliffe Hall* of the Canadian fleet, built in Scotland during 1961, had been lost as the result of a collision with the Greek steamer *Appalonia* on September 5, about 60 miles east of Quebec in the lower St. Lawrence River. Upbound with a cargo of iron ore, the first large Great Lakes ship ever built overseas went down with the loss of three lives.

The *Leecliffe Hall* took the place of the *Carl D. Bradley* as the largest Great Lakes vessel ever to meet with disaster on the St. Lawrence Seaway, although not the Great Lakes proper. In the 730-foot class, she was approximately ninety feet longer than the *Bradley* and, by a technicality of three inches, she had lost out to the *Arthur B. Homer* as the largest ship on the Lakes at that time (prior to the opening of the great new Poe lock at the Soo in 1968, ushering in the era of 1,000-foot boats, setting the stage for the 1,000-foot fresh-water freighters of the near future).

OMINOUS PORTENT

Reviewing the years of uneasy truce, the kinds of shipwrecks listed in the Annual Reports are of ominous portent. In 1959, the season of navigation following the *Bradley* breakup, the Liberian steamer *Monrovia* sank on June 26 as the result of a collision with the downbound Canadian ore carrier *Royalton* about eleven miles off Thunder Bay Island, Lake Huron, while upbound into Lake Michigan. The entire complement of the *Monrovia* was rescued and there were no casualties aboard the *Royalton*.

During the 1960 season of navigation, another Liberian steamer, the 236-foot *Francisco Morazan*, carrying 900 tons of chicken, lard, and machinery, stranded off South Manitou Island, northern Lake Michigan, on November 29, in a heavy gale. The crew of 14 and the master's pregnant wife were subsequently rescued by Coast Guard units, accompanied by the tug *John Roen V.*, a famed name in salvage operations. In due season the abandoned hull was salvaged and then the site was haunted by skin divers, some of whom no doubt also had wild hopes of locating a much older wreck in the near vicinity, the steamer *Templeton,* with a cargo of 350 barrels of whiskey, well aged.

In 1961, a growing trend of the times (reflecting the hazards incident to opening of the St. Lawrence Seaway and the consequent influx of ocean vessels unfamiliar with Lake customs and practices) witnessed an ocean ship involved in a minor collision with a Lake vessel. This season's incident occurred off Gull Island, Lake Michigan, August 9, when the Greek steamer *Zermatt,* downbound with scrap from Japan, collided with the small work ferry *Mackinac Islander,* livelier than ever and operating out of Charlevoix, but bound for Alaska.

As in the preceding season of navigation, the year 1962 saw another ocean vessel go to the bottom after colliding with a Lake craft. The motor vessel *Montrose,* of British registry, sank in the Detroit River just below the Ambassador Bridge, after collision with a loaded barge, and was not salvaged until late fall, after a continuing and arduous program spurred by the menace to navigation in heavily trafficked ship lanes. A historical footnote to the incident is that the *Montrose* thus became the first British ship sunk by an American ship in American waters since the War of 1812.

A PATTERN OF COLLISIONS

In this brief résumé of shipwrecks since the *Bradley,* a pattern of collisions is apparent and, in retrospect, the pattern seems to predict what inevitably took place — a collision between a Great Lakes vessel and a foreign vessel engaged in the transatlantic-Great Lakes trade, a collision involving more loss of human lives than all the collisions listed in the six years just reviewed.

During the six seasons of navigation under scrutiny, the St. Lawrence Seaway cleared the Great Lakes to the shipping of the world. Since the opening of the water-paved highway in 1959, the number of ships sailing into the northern Great Lakes, and on to western Lake Superior for grain, had steadily increased.

In 1964, 231 salt-water ships, flying the flags of 24 nations, made 392 round trips into and out of Lake Superior, and most of these ocean-going ships made other stops in virtually all the Lakes to take on general cargo. Previously fresh-water skippers had had the five inland seas all to themselves. Familiar with the often treacherous waters, these captains understood one another, and navigated on occasion by the seat of their pants. They were becoming increasingly apprehensive about the newcomers and derogatory of their seamanship, as is indicated elsewhere in this book (pp. 287-291).

The other side of the coin indicated that generally the newcomers played it safe on the Lakes by sailing strictly according to the rules, while some fresh-water skippers were accused of ignoring the rules or making up their own to fit the occasion. Whatever might turn out to be the real truth of the matter, the fact remained that foreign ships were all over the Lakes at all times during the season now. In the connecting channels of the St. Mary's, St. Clair, and Detroit Rivers, they required the services of a licensed Great Lakes pilot. But in the open Lakes, and in the Straits of Mackinac, they could operate on their own if one officer held the B certificate issued by the Coast Guard.

WEALTHY WRECKS AND HISTORIC HULLS

Sailors coming into the Straits of Mackinac are following the trail first blazed by Algonquin dugouts and birchbark canoes, the batteaux of the explorers, fur traders, and missionaries. In the Straits stood the Great Turtle Island of Michilimackinac, mecca of adventure, center of trade, key to the winning of the West.

Modern sailors, whether they come around the top of Michigan's mitten by way of the Beaver archipelago or "False Presque Isle" on Lake Huron or down the St. Mary's from Lake Superior, are voyaging upon a sunken graveyard of ships, a subterranean cemetery second to none on the Lakes. Here in the Straits or on its approaches may lie the historic bones of La-Salle's *Griffin* (pp. 36-37), and somewhere in the neighborhood the real *Westmoreland* rests with a reported $100,000 in her safe as well as a rich cargo in her hold. As this is being written, skin divers are readying their gear for the new season, to venture in quest of wealthy wrecks and historic hulls, including that of the three-masted combination power and sailing vessel *Minneapolis* that came through the Straits in heavy ice during the spring of 1894 with the schooners *Red Wing* and *San Diego* in tow. When the grain ship ran into trouble, the schooners were apparently cut loose and nothing more was ever heard of them; but the 300-foot hulk of the *Minneapolis,* discovered in 90 feet of water just west of the Mackinac Bridge, has yielded relics to make the eyes of skin divers sparkle and bring hope that the 85-year-old ship may be raised to become a museum to hold marine lore at the place where the waters of the three Upper Lakes come together, often in boisterous mood.

SHADOW OF COMING EVENTS

In a land where unusual weather is a commonplace, Mackinac weather has a habit of surprising even the natives. In the habitat of the original Peasoupers, the *voyageurs* and *coureurs de bois* of the Old Northwest, nature has seen fit to create a special fog, as thick as pea soup, and she specializes in this murky brew in late spring, ladling it out with a heavy hand to the Straits of Mackinac and environs.

On the night of May 6, 1965, a real peasouper fog descended on the Straits and cast the shadow of coming events — coming in less than twelve hours — across Grey's Reef, four miles west of Waugoschance Pt. (*Wobbleshanks* to sailors), at the Lake Michigan entrance to the Straits of Mackinac. A message phoned shortly before midnight from the life station to Coast Guard Group Headquarters at Charlevoix said:

"We've had a new experience.... we've been hit by a ship!"

Blundering through the fog-shrouded night, the 504-foot

S. S. J. E. Upson, bound out of Chicago for Silver Bay, Canada, had smashed into the rocky life station whose light and fog-horn were both working. But visibility ranged from "zero to 250 yards" and the three men stationed at Grey's Reef, twenty feet above the water, were startled to find their "crow's nest" rammed into by a confused ship.

The impact broke off iron hand rails, chipped cement, and caused considerable shock to the Coast Guard lookout team. The errant vessel took on water in a forward compartment but was able to proceed to Mackinac City where a marine inspection certified the *Upson* as able to proceed across the Straits and into Canadian waters.

BLINDFOLDED STRAITS OF MACKINAC

On the morning following the accident, the Straits of Mack-inac, blindfolded by the fog, seemed a lost world in which lonesome ships sounded plaintive cries as they passed one another unseen on the choppy waterway connecting Lake Huron with Lake Michigan. In the swirling mist the shapes of Mackinac, Bois Blanc, and Round Island had disappeared, as drowned from view as legendary Atlantis. Out of sight, too, were the mainland towns of Mackinac City and St. Ignace, separated by five miles of troubled water until the great Mack-inac Bridge had united them in a soaring rainbow of steel that arched from Michigan's Lower Peninsula to the adventurous Upper Peninsula. On this morning even the Paul Bunyan of bridges, visible for miles on ordinary days, could be seen only from scant yards away, carrying its traffic north and south at skyscraper heights above the crossroads of the Lakes.

Below in the Straits lone ships were passing east and west, foghorns blowing, lookouts straining to pierce the gloom, radars being scanned, radios on the alert to communicate positions. Among these busy merchantmen of the five Great Lakes and the Seven Seas was the 420-foot Norwegian motor vessel *Topdalsfjord,* heading up from Lake Michigan for Port Arthur, Ontario, to pick up a shipment of grain. With her bow pointed east the sturdy Norwegian passed under the Mackinac Bridge, apprehensive but unable to know that she was on a collision course with another ship, only minutes away. The time was approximately ten minutes to ten, the fog so thick that visibility was reckoned at barely fifty feet.

STEERING A COLLISION COURSE

Earlier that morning the other ship on the collision course had put out from Calcite, the port of U.S. Steel Corporation, near Rogers City on Lake Huron. Renamed the *Cedarville,* she had been originally built as the *A. F. Harvey* (2nd) at River Rouge by Great Lakes Engineering for Pittsburgh S. S. Co. She had Scotch boilers out of Manitowoc, Wisconsin, and her ladylike dimensions were 588.3, 60.2, 30.8 with 2200 h.p. and 8222 g.t. (gross tonnage).

The *Cedarville,* about 50 feet shorter than the ill-starred *Bradley,* hailed from the same port, was owned by the same company, carried the same cargo, limestone, and shipped the same complement of men, 35. Going out instead of coming home, steaming into a May fog instead of riding a November gale, the freighter plowed her way from Lake Huron, rounding the bend into the Straits of Mackinac, her ultimate destination Gary, Indiana, but her nose pointing toward Mackinac Bridge, due west.

Captain Martin E. Joppich, skipper of the *Cedarville,* reported passing the freighter *Benson Ford* approximately 13 miles east of what turned out to be the collision site. He told of contacting the Lakes freighter *Steinbrenner* by radio telephone and being advised of a ship that "wouldn't answer whistle or telephone."

The *Cedarville's* skipper also reported that his radar picked up an echo of a ship eastbound but on the west side of Mackinac Bridge. "I made a call to (that vessel) and the *Weissenburg* answered....I picked up a vessel clearing the Bridge. I called the *Weissenburg* again and asked for his position. He said he was west of the bridge but that there was a Norwegian ship ahead of him."

Leonard Gabryziak, a licensed mate, was at the wheel of the limestone carrier. He could observe everything in the pilothouse.

81

He could hear the captain and the third mate conversing and could hear all radio conversations. He could watch his compasses, the tachometer, and the telegraph signalling the engine room. He could not, however, see the radar screen, situated in a corner of the pilothouse.

The radar scope was being sharply watched by Third Mate Charles Cook, one of the crewmen who later went down with the ship. He knew that the *Cedarville* had had trouble with its radar and radiophones earlier in the spring; they had been serviced but there were still complaints.

Ahead, westward, in the mysterious unknown revealed only by eerie warnings, the eastbound *Topdalsfjord* searched her way through the eyeless fog. Captain Rasmus Haaland saw to it that his ship was sounding fog signals in accordance with Great Lakes regulations, himself operating the manual fog whistles and blowing three short blasts at intervals.

Shortly the crew on the westbound *Cedarville* began hearing the fog whistles of the approaching Norwegian ship. The wheelsman reported that the vessels were bare minutes apart when Captain Joppich ordered the speed cut from full ahead. He also reported that the skipper made repeated efforts to contact the foreign ship on the radio but failed.

The *Cedarville* began blowing its whistle.

Third Mate Cook looked up from the radar and said: "She's pretty close." Tension mounted in the pilothouse. Then a lookout on the port wing outside shouted: "There she is!"

Another lookout at the bow called it, "Half a block away."

Wheelsman Gabryziak said he looked out of the window and saw the bow of the Norwegian about 100 feet ahead. Captain Joppich immediately ordered the engine room to "slow."

GOING TO BE HIT

Third Mate Cook shouted: "Captain, we're going to be hit!"

The skipper then signalled the engine room for full ahead and hard right.

Aboard the *Topdalsfjord*, Jan Crostol, the radio operator, said later: "I sighted the *Cedarville* about four minutes after we passed the Mackinac Bridge, and it appeared that the ship would pass us on our starboard side.

"Suddenly the ship was so close I could no longer see it on the radar screen. I rushed out of the radar room to the bridge to warn the captain, and as I got there I saw the ship coming across our bow out of the fog.

"The captain saw it too and ordered our engines reversed, but we were too close. We struck the *Cedarville* about mid-ship, bounded off, and it disappeared into the fog again."

It was 9:55 a.m., the collision following a suspended moment of incredulity and horror as men on both bridges shouted and made gestures of fending the other ship away.

The *Topdalsfjord,* her crew unharmed but nursing a damaged bow, stood by for awhile, then managed to limp out of the Straits and up the St. Mary's River to Sault Ste. Marie.

Although the limestone carrier reeled with the shock of impact, not a single member of the crew was injured in the collision. As well as he could, Captain Joppich checked the extent of damage to his ship. Events were to prove that she had suffered a mortal wound, a 20-foot gash in the starboard side amidships, running vertically from the deck line to the keel.

RACE FOR LIFE

Instead of beaching his ship on the nearest shoal, the skipper decided to make a run for the safety of the Mackinac City beach and ordered full speed ahead. According to conflicting accounts the *Cedarville* lost the race for life when she rolled over and sank about 40 minutes later, two miles from shore. First Mate Harry Piechan testified that Captain Joppich never gave the order to abandon ship, although he did say: "Get ready." The last radio message from the stricken freighter said: "The *Cedarville* is sinking," and shortly thereafter a nearby vessel reported hearing "fellows in the water calling for help."

When the ship capsized, seamen were hurled into water where the temperature stood at a life-snatching 37 degrees. Lifeboats and rafts pitched around in the choppy seas, survivors clinging to them. The nearest ship to the scene, the *M.S. Weis-*

senburg, owned by the Hamburg-American Lines, with an all-German crew, came steaming to the rescue, braving the fog. In contrast to the wild night when the German ship *Sartori* tried in vain to find survivors of the *Bradley,* the *Weissenburg* picked her way through the overhang and saved 25 men, 12 of whom had been injured when the *Cedarville* keeled over.

Ivan Trafelet, a watchman from Rogers City, told his story of survival. He had been in the icy water almost half an hour when help arrived.

"I had swallowed a lot of water and had just about had it. They had to lift me into the boat. We were awfully lucky the German ship was so near."

Ten men were still to be accounted for. Carrying life rafts and other rescue equipment, 3 amphibians and 2 helicopters went up from the Coast Guard Air Station at Traverse City, ready to risk any danger, but they were blind and helpless in the fog. The Coast Guard cutters *Sundew* and *Mackinaw* steamed toward the scene. State police launched small rescue craft and asked private boats in the area to assist in the search for more survivors. Walking parties started a step-by-step survey of the rugged Straits coastline. The passing traffic on Mackinaw Bridge stared down at a scene that smoked like a witch's cauldron. With heavy hearts, divers readied cutting torches to probe the wreckage.

FORLORN VIGIL

That night, for the second time in seven years, the small Lake Huron town of Rogers City stood by to bury its dead if need be, as it had in the case of the *Bradley,* and to hope against forlorn hope — as again in the case of the *Bradley* — that the missing men would be found alive by morning. Among those who held vigil and endured the ordeal of waiting for her missing husband was a woman whose sister had been widowed when the *Bradley* went down.

One of the wives who waited long after rescue workers had lost heart was Mrs. Wilbert Bredow, whose husband had been a steward and Bradley Line veteran of 30 years. Somehow,

84

sitting in the living room of their neat brick bungalow in Rogers City, her hands clasped tightly together, she seemed to epitomize all the wives and mothers and sweethearts and "next of kin" who waited when hope had all but gone from their breasts.

Mrs. Bredow said that she never worried about the hazards of the Lake. "Until the *Bradley* went down there's never been an accident like that before." She said she drove her husband to Calcite at 2:30 a.m. Friday and saw him aboard the *Cedarville*.

"I thought nothing about it. The Lake was calm. There was fog, but that didn't bother me. Only storms bother me.

"And then I heard that the ship had sunk. At 5 o'clock two men from the Company came to tell me my husband was missing.

"I'm not thinking about anything. I don't think anything. I'm waiting for the Company to tell me."

The lost men were never found alive. Swept overboard and drowned, or trapped inside the ship when the *Cedarville* capsized, eight of the ten victims' bodies were recovered in the days and months that followed, the last identified by his dental chart.

Five days after the tragedy, the body of F. Donald Lamp, chief engineer, 46, Rogers City, father of two sons, was found by divers who cut through the door of the engine room. He was wearing a life jacket and offered mute testimony of the gallantry displayed by those who had sacrificed themselves to stay at their posts in the frantic race to beach the *Cedarville*.

SKIPPER PLEADS FIFTH AMENDMENT

In the wake of the disaster arose rumors that faulty radar readings aboard the Norwegian might have contributed to the collision. A Coast Guard Board of Inquiry heard conflicting testimony from witnesses about the speed and relative positions of the two ships. Karl Fagerli, chief officer of the *Topsdalsfjord*, testified that after clearing the Mackinac Bridge his ship never moved faster than four miles an hour, and most often between two and three miles an hour.

Yet Fagerli, when asked to calculate his ship's average speed during the 10 minutes it took to pass from the Bridge to the point of impact two miles east, came up with 6.5 miles an hour.

"And that," commented an attorney for U.S. Steel, "is just too damn fast for the heavy fog."

Surviving *Cedarville* crewmen told reporters earlier that their ship had sounded warnings to the *Topdalsfjord* just before the collision but that the foreign vessel did not answer them. The Norwegian's chief officer Fagerli conceded that his ship never answered the American's one-blast signal, which would indicate that the limestone carrier was trying to pass on the left. He said the *Topdalsfjord's* engines had been brought to full stop, though he could not tell whether the ship had ceased moving. It seemed to him that the *Cedarville* appeared to be crossing in front of the *Topdalsfjord*.

Conspicuous by his absence at the preliminary hearing in the Sault was Captain Rasmus Haaland, whose ship's bow had cut a fatal hole in the Lakes vessel. It was said that he stayed away on physician's advice because of exhaustion from lack of sleep, and that he had remained under sedation since the fateful crash.

There were cynical observers who drew their own conclusions about the Norwegian skipper being treated for a nervous condition. The case for the American skipper seemed going well until Captain Haaland finally appeared before the Board of Inquiry. He testified that the limestone carrier had been traveling at high speed and he charged the master of the *Cedarville* (absent and reportedly being treated for a nervous condition developed following the collision) with poor seamanship. Then he leaned over with tears in his eyes and asked the attorney for U.S. Steel to extend his deepest sympathies to Captain Joppich.

Charges and countercharges followed Captain Haaland's testimony. There were demands that Captain Joppich appear for cross-examination. Roman T. Keenen, who also had served as counsel in the *Bradley* case, invoked the Fifth Amendment for his client.

GUILT IN THE FOG

As the Board of Inquiry shifted here and there on the Lakes the drama unfolded. One hearing was scheduled in Chicago in mid-July, 1965, to coincide with the arrival in that port of the *Topdalsfjord,* which was making her second trip of the season into the Great Lakes, and her first return trip since the May 7 collision.

At Grand Rapids a federal judge held that Captain Joppich had no legal grounds on which to invoke the Fifth Amendment and ruled, under federal maritime laws, that he must answer questions dealing with the disaster. Attorney Keenen contended that Coast Guard policy in the past had denied representatives of foreign flag vessels opportunity to cross-examine American seamen before boards of inquiry.

The court overruled and the *Cedarville's* master underwent cross-examination. Much of the ground had been covered in earlier sessions of the hearing, recalling testimony that Captain Joppich had made three course changes in the minutes and seconds before the collision to stay clear of shoals and other traffic.

But as the inquiries continued, the American skipper surprised investigating officers by changing an earlier plea of innocence to guilty. He testified that he computed the *Cedarville's* speed in the last 63 minutes before the crash to be 12 miles an hour — almost full speed. He amazed himself with his own computation and confessed that he could not explain such high speed during the fog.

The Coast Guard case against Captain Joppich was solely against his master's license and not against the man (his person, money or property). Punishment could be handed down in several forms: a revocation of his license, a suspension for a period of months or years, or certain conditions might be attached to his return to the Lakes. Charges alleged recklessness, negligence, and poor seamanship.

SURVIVORS GO TO COURT

While the inquiries were underway, the survivors went to

court to wage a multimillion dollar ($15 million) fight against the three principal ships connected with the tragedy, even the rescue vessel *Weissenburg*, which the litigants claimed had given out radio signals that created confusion in the Straits. The case dragged through the courts for almost two years.

Meanwhile, the collision had claimed another life indirectly when a teenage diver drowned while trying to recover the name plate from the *Cedarville*.

At Cleveland the Coast Guard found that Captain Joppich failed to operate his ship at the safe speed warranted by low visibility and also failed to take the proper action when the *Cedarville* was approached at one-half mile by another vessel, or when it heard the fog signal of the other ship. The Commandant of the Coast Guard, Admiral W. J. Smith (onetime schoolboy at Charlevoix near the Straits of Mackinac), approved the investigation board's report blaming an American ship captain for the fateful collision with a Norwegian vessel. The Board said the captain "judged poorly the peril to his crew and vessel and the time remaining for him to beach his ship," that he should have beached the ship on the nearest shoal, that the beaching course picked by the captain was incorrect and he "should have immediately realized this," that had the ship steamed for the closest beaching point, it would have made safety before it capsized.

The *Topdalsfjord's* master, Captain Rasmus Haaland, was found to have operated in complete accordance with Coast Guard and Great Lakes sailing recommendations.

Captain Joppich lost his master's license for one year.

During the Indian summer of 1967 at Cleveland, U.S. District Court ruled that U.S. Steel would have to pay punitive damages to the families of the 10 dead seamen, thus awarding more than $10 million to those bereaved by the disaster. In an 80-page decision the Court said the *Cedarville's* captain, Martin Joppich, was "guilty of wanton and almost grotesque indifference" of the safety of his crew, charging that he had failed to abandon ship when the hopelessness of the attempted beaching became apparent, failed to release his crew when the very decks of the *Cedarville* were awash, failed to accept assistance from the German ship *M.S. Weissenburg* when its captain, Werner May, offered to remove sailors from the sinking vessel.

Judge J. C. Connell charged U.S. Steel with entrusting the safety of the crew to a "reckless and incompetent master." He also said that the ship was dangerously overloaded with limestone and the company failed to provide watertight bulkheads.

Both the Norwegian owners and U.S. Steel already had admitted joint liability for compensatory damages, but attorneys for the American corporation appealed the federal court decision, stating it was the first one ever calling for punitive damages in a maritime collision resulting in loss of life.

Whatever the final settlement, the case of the *Cedarville* was red-inked in maritime history for all time one foggy May morning not so long ago in the impatient Straits of Mackinac, when almost a third of her crew lost their lives and another full third were injured. Even that is an understatement.

No real man ever survives a shipwreck unharmed, unchanged, unawed by the prayerful question: "Why them, O Lord, why them instead of me?"

STORK DELIVERY IN THE STRAITS

As a reminder of the eternal Eastertide in life, the same spring that brought death to the Straits also brought birth. A young lady from St. Ignace, on the Upper Peninsula side of the Straits, went visiting her parents on Mackinac Island. On Sunday, May 7, two days after the *Cedarville* capsized, she felt her time was near and sent for the island doctor. He recommended that she be taken immediately to medical facilities on the mainland, so he put in an urgent call for the Coast Guard.

Fog still hung like a funeral pall over the Straits of Mackinac, but a Coast Guard crew in a 36-foot lifeboat piloted their way through the gloom and put into the island late that evening, taking the expectant mother aboard. They departed at 11:25 p.m., insisting that the doctor go with them because of the heavy fog and the possibility that the six-mile trip might take longer than usual.

About midway to land, somewhere between Michigan's mitten and her copper-plated iron derby, the doctor delivered a daughter, assisted by an able seaman, with a BM2 operating the boat and an EN1 in the bow on fog lookout.

The infant uttered her first sounds of life across the waters where drowning men had given their last cries for help two days before. The lifeboat made the mainland at one minute past midnight, mother and daughter doing fine, a promise for the future from the Straits of Mackinac.

BOOK TWO

LOST OFF LAKE HURON'S SHORE

Around the beach the sea gulls scream;
Their dismal notes prolong.
They're chanting forth a requiem,
A saddened funeral song.

They skim along the waters blue
And then aloft they soar
In memory of the sailing men
Lost off Lake Huron's shore!

(Popular Lake song, 1869)

The song on the preceding page originally commemorated the loss of the schooner *Persia* with all hands in the great November storm of 1869, one of the wildest ever to hit the Lakes. The *Persia* was bound up from Chicago and had "sailed the horseshoe" around the Straits of Mackinac when her good fortune spilled out.

1. Summertime and the Living

Second only to Superior among the Great Lakes, Huron has a single bay larger than Lake Ontario and only a few hundred square miles smaller than Lake Erie. In her southernmost reaches along the St. Clair River she runs a busy thread between the United States and Canada where her shore lines present a civilized gauntlet of power plants, vacation resorts, boat works, and towns that reach out and join hands with other towns.

But when Huron begins to swell out in all her broad blue glory beyond Port Huron and Sarnia, towns stretch few and far between. The thumb of Michigan's mitten juts out to form Saginaw Bay, with as notorious a reputation for rough seas as the Bay of Biscay, and the Canadian Saugeen Peninsula seems to aim a jagged fishing spear at storied Manitoulin, largest fresh-water island in the world.

Upward bound, the landmarks to port of the international boundary line are long to reach but short to sing out: Harbor Beach, Pointe aux Barques, Tawas City, Au Sable Point, Thunder Bay, Alpena, Rogers City, Calcite, Cheboygan, the Straits of Mackinac, Drummond Island, Detour Passage, Sault Ste. Marie; while off to starboard are the Canadian ports of call: Kettle Point, Grand Bend, French Settlement, Bayfield, Goderich, Kincardine, the shipwreck-haunted Saugeen; and beyond and around this peninsula Huron looms into what amounts to another Great Lake — Georgian Bay and North Channel.

Every sailboat and cruiser worth naming on the upper Lakes has a heart set on a holiday trip into the northern reaches of Lake Huron where the Thirty Thousand Islands run as thick as mice at the foot of the oldest mountains in creation, the Laurentian Shield, and against a backdrop of the wildest scenic beauty left on earth.

By the way a sailboat or cruiser is fitted out and by the smiles on the faces of those aboard, a veteran harbor master knows the answer before he hurls the question, "Where you headed?"

The reply always carries a note of pride: "We're going up to Georgian Bay and into the North Channel."

These are good vacation sailors and some of them have hired expert captains because picturesque north Lake Huron is a jigsaw puzzle of islands and peninsulas scattered across the chart from Owen Sound and Collingwood and Penetanguishene to Parry Sound and Little Current and Blind River, the uranium country.

On lazy days with a schooner gliding across a bay that holds a mirror to pine-clad hills, or a cruiser loafing through the inlets separating the islands, it takes no imagination to hear a baritone slung in a deck hammock complete the picture by singing out, "Summertime, and the living is easy . . . ."

The waters of the upper Lakes are indeed summertime playgrounds, but the season is from the Fourth of July to Labor Day. The rest of the year they are no place for a picnic, and even during the vacation months they must be treated with uninterrupted respect by the summertime sailor who wants to enjoy another season.

The financier, J. P. Morgan, whose *Corsair* was the largest yacht ever to sail these waters, also had another hard-and-fast rule for survival: "It makes no difference whom you do business with, but don't step aboard boat until you've made sure you're setting sail with *gentlemen!*"

2. Ghosts in Georgian Bay

The summertime sailors of to-day may cruise waters and enter harbors that are no more than names on the charts to captains of the larger liners and bulk carriers of the present but that are still haunted by the ghosts of the smaller steamboats and schooners which performed the necessary chores of the past century, trans-porting the supplies, the equipment, the tools, the work gangs, and the settlers, to establish communities in the wilderness, to clear the forests, to open the mines, and to build the Soo Canal and the Canadian Pacific Railway.

In their eagerness to get the job done, these Lake Huron vessels were no different than their Lake Michigan sisters. They went out on the heels of the spring breakup and came in only when winter locked up the Lake with death-sharp, looking-glass ice. Rival shipping lines and captains vied so strenuously in making record hauls and fast passages that a Manitoulin Island newspaper editor reported one of the classic contests with appropriate embellishments in the style of Mark Twain (himself a steamboat man, be it re-membered):

Captain Pete Campbell of the *Pacific* came in Wednesday with three darkies and a Sheguiandah cheese on the safety valve and the keel carefully greased to prevent friction. The story they brought was that they had beat the *City of Midland* by five minutes and 37.12076 seconds between Collingwood and Owen Sound.

You could see the Cap's smile halfway to Strawberry shining like the church steeple, and his chin whisker was sticking out at an angle of 90 degrees with excitement, while his hat was tied on with a stout piece of hawser, and in each boot was a flat iron to keep him from blowing off the hurri-cane deck. Few and short were the words he said and his story was briefer than a guinea pig's tail. Then the *Pacific* steamed out, making 22 knots and smoking at every seam.

95

Two hours later, the *City of Midland* hove in sight, throwing the foam from her bow six feet into the air and twenty feet on each side of her like great white wings, belching forth rolling masses of smoke and looking thoroughly businesslike in her neat black coat. Her story was also brief, and Captain Bassett once more started on the trail of the *Pacific* with blood in his eye. All the paint was burnt off her smokestack.

The old saw about many a truth being spoken in jest applies to the Manitoulin editor's good-natured poking fun at Captain "Black Pete" Campbell, so called from the color of his goatee and not for any fault in his character, which he proved to be of solid gold in a full-steam race with death itself when he brought his ship in with more than the paint burnt off and literally smoking at every seam.

The three years with the blackest borders in Lake Huron's history are 1865, 1882, and 1913; the first for a single disaster and the other two seasons of navigation for multiple shipwrecks. There are other grim dates in Huron's record books, but these have gripped generations with the strange fascination that tragic events arouse.

Bound out of Collingwood with a full passenger list and a heavy cargo for Manitoulin Island and the north shore, the smart propeller *Manitoulin,* with an expert crew that jumped lively when Captain Black Pete Campbell barked, was steaming up Manitowaning Bay in fine weather along about noontime on Wednesday, May 17, 1882. The captain had a napkin tucked under his chin and was enjoying lunch at the head of the passenger table when someone cried: "Fire!"

There followed one of the finest exhibitions of seamanship in the annals of the Lakes. With the napkin still under his chin and streaming in the wind of his passage, Black Pete raced for the engine room and found it in flames. He gave one look at Chief Engineer William Lockerbie, whose helpers already were being driven from their posts by smoke and fire, and that was order enough for the Chief to hold full throttle while there was life below.

Climbing to the hurricane deck and the pilothouse, Black Pete roared commands as he went:

"Hard starboard at the wheel and steer for shore!"

The beach loomed two miles distant, and it took the blazing *Manitoulin* a bare six minutes to make the trip. On the way the crew leaped to carry out Black Pete's life-saving decisions:

"Swing out the lifeboats on the ready! Lower hand lines over the bows!"

These precautions were never needed. Down below Chief Engineer Lockerbie had remained at his post when all others had been driven off by sparks eating up their clothes and smoke searing their lungs. He got a death grip on the throttle with his left hand and held it wide open until he felt the *Manitoulin* scrape under him as she hit the beach. Then he made his bid for last-minute escape.

Up above First Mate George Playter and Captain Campbell had fought the wheel until it blistered their hands. When the steamboat struck the shore, the roof of the pilothouse was in flames over their heads. They had brought the boat so close to safety that everyone could have waded ashore.

But in the final split seconds a number of passengers went into panic and made frenzied leaps for life overboard. At least eleven perished needlessly despite the crew's brave exhibition of skill in crisis, and various other estimates put the death toll as high as forty. Passenger lists in those days were as uncertain as the weather and the sudden violence that lay in wait on the Lakes.

However, one thing is certain and a matter of proud record on Georgian Bay. Captain Black Pete Campbell was the last man to leave his blazing steamboat, and he went over the side with a child cuddled safe under one brawny arm.

3. Wonders of the Deep

Sailor yarns go hand in hand with superstition and psychic phenomena, and Lake Huron's Georgian Bay has its own story of the Bride's Dream to contribute to the occult library of the Lakes.

Oldest of the fresh-water supernatural legends is that of the Indian drum which, during the height of every great storm, supposedly sounds out the death toll in every shipwreck, one beat for each victim. Rarely heard by summer resorters but always listened for by Lake men and by the Ottawas, whose ancestors once coasted the inland seas and who used crooked trees along the shore for navigation guides, the Indian drum is said to have beaten thirty-three times all night long in the gale that lashed through Michigan's mainland pines when the *Bradley* sank. The phantom Ottawa drum thus had foretold there would be two survivors found.

VISION OF GRANDFATHER CAPTAIN

A curious instance of psychic phenomena was reported in an Ontario newspaper in 1869, the memorable year in which the schooner *Persia* went down with all hands, a tragedy that inspired the ballad dedicated to Lake Huron and a long-time favorite sailor song.

During the same November storm that swallowed the *Persia,* the little granddaughter of Captain Disbrow, sailing master of the schooner *Volunteer,* awoke her mother about midnight and asked to have a lamp lighted, because she had seen "grandfather captain" standing by her bedside.

The grownups tried to dismiss the youngster's vision as no more than a nightmare, but they themselves were seized with uneasy foreboding because it was the ominous night before Thanksgiving and one of the worst November storms on record was raging across the Lakes. Several days later their secret fears, and the child's dream, became realized when news arrived that the schooner *Volunteer* had been wrecked by the storm and that Captain Disbrow had gone down with his ship.

A SAILOR'S HUNCH

In the lull before the murderous storm of 1913 on Lake Huron, Milton Smith, assistant engineer aboard the ore carrier *Charles F. Price,* one of the great long ships in the Hanna fleet, was whiling away time in port by reading a Cleveland newspaper. Instead of being able to concentrate on other items of interest, he found himself turning back, again and again, to the government weather forecast for the upper Lakes:

> November 8, 1913 — Snow or rain and colder, Saturday, with west to southwest winds. Sunday, unsettled.

There was nothing worrisome in such a forecast at that season of the year, but something gave Milton Smith a feeling of dread in his bones. A sudden hunch made him decide to get off the *Charles F. Price,* right there and then, while the getting was good. He packed his kit and asked for his time.

Chief Engineer John Groundwater tried to argue his young assistant from making a foolish move. "Get that wild hair out of your nose and stick aboard. Why throw money in the bilge? The *Price* will be tied up for the winter inside of three weeks and you'll collect crew bonus on top of regular pay. Take my advice, son. Think it over."

But thinking had nothing to do with Milton Smith's action. Some primeval sixth sense had advised him what to do. He walked off the *Charles F. Price* as if he could not leave her fast enough. Five days later he was called from Cleveland to Port Huron to identify the bodies of his shipmates. The *Price* had gone down with all hands.

THE BRIDE'S DREAM

The shipping notice of 1879 states that the most serious disaster of the season of navigation was the loss of the Canadian steamer *Waubuno,* which floundered on Georgian Bay in November with a loss of thirty lives, the manner of her destruction remaining unknown. The notice goes on to report that the series of storms which swept over the Lakes from November 15 to November 24 proved unusually destructive to shipping and life. No less than sixty-five vessels met with disaster between those dates.

This prolonged storm had held up the sailing of the *Waubuno,* a 150-foot, side-wheel type steamboat heavy laden with merchandise and supplies that were long overdue in Parry Sound. The crew and passengers were getting tired of the delay. They wanted to get out of Collingwood. After all, it was a short trip with very little risk and, even in the gale now blowing, the *Waubuno* would not be exposed to the open Lake except on the twenty-mile stretch between Hope Island and Lone Rock, and Captain Burkett could avoid even this by heading for Moose Point and running into Parry Sound by way of another channel.

There were summertime sailors among the *Waubuno's* crew and passengers who grumbled at the captain for staying alongside the dock. They hinted that something more than November weather might be giving him cold feet. He might even have been superstitious enough to swallow, hook line and sinker, that silly dream of the young bride.

All this was going through Captain George Burkett's thoughts in the short black hours after midnight on November 22. Back and forth he paced his pilothouse, trying to make up his mind, scratching his fingernails now and then on the frosty windows to take a look at the snow squalls driving at the *Waubuno.*

Two nights ago the young bride had come aboard with her doctor husband. The newlyweds were headed for the North Country, he to set up a medical practice and she to

100

set up housekeeping, the very type of people the upper Lakes needed.

But the bride had come out of her cabin the next morning and sat down at the breakfast table still full of a wild dream in which the *Waubuno* got shipwrecked and all on board drowned. She had implored her husband to leave the steamboat and make the trip overland. Of course, like any sensible man, the young husband had done his best to calm down his impressionable wife. It was only a dream. But the bride remained worried and the story spread from the boat to the town. And it was enough to set a man's teeth on edge to have the crew and passengers muttering behind the captain's back that *he* must believe in such nonsense or else why did he keep the *Waubuno* snug in harbor.

Captain Burkett stopped his pacing and stared at his watch. Four o'clock. The wind had abated. The storm seemed to be blowing itself out. Suddenly he resolved to get the whole thing over and done with, and no more stewing around. He clanged the engine room, roared orders to clear the lines, and moved so fast out of Collingwood that he never took time to blow the departure whistle for those who had taken rooms in town for the night. If they weren't aboard the *Waubuno*, let them wait for the next boat, if any, the backbiters!

But the frightened bride and her sensible husband were asleep in their cabin when the side-wheeler paddled into the rolling seas, her engines gasping with the effort of bucking the waves that dashed aboard in spray that was hard to distinguish from the wind-whipped snow.

The last ever heard of the *Waubuno* was the mournful sound of her whistle several hours later, a familiar signal recognized by loggers working near Moon River. "There she goes," they said. "There goes the *Waubuno*. Takes more than bad weather to stop that old girl."

What stopped the *Waubuno* remains unknown to this day. Eventually almost every one of her life preservers washed ashore with wreckage, and so it is presumed that whatever happened came fast. When she failed to arrive in Parry Sound on Monday, a rescue tug went out into Georgian Bay. A lifeboat with no one aboard was found right away, and later a part of the steamboat's paddle box with her name painted on it. The following March an Indian discovered the hull bottom side up in a small bay behind Moose Point. Years afterwards portions of the machinery were located on the Haystack Reefs. Other wreckage was hauled up in commercial fishing nets. It seems obvious that the storm simply tore the *Waubuno* to pieces and then scattered those pieces across Georgian Bay. No bodies ever appeared. Variable estimates place the death toll from twenty-four to thirty.

Although not listed as one of the great disasters of the Great Lakes, the story is one of those most often told when sailing people get together, perhaps because it has the tragic inevitability of classic drama, this classic tale of the bride's dream of shipwreck that turned out to be true on Lake Huron's Georgian Bay, where the terrified girl who had a vision of drowning with all those aboard the *Waubuno* now sleeps forever in her own haunted dream on the bed of the inland sea.

4. Huron's Story of Two Survivors

Lake Huron has a nineteenth-century story of two survivors to match Lake Michigan's modern story of two survivors, and a toll of lives lost which more than matches the *Bradley* disaster. The tragedy produced such an effect in the vicinity of its happening that another genuine ballad of the Lakes was inspired, printed anonymously in a local newspaper, and sung for years thereafter by sailing crews:

Loud raged the dreadful tumult,
And stormy was the day,
When the Asia left the harbour,
To cross the Georgian Bay.

One hundred souls she had on board,
Likewise a costly store;
But on this trip, this gallant ship
Did sink to rise no more.

With three and thirty shanty men
So handsome, stout and brave,
Were bound for Collin's Inlet
But found a watery grave.

An exact record sets the number aboard the *Asia* at 125. This year was the ominous one in which Captain Black Pete Campbell had started the disastrous season of navigation with his race to the beach against flaming death. The *Asia* was one of the small steamers that ran the big errands across Georgian Bay, and she had a captain as reluctant to waste time in port in bad weather as Captain Burkett whose *Waubuno* had met its destiny three years earlier.

Captain John Savage took the *Asia* out of Owen Sound on the night of September 13, 1882, while a boisterous wind already had begun to build up mountainous seas. The vessel was top-heavy when she left the dock, because it was easier and quicker to throw stuff on deck rather than pile it in the hold. Even up on the hurricane deck there were barrels and boxes of supplies and provisions. A number of horses snorted and pawed in alarm as the main deck lurched under them.

Every cabin on the *Asia* was filled with passengers, and there were others sleeping in every corner of the boat where a carpetbag or grain sack could cushion a head. Those not asleep were too sick to lift up their heads in alarm even when the cargo started to shift and roll about as the steamer

103

came from behind the shelter of the Saugeen Peninsula into the open Lake.

Bound for French River and Sault Ste. Marie, Captain Savage realized long before noon the next day that he would be fortunate to bring his boat ashore, even if he tore the bottom out of her, on Lonely Island off Great Manitoulin.

At eleven o'clock, with the storm at its height, Captain Savage saw a glimmer of hope from his pilothouse as the outline of Lonely Island began to take shape across the white-capped waters ahead. He realized that the *Asia* was foundering under him, and he shouted last-minute emergency orders to lighten the boat by throwing overboard everything that was loose. While crew members hastened to carry out these commands, the passengers started to panic. A clergyman moved through the confusion with words of comfort and prayers to calm the terrified.

With Lonely Island dead ahead and plain to view, the *Asia* wallowed into her death struggles. One of the two survivors, seventeen-year-old Duncan A. Tinkiss, saw the pictures of those final moments aboard the doomed vessel in nightmares to his own dying day:

"The aft gangway leading from the promenade to the main deck was jammed with men, women, and children who could get neither up nor down. At every pitch of the ship this mass would writhe and twist like a serpent while the waves broke over them from above. The horses in the meantime had broken loose and at every roll they were thrown from one side of the main deck to the other. The cabin was already broken at several points but still the craft floated. At last, about 11:30, she pitched up at the head and went down stern first, the cabins breaking off and the boats floating off as she did so."

Three overcrowded boats had been shoved off, barely in time, and young Tinkiss happened to clamber into one that was quickly swamped with frenzied and clinging humanity. With amazing presence of mind in the midst of disaster, he jumped off and took another desperate chance:

"As she was about to sink, I sprang over and swam for the captain's metallic lifeboat. There were great combs on every wave, and these, loaded with floating debris, broke over my head every time I came up on the crest. My hands and head were both cut and bleeding, but I reached the lifeboat and managed to clamber in. We were driving fast before the sea and soon lost sight of the wreckage and other boats as well."

By fortunate accident, young Tinkiss had climbed in at one end of the boat and at the other end was equally fortunate Miss Christina Ann Morrison who had leaped for life when the deck of the *Asia* went awash and who had been carried by a wave close to the captain's boat where the mate, her own cousin, hauled her in.

> *Of all the souls she had on board,*
> *Two only are alive;*
> *Miss Morrison and Tinkiss,*
> *Who only did survive.*
>
> *Miss Morrison and Tinkiss,*
> *Their names I'll ne'er forget,*
> *Protected by a lifeboat*
> *Which five times did upset.*

No doubt their youth contributed to the survival of the two celebrated in the ballad called "The Wreck of the Asia," but fortunate placement in the boat may have been a more important factor than their ages, each being less than twenty years old. Every time the lifeboat upset — and it did so repeatedly — there were fewer survivors in the craft that had headed for shore with more than twenty. When the boat overturned, the two young people at the opposite stations could get a grip on the ends, hang on until things quieted down and the boat righted itself, and then pull themselves in again.

From stormy noon to raging dusk the lifeboat drifted wildly across Georgian Bay. Apparently the oars were lost early. As darkness came, only six remained alive, and there was one lifeless body aboard, that of a French Canadian deck hand who had died an hour before.

> *The cabin boy next passed away,*
> *So young, so true, so brave;*
> *His parents weep while his body sleeps*
> *In Georgian's watery grave.*
>
> *And likewise Billy Christie,*
> *With his newly-wedded bride,*
> *Were bound for Manitoulin*
> *Where the parents did reside.*
>
> *"Oh, had we only left this boat,*
> *Last eve at Owen Sound!*
> *Oh, Willie dear, why came you here*
> *To in these waters drown?"*

The wind had died down but the waves were still rolling high as evening lengthened across the black Lake. In addition to young Tinkiss and Miss Morrison, the names of the living were John Savage, captain, John McDonald, first mate, a man named Little and a man named McAlpine. They cheered weakly at a flash of hope in the distance, which the ship's two officers identified as Byng Inlet light.

The young girl's cousin, First Mate McDonald, started the old revival hymn, "Pull for the Shore, Sailor," but the voices were feeble, partly because they were in shock and already half dead from exposure, partly because they realized the terrible irony of the words coming from a boat without oars. The song died out but later they sang very softly together one last time — lost voices reaching out for companionship in the final darkness that was closing around four of them. They harmonized: "In the Sweet By and By."

The man named McAlpine was the first to go in the raw and bitter night on troubled Lake Huron; he died at eight o'clock. Then the man named Little, to use the expression formerly given in shipwreck notices, "went out of time." At eleven o'clock the gallant mate who had pulled his young cousin aboard and then buoyed up the hearts in the darkness with his singing, lost the last spark of life.

> The men cried, "Save the Captain,"
> As the waters round him raged;
> "Oh, no," cried he, "ne'er think of me
> Till all on board are saved."

Sometime after midnight young Tinkiss noticed that the captain seemed to be falling asleep. Tinkiss shook him until finally he murmured, "All right, I'll be up in a minute."

At that instant a huge wave crashed over the boat and when Tinkiss had time to look again, Captain John Savage was dead. The youth carefully placed the body under the seats, where he had placed all the others to keep them from being washed away. Then he and the girl, who was also in her teens, waited out the night, adrift in a boat half filled with water and the company of five dead men, fighting to keep their eyes open against the sleep that meant death.

At dawn they sighted land, and the hope of drifting ashore kept them alive all morning. Toward noon the lifeboat beached itself on one of the countless islands in Georgian Bay. The two young people had been exposed to the elements in an open boat for about twenty-four hours; they had been without food or rest in the storm for more than thirty hours; and it would be another full twenty-four hours before help arrived to save them from starvation.

At that time, with himself and the girl on the verge of delirium, Tinkiss sighted a small sailboat. He put his coat on the torn-off branch of a tree and waved it to attract attention. An Indian in a Mackinaw boat came scraping on the beach. He had some fat pork and "choke dog" which the two survivors looked upon as a banquet, and he accepted the offer of Tinkiss' watch to carry them safe to Parry Sound, where they brought the story of the shipwreck which

107

ranks eighth among the great disasters on the Great Lakes and second in the annals of Lake Huron:

> Around each family circle,
> How sad the news to hear,
> The foundering of the Asia
> Left sounding in each ear.

Tinkiss lived, at Manitowaning and Little Current, until 1910. But the young girl lived to tell her story for fifty-five years after surviving the most terrible shipwreck in the history of Georgian Bay, the body of water with the longest history of sailing on the Great Lakes, dating back to nameless Vikings and to the French explorers whose paddle-and-portage *batteaux* first ventured upon the ocean-blue expanse of this sweet-water sea.

5. Ship-to-Shore Spirit

In the same year of multiple shipwrecks on Lake Huron that recorded 123 lives lost in the foundering of the *Asia*, the schooners *Clayton Belle* and *Thomas Parsons* collided on the open Lake, ten miles above Port Huron and Sarnia, and the former sank to the bottom in seven minutes. Three of the crew escaped by leaping aboard the *Parsons*. Captain Fred Colvin and three others were below when the *Parsons* struck the *Clayton Belle* on the quarter. They rushed up and launched a boat, but it became entangled in the wreck and went down. The *Clayton Belle* was bound down from St. Ignace to Erie with pig iron and the *Parsons* was bound up with coal.

This routine notice in the shipping news of 1882 draws the pattern of a thousand wrecks on the Lakes in the nineteenth century. In those days people caught boats as casually as they were to catch streetcars and buses in the century to come. They treated boats as carelessly as today's crowds jam into subway cars or race for commuter trains. Water was the quickest way to get from one place to another, and whatever craft happened to be handy was fine.

The people who drove the boats, the captains and the crews, might well be compared with modern motorists. Traffic was so heavy and speed was such a mania that their steamboats and schooners collided head on, side-swiped, or rammed one another amidships all the way from the tiptoe of Ontario to the topknot of Superior.

There were captains on the Lakes who no more thought of carrying a barometer than today's car driver thinks of an extra accessory such as radar. A typical skipper wet his thumb to tell which way the wind was blowing and he relied on such optimistic weather forecasts as "evening red and morning gray will set the sailor on his way" or "rainbow at night, sailors' delight," but he ignored all the pessimistic weather jingles because he was bent on going places and he intended to get there, weather or not.

Instead of bothering with nautical frippery like a compass, the fresh-water captains often navigated by watch, pointing the hour hand at the sun and estimating due south to lie exactly midway between the hour hand and the figure 12 on the dial. At nine o'clock in the morning, for example, the captain might interrupt his endless game of cribbage with the first mate to pull a dollar watch out of his vest, squint at the sun, point the hour hand in that direction, and estimate due south to lie just between the 10 and 11 on the dial.

As for such safety refinements as fog horns, the attitude of old steamboat captains is expressed in the tart reply given by one of them to a commercial traveler:

"Buy a fog horn? For why? If I got steam up, I can whistle. If I haven't got steam up, I'm not there!"

The first government charts were scorned by Great Lakes captains on the grounds that they were made up by a lot

109

of desk pilots who had never sailed the waters these fancy maps were supposed to cover. Any veteran fresh-water skipper would prefer to check his position by more reliable aids, ranging from the smell of cherry blossoms in the wind off Grand Traverse Bay to the time it took his whistle to echo back from the Pictured Rocks. In order to get the original Lake charts into circulation, the government had to give a set away to every vessel.

The Lakes and the land, the sailors and the people along the shore have always been intimately associated. Perhaps the word is *homey*. Today's great bulk carriers clear the iron and grain ports with a housewife's garbage can at the stern rail and a kitchen broom leaning against the door jamb of the aft cabin, just as at the back porch of any home ashore. Down along the St. Clair River, the blue ribbon that Huron wears for a sash, wives and sweethearts and mothers wave and blow kisses and call out the latest household gossip to their men aboard the long ships that are passing.

CLEVELAND TO CALIFORNIA

As of recent date there were 281 U.S. flagships of 1,000 gross tons and over operating on the Great Lakes, including 146 bulk freighters in the iron-ore trade, 11 bulk freighters in the mixed trades, 56 self-unloaders of various kinds, 5 bulk freight barges, 41 oil tankers (including New York State Barge Canal craft), 20 car ferries, and 2 passenger steamers. Canada's flagships numbered 196, including 151 bulk carriers, 29 tankers, 13 freighters, and 3 combination passenger and cargo ships. A comparison with statistics published in the first edition of this book (p. 96, 1960) points up the diminishing numbers of United States and Canadian flagships on the Lakes. But the St. Lawrence Seaway continued to expand trade as foreign flagships made 1,109 trips into the Great Lakes during the 1967 season of navigation. And so busy were American shippers with important cargoes that their request to extend the 1968 season into the icebound passages of January 1969 was granted.

Great Lakes sailors had carried patient smiles for the hullaba-loo of publicity that had attended the opening of the St. Law-rence Seaway back in the mid 1950's. Lakelanders had done the real opening long since. They have been sailing out the Lakes and across the oceans for more than a hundred years. They have made countless such trips without any fuss or brag. It was all in the regular line of business, and often not as much trouble as hauling between Buffalo and Chicago or Cleveland and Duluth.

One of the sailing notices of the 1849 season of navi-gation was the departure from Cleveland of the bark *Eu-reka,* with fifty-nine passengers aboard bound for California where they all arrived safely. This did not mark the first ocean trip by a Great Lakes vessel. In 1844 the brigantine *Pacific* had cleared Toronto with a cargo of wheat and flour for Liverpool. After that there was a parade of ocean crossings from Toronto and Kingston and Milwaukee, and in 1850 another gold-rush boat, the propeller *Ontario,* went from Buffalo to San Francisco.

During the 1858 season of navigation, fifteen vessels sailed out the Lakes and across the western ocean. After that, even the shipping notices began to lose count, it was such a common occurrence.

Just to make it unanimous and to prove that Great Lakes boats, like the proverbial Western hero, could ride off in all directions simultaneously, a trail-blazing steamer churned out of Oshkosh, Wisconsin, in 1871, and proceeded by way of the Fox and Wisconsin rivers to Prairie du Chien on the Mississippi, thus serving notice to the world that Lake sail-ors were able to reach the sea via the "Father of Waters" too. Given the urge, Lakers could sail from Atlantic Ocean salt water at Quebec to Gulf of Mexico salt water below New Orleans, from the land of the French Canadian to the land of the *bayou creole,* and still consider themselves on their own inland waterway.

In this same decade, a notice in the shipping news had mentioned the following:

> *Arrivals from Norway* — A sloop named the *Skjoldoman,* from Bergen, Norway, arrived at Detroit, July 14, en route to Chicago, and returned on her homeward voyage, passing Detroit, August 1, freighted with provisions. The barge *Sleipun,* also a Norwegian vessel, arrived at Detroit, June 27. with one hundred passengers en route to Chicago. She passed on her return voyage August 23, with a cargo of wheat.

By 1870 the number of Lakers making hauls to Europe was not news, unless the number was unusually small, as instanced in the following shipping notice:

> *Departures for Europe.* — On July 27, the bark *Thermutus* departed from Cleveland on a voyage to Liverpool with a cargo of oil and staves. She and the *Wirralite,* which sailed earlier in the season, were the only vessels to make European voyages during this season.

In 1892 there were 1,700 steamboats and 1,500 sailing vessels bustling along the fresh water seaway compared with the combined total of the United States, Canadian, and foreign flag vessels of 754 in 1960. The United States and Canadian fleets on the Great Lakes by 1968 had dropped from the 1960 total of 638 to a low of 477 vessels.

Times have changed, certainly for the better on the practical side of the shipping ledger, but with red-ink losses on the romantic columns. Trains, family cars, trucks, and planes have reduced the hundreds of passenger liners and excursion boats to a handful. Fast new bridges have driven quaint and pleasurable ferryboat runs out of service. Each year the long bulk carriers get longer to carry more and more profitable tonnage, but the size of the fleet goes down.

Even so, with this tremendous reduction in traffic, there were still collisions, and major ones, on the Lakes in recent years.

On a single day in 1943, June 15, there were three collisions resulting in two sinkings. The freighter *Goderich* on the St. Marys River rammed the brand-new 621-foot ore carrier *Frank Armstrong;* the 12,000-ton ore boat *George M. Humphrey* was sunk in seventy feet of water off Old Fort Mackinac Point twenty minutes after a collision with the 600-foot *D. M. Clemson;* and the grain carrier *Brewster,* deep laden with 90,000 bushels of Lend-Lease wheat to England, was sunk near Walpole Island in the St. Clair River where the swelling of her cargo soon buckled her plates, a phenomenon that has resulted in many a shipwreck on the Lakes during storms when water gets into a hold full of wheat or corn and turns it into a rustling monster of fast malignant growth.

In 1966, the German freighter *Emsstein* collided head-on with another freighter in the St. Clair River between Michigan and Ontario. The other freighter, *Olympic Pearl,* from Liberia, suffered a gash in the bow but continued on toward Montreal. Thirty-five were rescued from the *Emsstein,* whose smoldering hull was tilted over in the water.

In 1953, a year of record hauls on bulk carriers, a German-owned ocean-going freighter, the *Wallschiff,* sank in the St. Clair River on October 2, after being struck amidships by the loaded Cleveland Cliffs ore boat *Pioneer.* A Canadian pilot lost his life and there were long carriers lined up and blowing off steam along both channels of the busy international river until the wreckage could be cleared.

Considering such collisions in these days of amazing navigational aids and decreased traffic on the Lakes, the number of collision disasters reported in the nineteenth century no longer seem fantastic. With more than three thousand steamboats and sailing vessels running loose, fatal accidents were as inevitable as they are on crowded modern highways. The rules of the road were tailor-made for accidents. Schooners were not required by custom to carry running lights and they always had the right of way over engine-driven vessels. When sail approached steam, let the rival beware!

113

6. Death at the Wheel

With shipping traffic at its peak in the nineteenth century, and much of it up and down Lake Huron's busy waterway, it was not until 1911 that separate sailing courses were laid out on her chart to prevent accidents between the up- and the down-bound boats. But one of the greatest hazards to navigation was the very intimacy, the casualness, of the way you made a trip.

You got aboard a boat with no more thought than you hail a taxi. Instead of leaning out the window to buy a paper from a corner newsboy when the cab stops for a red light, you met an up-bound boat on Lake Huron and reached across the rail to get a Detroit newspaper, to find out the latest word in the place you were headed for.

Sometimes, in reaching out to grab the headlines, there was an accident that itself made the headlines — an accident resulting in shipwreck and heavy loss of life, such a collision perhaps as that between the *Pewabic* and the *Meteor* when 125 people were lost in the seventh worst disaster in Great Lakes history.

The exact cause of the tragic collision has never been proved, but the two propeller-type steamboats were sister ships and it is known that they were in the habit of coming close together so that mail bags, personal notes, and the latest newspapers could be exchanged over the rail.

It was a balmy summer evening, August 9, 1865. The heat of the day had been washed fresh by a Lake shower. A golden spell of sunset drowsed on the calm waters as the steamers began to approach each other about seven miles off Thunder Bay Island and abreast of Alpena on upper Lake Huron.

They were good stout boats, the *Pewabic* and the *Meteor*, but fancy enough to attract the passenger trade in the Civil War era with their elegant salons, handsome stained-glass domes, playing fountains, gorgeous satin and lace drapery,

exquisitely architectured joinery, enormously splendid mirrors, rosewood furniture, marble-topped tables, dining rooms ample enough to seat a hundred, and silverware made to order at a cost of $15,000.

Bound down from Houghton, Michigan, in Lake Superior where she had picked up 250 tons of virgin copper consigned to Cleveland, the 225-foot *Pewabic* was on the home leg of her trip and many of the passengers had already retired to their cabins. But the *Meteor,* not many hours out of Detroit and headed for Sault Ste. Marie, had a list of lively passengers, quite a number of whom could be seen from the *Pewabic's* deck, dancing to the steamer's band.

In plenty of time the lookout aboard the *Pewabic* saw the *Meteor* and called to the pilothouse: "Steamer ahead, sir, bound this way."

Closer they came together, dangerously close. In the final instant of decision, the wheelsman on the *Meteor* apparently became confused and turned sharply in the direction opposite to what he had been ordered. The two steamboats collided with a crash that killed many aboard the *Pewabic* at the moment of the impact and hurled scores into the water. Children and grownups struggled to hang onto wreckage until the survivors were rescued at dawn.

Captain George Perry McKay, only twenty-seven years old, whose distinguished career after the disaster included becoming first treasurer of the Lake Carriers' Association, has handed down his own account of the collision:

"There was no storm the night the *Pewabic* sank. It was clear weather and just beginning to get dark. I was on the main deck near the engine room when I saw the lights of the *Meteor* approaching us. I went up to the pilot house. The *Meteor* drew closer. She was trying to avoid us. I gave orders to stop the starboard engine and hold the steering wheel hard. We shifted wheels three times to clear the *Meteor*. Then came the crash. The *Meteor* didn't sink. The *Pewabic* did.

"The passengers on the boat rushed up from the salon

where they had been dancing. Some were trapped in their staterooms. I helped them all I could and succeeded in getting some of them over to the *Meteor,* which was beside us unhurt. Our boat was sinking rapidly, and the upper cabins were being forced off by the expulsion of the air and drifting out into the Lake. The crew of the *Meteor* were manning the lifeboats and going to rescue the people in the floating cabins. The *Pewabic* sank slowly, and when the water reached the deck where I was working I seized a rope from the *Meteor,* tied it around me, and as the vessel sank beneath me was hoisted to the deck of the *Meteor.*"

Captain Thomas Wilson of the *Meteor,* another twenty-seven-year-old commander, and a born Scot like so many of the fine Great Lakes sailing masters, also conducted himself with credit that black night. He kept his vessel at the scene and did everything humanly possible to save those who were fighting for life in the water. Captain Wilson in later years became the owner of a fleet and founded a freighter line still in existence, the Wilson Transit Company, whose black stack with the white *W* is a familiar sight today on the inland seas.

We have another eyewitness account from a passenger's viewpoint, one of those who survived the night on the water, thanks in good part to Captain Wilson's remaining on hand with the *Meteor* as a sign of hope and eventual rescue. This witness was Samuel Douglas, a small boy at the time and a son of the first professor of chemistry at the University of Michigan, Silas H. Douglas. More than sixty years later Samuel Douglas wrote down his recollections of the disaster:

"We all ran to the stern of the boat on the starboard side, my father and the women in advance. When we reached the stern my father, realizing that the vessel might go down at any minute, ordered the women to jump into the Lake, and he did likewise. We were all equipped with the ordinary cork life preservers, used at that time. Running around the stern of the boat to the port side I saw that the *Meteor* had swung alongside the sinking *Pewabic,* and it seems to me today the sides of the vessels were not more than six to eight feet apart. As I jumped I touched one of the hands outstretched, my body striking the side of the *Meteor* and I fell between the two boats. So close were the vessels together that I could almost touch the sides with my hands.

"I was in the water from one-half to three-quarters of an hour, but finally the hurricane deck of the *Pewabic,* wrenched off as she made her final plunge, was floating some distance from where she went down. It was to this that my efforts were directed and I was finally pulled onto this raft by the steward of the *Pewabic,* John Lynch. My father, sister, brother and myself were all rescued at different times. A number of passengers were saved by jumping from the deck of the *Pewabic* to the deck of the *Meteor.* After passing through the horrible night of rescue, the saved passengers were taken on board a passing propeller called the *Mohawk,* bound for Detroit."

So ended the *Pewabic* disaster, but it was by no means the end of the *Pewabic's* story.

7. Strike It Rich Below

The Greek philosopher Diogenes, who held a lantern aloft in search of an honest man, might as well have gone below in search of a shipwreck that did not leave behind a tale of sunken treasure. Even the *Bradley* left a still-alive rumor in the wake of her last trip, a wild yarn that she carried $100,000 to the bottom of Lake Michigan.

Faced with this story by inquiring reporters, transportation line officials explained that this could not have been the company payroll because they paid their men by check. With the payroll theory blasted, rumor then circulated the idea that the money represented the captain's personal fortune which he kept in a strongbox or the ship's safe.

Befitting their responsible duties, Great Lakes sailing masters on the large fleets are well rewarded. They make upwards of twenty thousand dollars per nine-month season of navigation. But even if one of them had a personal fortune of $100,000 in cash, he would hardly carry it around with him. Men smart enough to accumulate that much ready money either put it to work or put it in the bank drawing interest.

However, the rumor about the *Bradley's* captain will not die and, with the limestone carrier lying at a depth of 365 feet, both the money and the story about the money are in safekeeping, until new methods of deep-sea diving are perfected.

Since the date she went down (1865), the *Pewabic* has continued to make headlines and stir up rumors for ninety-odd years. In addition to the fortune in copper that she was known to have carried to the bottom, there were persistent rumors concerning $40,000 in cash reputedly stored in the strongbox in the purser's office.

Standard accounts of salvage attempts on the *Pewabic* wreck start with World War I and its resulting upsurge in copper values, but interesting is this curious, and illuminating, fragment of history tucked away in a Great Lakes shipping notice of 1897:

> *Wreck of the Pewabic Found.* — The wreck of the long-lost steamer *Pewabic* was located after a casual search extending over thirty years. The wreck was found by a wrecking expedition from Milwaukee in the steamer *H. A. Root.* It lies six miles southeast from Thunder Bay Island, Lake Huron, in twenty-seven fathoms of water, and is in the regular course of steamers, on almost an even keel. The upper works are entirely gone, but portions of the bulwarks are standing, and the main deck appears to be intact. The

118

American Wrecking and Salvage Co., of Milwaukee, under a contract with the underwriters, worked for the recovery of the wreck and cargo, consisting largely of copper in barrels, recovering copper to the value of $7,000. For several years from one to four expeditions had been sent out to locate the *Pewabic*, and several lives had been lost in the search. There was always a belief that the safe of the steamer contained a large amount of money.

The notice is significant, among other aspects, for its mention of underwriters. The wreck of the *Pewabic* had ruined the transportation company founded by John Tallman Whiting, one of the Lake Superior stalwarts responsible for building the Soo Canal. The insurance underwriters had become the owners of the sunken vessel and therefore any salvage operations had first been obliged to get a contract with them. Salvage law on the Great Lakes, as impulsive skin divers have learned to their embarrassment and sorrow, is not the same as that on salt water. At sea the law more or less follows the jingle "finders keepers, losers weepers," but here on fresh water all salvage rights belong to the owners. They have a right even to the floating debris and wreckage, no matter where it may be picked up, or when, or by whom.

Owners on the Great Lakes continue to have all rights in a shipwreck until and if they relinquish them in writing to the U. S. Corps of Engineers, which may then assign the rights to another party upon request. Because of this law and because of the whack that governments insist on getting from at least certain kinds of sunken treasure, there is always an air of stealth and secrecy surrounding salvage operators, and at times the manner and method of their coming and going is remindful of Mark Twain's laconic history of certain characters on the frontier:

"They stole into the Territory; they stole the Territory; they stole out of the Territory."

Great salvage operations have been conducted on the Great Lakes, notably the modern raising of the ore carrier

George M. Humphrey in 1944 by Captain John Roen after it had sunk in the Straits of Mackinac. This was a million-dollar piece of work by a onetime Charlevoix sailing master whose first tug was built in Charlevoix harbor by Captain Roy A. Ranger, last of the famed Mackinac-boat builders. But by the very nature of its get-rich-quick formula a certain dubious cloud hovers around most searching expeditions for sunken treasure.

Another recent case that put the *Pewabic* back into the headlines and revived her ninety-year-old story, was the news of the rival outfits off Tawas Point in Lake Huron who were racing each other to locate the bones of the *Kitty Reeves*. She supposedly went down in that area in 1870 with 450 tons of copper ingots, almost double the *Pewabic's* load, and worth a quarter of a million dollars on today's market. A retired Ohio grocer named Julius Roth claimed to hold a federal permit that entitled him to search for the copper cargo, but this failed to daunt the other search party from Saginaw aboard a two-masted schooner combing the scene. What finally happened is a mystery. They may have located the treasure and divided the loot or perhaps they quietly folded their sails and stole away.

There remains, however, little mystery about the *Pewabic*. The secret of her strongbox was at last unlocked after more than half a century. Money was found, quite a lot of money; in fact, a heartbreakingly large amount.

To find that money and to salvage the copper, five men had given their lives, strangled to death inside iron hats and clumsy underwater gear. Then, in the year 1914, two men went down in a diving bell that measured eight by seven feet. One of the glass windows in the bell cracked and the treasure hunters were drowned before they could be hauled to the surface.

Finally, in 1917, with copper at premium prices, Captain Fred Ermish of Sandusky brought to the historic scene an expedition fitted out with excellent salvage equipment and new-type Leavitt diving suits. He was guided to the exact spot of the shipwreck by an extraordinary throwback in time.

On the evening when the *Meteor* rammed into the *Pewabic,* a boy happened to be walking the beach on Thunder Bay Island. He watched the steamboats collide in fascinated horror, and the place where the *Pewabic* sank was branded on his memory. The boy's name was John Persons. He grew up to become a sailing master and a member of the lighthouse department at Thunder Bay Island. To members of the latest salvage expedition he pointed out the place marked forever on his mind that ill-fated evening fifty-two years before, and they located the wreck right where he had told them it would be.

Divers were lowered from the 130-foot salvage boat in suits that had been tested off Grand Traverse Bay in Lake Michigan at depths of 265 feet. There the terrific pressure had flattened out the gear until the men looked like cardboard cutouts stuck to the bottom, able to survive, but helpless to move their legs or arms which had stiffened into grotesque poses. Since then the suits had been improved, and the divers on Thunder Bay in Lake Huron were able to make successful descents to a depth greater than had ever been reached on the Great Lakes.

At 175 to 185 feet below the surface, the divers explored the *Pewabic,* careful not to snag their air hoses in the wreckage, carrying on a running conversation with the men above at the pumps. They reported huge chunks and slabs of solid copper, and fastened lines to the stuff.

The rig aboard the salvage boat included a derrick with a one-hundred-foot boom capable of hoisting a hundred tons, with a five-fingered crab that could take a twelve-foot bite out of anything on the bottom. Up from their ninety-year-long submersion came huge nuggets of pure copper from the Keweenaw bonanza range, the largest of these North Country nuggets weighing five tons.

Salvage operations extended over the spring of 1917, depending on weather which, although reasonably moderate for the season on Lake Huron, allowed the men to work only an average of two days a week. Final results of the copper salvage from the original cargo of 250 to 350 tons yielded fifty-five tons, which brought over $30,000, enough to pay all expenses and leave a small profit. The big expectancy, the bonus to boot, the real treasure that everyone anticipated and awaited in finger-crossed suspense was, of course, what rumor had reported, in the *Pewabic's* strongbox. Let Captain Ermish tell the story in his own words:

"Our big disappointment came upon our fourth trip. The very much coveted ship's strongbox was located and brought to the surface. I hastily opened it with bars, hoping to find the $50,000 (treasure always increases in the telling), which we had expected would be in gold. Imagine our feelings when we saw that it was paper money, put up in sealed packages. The paper had been so thoroughly saturated that it had become a soggy mass of pulp which resembled somewhat the scales found on the bottom of a well-used teakettle. A part of some of the bills could be identified but not enough, we believed, to be of any value."

A five-dollar bill was found intact aboard the sunken *Pewabic,* and a host of other items saw the light again after that night of terror off Thunder Bay Island so many years in the past: a dollar gold piece, a ruby ring, a ring set with sapphires, little jade ornaments, a jewel box containing two watches, box-toed shoes and slippers, spectacles, walking sticks, padlocks, Civil War revolvers, rubbers, buttons, tintypes in a perfect state of preservation, books that could still be read, dishes, knives and forks bearing the name *Pewabic,* skeletons waiting patiently in cabins, an unfinished game of cards on a folding table, coins jingling in pockets, hairnets, woolen shawls, horses' hoofs, canned sardines, salted fish in barrels, mixed pickles, and a considerable amount of sarsaparilla pop.

Captain Ermish reported that members of his expedition

drank some of that ancient beverage on top of the sardines and thought the combination, intended for snacks aboard the *Pewabic* in the 1865 season of navigation, not so bad in the twentieth century.

Indeed, the pure and ice-cold waters of Lake Huron had preserved all but the human lives, 125 of them, that had been lost with the *Pewabic* in the seventh worst disaster in Great Lakes history.

8. November 7 to 12, 1913

Seldom a November blows itself off the calendar without having brewed a great storm on the Great Lakes, such as the November 18, 1958, gale that spelled doom for the *Carl D. Bradley*. But among these great storms there have been four giants of their kind creating epics of violence and destruction, leaving in their wake incredible legends that are too wild for fiction and therefore must be confined to the naked bones of stark truth.

Although these storm kings raged across the Great Lakes in general, each of the four giants chose out one particular Lake on which to visit such a preponderant loss of life and shipping that the name of the mass murderer has been attached to the scene of his greatest crimes. The big blows that dealt unparalleled disaster are known simply as the Lake Huron storm of November, 1913; the Lake Superior storm of November, 1905; Lake Erie's Black Friday of October, 1916; Lake Michigan's Armistice Day storm of November, 1940.

Sailors who were in these storms speak of them with a fierce pride. They may argue the force of Lake Superior's 1905 storm against Lake Huron's 1913 storm, but they deny anyone the right to mention any other storm in the same breath with these four.

During an interview with the two survivors of the *Bradley*

at Charlevoix hospital, a reporter asked First Mate Fleming if he had ever been in a worse storm. The forty-two-year-old veteran officer looked sidewise at young deck watchman Frank Mays over on the other cot and then smiled as if the newsman had asked a foolish question.

"I was in Lake Michigan's 1940 storm," he said, "when seas broke spray sixty, seventy, eighty feet high aboard the *T. W. Robinson* on Lake Huron."

On November 7, first day of the long storm on Lake Huron in 1913, many a home and apartment along the Detroit and St. Clair rivers held anxious occupants when the wind began to rattle at the windows and pile up snowdrifts on the cobblestoned pavement of water-front Jefferson Avenue. An atmosphere of dread and fearful waiting prevailed in every sailor's home throughout that storm, a lamp-lit vigil as if by a sick bedside where wives and families whisper out the doubtful hours in the suspense of wondering whether the patient will survive the crisis. This tension communicated to the youngest child, nursing infants drawing it in from their mothers' breasts.

Lakemen of today, who were small boys at the time, seem to remember two pictures vividly, the way two separate lightning flashes might momentarily illuminate an eery darkness — the gray haunting vision of a huge long freighter wallowing upside down in angry water and floating closer and closer to shore, and the wind-swept vision of another great freighter broken in half, with the captain and crew afloat on the aft section, weighted down with tons of ice sculptured into weird shapes by freezing spray as the waves drive relentlessly aboard.

These are impressions of disaster, not photographs, but they paint a backdrop for the scenes to come.

There are times when the casual bad-weather greeting of the Great Lakes region — "God help the sailors on a night like this" — becomes an earnest and fearful prayer. The second week in November, 1913, is marked on the calendar as one of the fateful times.

124

No attempt to dress up the stories about Lake Huron's 1913 storm could improve on the original. They have been told by sailors and retold by historians, and they will be worth the telling as long as there are hero worshippers who want to be lifted from a humdrum world on the wings of brave deeds. These tales afford raw glimpses of life itself at the supreme moment of crisis. They tell of the eternal battle of men against the elements, of courage shining in a dark hour, of sailors going down with their ships as soldiers have gone down on distant battlefields, not without fear perhaps but fighting to the last. Lakemen of today, whose boyhood was inspired by such books as *Heroic Deeds of American Sailors,* know these stories by heart.

It is generally agreed that Lake Huron's 1913 storm was the greatest ever to strike the Lakes. Beyond all argument it must be called the worst in loss of life and in loss of shipping. No other Lake storm in modern history even begins to compare with its toll of 235 lives and forty shipwrecks. No less than eight giant Lake freighters went to the bottom of Lake Huron, disappearing with all hands. Not one survivor reached shore to tell what finally happened to any of the long stout carriers.

This king of storms kept building up strength over a period of days before exploding across Lake Huron in all its savageness. As early as midnight on Thursday, November 6, the steamer *Cornell* ran into bad weather conditions suddenly when fifty miles west of White Fish Point in Lake Superior. With the wind light from the southeast, the steamer all at once ran into an unusually heavy northeast sea. Shortly thereafter the wind backed to northerly, blowing a gale that badly damaged the *Cornell.* This gale lasted until Monday night, November 10, almost driving the steamer on shore.

At noon on Friday, November 7, Coast Guard stations and weather bureau offices in ports along Lake Superior hoisted white pennants above square red flags with black centers. Streaming in the wind, these warnings of a northwest storm spurred freighter crews into a hustle down at the loading docks. Captains and mates gave appraising looks at the sky as they ordered hatches battened down and tightly clamped.

Late in the afternoon lighted lanterns replaced the flags at Coast Guard stations and weather posts. But instead of white lanterns above red ones, carrying word that the storm was still a nor'wester, there were red lanterns, one at the top and one at the bottom, with a white lantern in between. This warning, not often hoisted, told that a hurricane, with winds of seventy-four miles an hour and over, was on the way.

That afternoon on Lake Superior the wind already had a fifty-mile velocity and, as it picked up momentum for a visit to Lake Huron, it was driving a blizzard along, too.

The next morning, Saturday, November 8, Assistant Engineer Milton Smith of Port Huron took a look at the weather forecast in Cleveland and walked off the huge 524-foot carrier *Charles S. Price*. He hated to leave his mates at a time when risks were greater, but a man has to make his own decisions and stand or fall by them. He especially hated to say good-bye to his good friend and neighbor, Arz McIntosh of St. Clair, a wheelsman, who was having trouble with his eyes and wanted to quit, too. He almost got Arz to walk off the *Price* with him, and then the wheelsman made his own decision, based on his needing the money for a possible operation:

"No, Milt. I'm sorry. I wish I could get my time and go with you, but I guess I better stick it out for another trip. So long, sailor. See you in Port Huron."

Meanwhile, up on Lake Superior, there had been a false lull in the storm. Carriers that had remained in port or stayed in the shelter of the St. Marys River started to move *down* into Lake Huron. At the other end of the waterway, freighters in Lake Erie and along the Detroit and St. Clair rivers started to move *up* into Huron.

The shipmasters figured they could weather what seemed

to be just another early winter blow. When November rolls around on the Lakes, every minute counts before close of navigation, and chances are taken. As the steamboats ventured out across the troubled waters under a hurrying sky, there were gale flags hoisted in more than a hundred ports, but the long carriers, attending to the nation's business, had been built to ride out storms.

As for the crew, sailors are not a worrisome breed. They had faith in the old man in the pilothouse, faith in the old girl under their feet, and faith in their own fortune. They stretched their lifelines from the fore spar to the boiler-room bulkheads, and in their hearts, if not on their lips, was an old sailing song that spoke their philosophy:

> *A strong nor'wester's blowin', Bill!*
> *Hark! don't ye hear it roar now?*
> *Lord help 'em, how I pities them*
> *Unhappy folks on shore now!*

The storm had, indeed, made folks ashore unhappy. Blizzards paralyzed traffic. Streetcars were stranded by heavy drifts. Train schedules had to be cancelled. A twenty-two-inch snowfall put Cleveland out of business for two days. A park project that had taken Chicago eight years to complete was destroyed by the storm in as many hours. At Milwaukee a new breakwater was smashed to rubble by sledge-hammer waves. Throughout large sections of Michigan and Ontario telephone and telegraph communications were completely out by Sunday, November 9, and it took several days before power lines were working again. The snow was four feet deep in places surrounding Lake Huron.

While the storm was battering the shore line and the harbor cities, causing hundreds of thousands of dollars worth of damage, the violence on Lake Huron is best summed up in the report made by the Lake Carriers Association in the wake of the hurricane:

> No lake master can recall in all his experience a storm of such unprecedented violence with such rapid changes in

127

the direction of the wind and its gusts of such fearful speed. Storms ordinarily of that velocity do not last over four or five hours, but this storm raged for sixteen hours continuously at an average velocity of sixty miles per hour, with frequent spurts of seventy and over.

Obviously, with a wind of such long duration, the seas that were made were such that the lakes are not ordinarily acquainted with. The testimony of masters is that the waves were at least thirty-five feet high and followed each other in quick succession, three waves ordinarily coming one right after the other.

They were considerably shorter than the waves that are formed by the ordinary gale. Being of such height and hurled with such force and such rapid succession, the ships must have been subjected to incredible punishment.

Masters also relate that the wind and sea were frequently in conflict, the wind blowing one way and the sea running in the opposite direction. This would indicate a storm of cyclonic character. It was unusual and unprecedented and it may be centuries before such a combination of forces may be experienced again.

Such a combination of forces came sooner than the Lake Carriers Association expected, only twenty-seven years later, when three large freighters went down, two of them with all hands, in Michigan's November storm of 1940.

Through the storm of 1913, there were long ships passing all day Saturday through the St. Marys River from Lake Superior into Lake Huron; there were long ships passing all night Saturday through the Straits of Mackinac into Lake Huron from Lake Michigan; and there were long ships passing early Sunday morning, November 9, up the Detroit and the St. Clair rivers into Lake Huron from Lake Erie.

Early Sunday morning Howard Mackley, second mate aboard the *Charles S. Price,* mailed a letter to his wife as his boat was passing Detroit. Later that same morning, while the *Price* moved her long length up the St. Clair River toward Lake Huron, he stood in the pilothouse and pulled the whistle in customary salute to his young wife who had come down to the dock at their St. Clair home to wave until the boat was out of sight. There were many others who went to the docks that day, heedless of bad weather, to wave good-bye from Marine City, Marysville, Port Huron, Sarnia, and the other ports that last saw the doomed ships before Lake Huron swallowed them forever. Nor was she the only sailor's wife never to sleep a wink that night.

The newspapers of Monday morning, November 10, were full of the damage done by the storm on land, and concern was expressed that some Lake vessels might have been caught out on open water and run into trouble, but there were no reports of disaster.

Unknown to the world ashore, at least eighteen stout-hearted boats struggled on Lake Huron all day Sunday and into the wild night. A few of them may have ridden out the storm all day Monday and even survived that night until Tuesday, November 11. But all of them were wrecked at one time or another. The more fortunate ones crashed ashore and most of the crews were saved. Eight of the proudest and longest and costliest sank, no one knows exactly where or when, because of the grim adage: "Dead men tell no tales."

After scanning his Monday-morning newspaper, Captain Plough of the Lakeview lifesaving station north of Port Huron swept the heavy seas with his glass. Far out on the Lake he saw what appeared to be the hull of a vessel from which the sticks and the smokestacks had been lost. He sent out a tug to investigate.

The tug skipper had to rub his eyes and pinch himself to believe what he saw. In the strangest wreck sighted in all his long Lake experience, a huge steel freighter was floating bottom side up, the bow about thirty feet clear of water but the stern dipping down until it was impossible to tell the length of the carrier. Every visible part of the hulk was coated with ice and there were no identifying marks in view.

129

Baffled, the tug skipper circled the wreck for hours and even went after a diver finally, but the water was too rough for a descent. Its name plate lost or below the surface, the wreck was nicknamed the mystery ship and a mystery ship it remained for almost a week, afloat in the Lake outside Port Huron.

On Tuesday a farmer, looking out from a high cliff near Grand Bend along the Canadian shore, sighted the first body given up by the storm. Washed in and then out by successive waves, the body's arms were extended from the elbows in such a way as to create the impression of a dead man pleading for help.

Farther along the beach two more bodies were found. All three bore life jackets with the name *Wexford*. A smashed lifeboat with the same identification turned in conclusive evidence that the sturdy 270-foot Canadian package freighter, a typical British tramp built in Scotland to weather the gales of the seven seas, had gone down with her crew of seventeen on Lake Huron after riding out many an ocean storm.

With telephone lines still down and roads almost impassable with snow, a railroad conductor brought news into Sarnia that more bodies were coming ashore up the Lake. The next identifying life jackets came from the giant 550-foot grain carrier *James C. Carruthers*, Canada's largest and newest in the trade. She had been bound down from Lake Superior, out of Fort William with 340,000 bushels of wheat, making only the third trip of her first season when she met the end with her crew of nineteen.

All week long the dying storm carried wreckage and bodies into the Lake Huron beaches. Many of the scenes of discovery spoke their own mute stories of heroism. Men were found with their heads bowed across life preservers as if praying, men with ice in their hair. Men were found wrapped in each other's arms and men were found in frozen clusters. Herbert Jones, a steward aboard the *Charles S. Price*, was found with his apron frozen stiff around him, as

130

though he had been about to prepare a meal when disaster struck.

Mrs. Walker, stewardess on the 440-foot freighter *Argus*, must have had her last moments heartened by sailor deeds as gallant as anything celebrated in the courts of chivalry. Her knights in shining armor were the engineer and the captain. The body of the stewardess came ashore near Kincardine wrapped in the engineer's heavy coat and buoyed up by the captain's own life preserver. When the body of Captain Paul Gutch, master of the *Argus*, washed into the beach, it was without a life preserver.

Hope for missing vessels dwindled throughout the week and they had to be counted lost as bodies in marked life preservers identified ill-starred ships. Wrecked on Lake Huron with all hands, besides the *Wexford*, the *Price*, the *Carruthers*, and the *Argus*, were the 440-foot freighter *Hydrus*, the 269-foot Canadian package freighter *Regina*, the 452-foot *John A. McGean*, bound out of Sandusky with coal for South Chicago, and the 524-foot *Isaac M. Scott* which was sailing up the open horseshoe and heading around for Milwaukee when her good fortune spilled out. A total of 178 sailor lives, men and women, came to an untimely end when these eight carriers disappeared in the storm, none of them to be seen again except the mystery ship.

In one of its wild blows the storm created a chain of accidents that resulted in other shipwrecks but not such grave misfortune. *U. S. Lightship No. 61* was hurled ashore at the head of the St. Clair River during the early hours of the big wind. Then the steamer *Matthew Andrews*, heavy with iron ore, came plowing down Lake Huron in the dark late afternoon. She had safely breasted the mountainous seas and met every buffet of wind across the open Lake. Another few minutes of tricky steering and riding the waves and she might have been snug in the sheltered bottleneck of the St. Clair River, but Captain Lampoh saw the lightship through the snow squalls and decided to anchor for the night rather than take any further chances. However, the lightship was not on the place where it should have been, and his boat went crashing on the Corsica Shoals.

On that identical Sunday, early in the morning, Captain A. C. May had taken the 550-foot *H. B. Hawgood* out of the St. Clair River into Lake Huron. About noon he sighted the *Charles S. Price* a little bit north of Sand Beach and he observed that she was making bad weather of her passage. After watching how the *Price* worked in the heavy seas, he decided to take no further chances and turned the *Hawgood* back toward Port Huron to get her off the open Lake. As he was returning he met the up-bound *Regina* fifteen miles south of Harbor Beach and at 3:30 in the afternoon he saw the *Isaac M. Scott* five or six miles north of Fort Gratiot light. That was the last time the *Regina* and the *Scott* were seen by the living. They vanished without trace.

Soon after meeting the *Scott,* Captain May himself ran into trouble. Also shaping his course by the Huron lightship that had broken from its anchorage, he drove the *Hawgood* aground two miles above the mouth of the St. Clair River.

Two of the doomed vessels that the cautious skipper had seen were to figure, not once but several times, in the grim week to come as farm wagons lumbered through the deep snow with bodies recovered on remote beaches to the little Ontario towns where inquests were held and relatives or friends could identify the dead. One of these places was Thedford, about thirty miles from Sarnia, where the bodies were lined up under blankets on the floor of a typical combination furniture store and funeral parlor, with couches and upholstered chairs and four-poster beds moved aside to make way for drowned sailors.

Men and women, faces sharp with sorrow or swollen in grief, filed past the bodies and gazed intently at each face as the blankets were lifted one by one. The young wife of the second mate, who had blown the whistle to her as the *Charles S. Price* passed up the St. Clair River into Lake Huron Sunday morning, had to rub the tears from her eyes every time she looked; but she shook her head all the way down the line. Her husband's body was never found.

Milton Smith, the assistant engineer who had quit the *Price* in Cleveland, also came to Thedford. The first body he was asked to identify gave him a shock. Despite the ruthless battering of the storm, he recognized his former chief, John Groundwater.

"That's big good-natured John," he said. "All the boys liked him."

"Are you sure?" demanded the coroner.

"Sure I'm sure. I worked under him all season. I saw him just last Saturday. I ought to know. Why? What's the trouble?"

"If he was chief engineer aboard the *Price*," said the coroner, "then why has he got a *Regina* life preserver wrapped around him?"

The question has echoed from 1913 to this day. Other bodies identified as from the crew of the *Price* were picked up also wearing life preservers marked *Regina*. It may be speculated that the two boats were slammed together in the storm so that men passed from one deck to the other, seizing any life preserver handy. Perhaps, as the ships were sinking, life preservers thrown to those knocked into the water by the theoretical collision were grabbed at by members of both crews struggling to stay afloat. All this granted for the sake of argument, why were no *Regina* men ever found wearing *Price* life preservers? Somehow the crews must have met and intermingled in that hurricane-blizzard. Perhaps the *Price* went down so suddenly that her crew had no time to put on life preservers and the crew of the nearby *Regina*, sinking more slowly, had a chance to toss the drowning men extra life preservers that were aboard their boat. Perhaps a thousand things. Only Lake Huron knows what really happened and she has kept her secret forty-seven years.

Another strange case involving identification, but one quickly solved, came when a sister of young John Thompson heard that bodies from the wreck of the *James Carruthers*

133

had washed ashore. From Sarnia she notified her family in Hamilton, Ontario, and her father hurried to the port of Goderich where he identified a body which bore every resemblance to his son, even to the tattooed initials "J. T." and a well-remembered scar. He brought the body home.

Meanwhile, the young sailor himself had changed ships without notifying his family. Safe on Lake Ontario, he had the experience of reading in a Toronto newspaper that his body had been found on a Lake Huron beach following the *Carruthers* disaster. He hurried home to find a coffin in his father's parlor and preparations underway for his own funeral.

Some of the bodies scattered along the Lake Huron shore and marked by the mournful circling of sea gulls never were identified. In the cemetry at Goderich may still be seen what might well be called "the tomb of the unknown sailors." Here five men lie buried at the foot of a red obelisk on which an anchor is carved above the inscription: "A memorial to the unidentified seamen whose lives were lost in the Great Lakes disaster of Nov. 9th, 1913." On the opposite side of the obelisk there is only a single word, but it carries the highest title on the Lakes: SAILORS.

On Saturday, November 15, at the close of the most disastrous week in Lake Huron's history, the secret of the mystery ship was at last unlocked. Still floating upside down in the open Lake above Port Huron, she had been the object of much guesswork. There was even wild conjecture that another vessel might be found under her bow.

A diver ended this theorizing by going down and working his way around the hull. He located the name plate and it identified the long carrier that had figured in the story of the Lake Huron storm from start to finish, the 524-foot ore boat *Charles S. Price* on which assistant engineer Milton Smith had decided not to take the last trip.

There was no other vessel under the bow of the *Price*. The diver found that the buoyancy of the hull was due to imprisoned air, now slowly escaping in two streams of bubbles. Careful investigating revealed not a sign of any collision and so the mystery of why *Price* men had been washed ashore wearing *Regina* life preservers was deeper than ever. Finally, on November 17, the huge three-year-old freighter which had been considered capable of withstanding any storm and which had been equipped with every known device to insure its safety, sank from sight and joined the seven of her sisters who had preceded her by going down with all hands a week before.

In 1957 a historical marker was erected at Port Sanilac, Michigan, along the highway overlooking Lake Huron. This maritime plaque is inscribed:

THE GREAT STORM
OF 1913

Sudden tragedy struck the Great Lakes on November 9, 1913, when a storm, whose equal veteran sailors could not recall, left in its wake death and destruction. The grim toll was 235 seamen drowned, ten ships sunk, and more than twenty others driven ashore. Here on Lake Huron all 178 crewmen on the eight ships claimed by its waters were lost. For sixteen terrible hours gales of cyclonic fury made man and his machines helpless.

A sign along a Michigan highway, a memorial in a Canadian graveyard across the Lake — these are the aftermath of the storm, these and the haunting cries in every shrill November wind.

9. Huron Rescues and Flying Dutchmen

There have been great rescues on Lake Huron and the great storm of 1913 set the stage for many a heroic venture by lifesaving crews and tugboats. At the very tip of the thumb of Michigan's mitten, on the verge of the thumbnail, so to speak, is Pointe aux Barques, which is often called Point of Arks, thoughtlessly no doubt, but giving the French name a sound Biblical echo.

From here went out one of the gallant rescue teams when the giant coal carrier *Howard M. Hanna, Jr.* was shipwrecked by the lunatic seas off Saginaw Bay on Sunday night. She had cleared Lorain, Ohio, with a full load for Milwaukee where she was to have laid up for the winter — another last trip of the season.

Not far from where the *Price* and the *Regina* were last sighted making bad weather on the Lake, Captain Richardson ran into serious trouble with the big *Hanna*. He was unable to keep the steamer's head to the sea. She rolled and pounded in the trough of the mountainous waves. Half an hour before she struck the shore off Pointe aux Barques, the *Hanna* lost her rudder and her smokestack crashed overboard.

Smashed aground, the long carrier began to break up, her decks lashed with icy spray, her crew, including thirty-two men and one woman, battling to escape death from exposure, and to keep from being washed away. Slowly the boat began to settle in deep water. The waves rolled heavily across her deck.

The lifesaving crew at Pointe aux Barques sighted distress signals and took off into the storm. In the finest tradition of the service, those Coast Guard men reached the *Hanna* when her deck was within six inches of being under water and they saved every member of her half-frozen crew.

This story gives the pattern of a dozen other rescues

136

during the storm that sent twenty other vessels careening into the beach here and there along Lake Huron's shore.

The story of the greatest modern rescue in Great Lakes annals, involving the quick thinking of a captain, the heroism of an engineer, and gallant action by others, properly begins during the storm of 1913 and continues to the end in 1945, because the complete story of the boat's career is the strange tale of a fatal nemesis, an avenging fury that pursued her across the Lakes and finally caught up with its victim.

The *Hamonic* was one of the floating palaces representative of an era fast disappearing on the inland seas. With her glistening black hull, her stately decks with white cabins, her huge single smokestack painted red and white with a black smoke band at the top, she was a familiar sight up and down the Lakes for almost half a century. In her day she carried untold thousands of happy excursionists who could enjoy a vacation cruise with all the comforts of life ashore: a barber shop, a beauty salon, a snack bar, banquet tables, lofty observation windows, and a ballroom.

Two sisters had the *Hamonic*, the flagship *Noronic* and the *Quebec*. All three were destined to die by fire, the *Noronic* in the ninth worst disaster in Great Lakes history.

The first foreshadowing of eventual doom came to the *Hamonic* up on Lake Superior during the 1913 storm which dealt out wholesale death and punishment across America's largest body of fresh water. Out very late in the season, and one of the few passenger boats still operating, the *Hamonic* was caught on the open Lake at the height of the storm. As the gale blew out her pilothouse windows, the captain, standing on shattered glass, decided to run her aground in Whitefish Bay in hopes of preventing further damage. She rode out the storm and, with her crew wielding axes to clear away the wreckage, she proceeded to her home port of Sarnia at the foot of Lake Huron.

Her second brush with death came in the same area and

in the identical month when, on November 6, 1925, about eighty miles above Whitefish Point on Lake Superior, the *Hamonic* ran into a howling gale and blizzard which snapped off her propeller in heavy seas. At once she dropped into the trough of the waves, wallowing and rolling out of control at the mercy of Lake Superior.

· The captain started to blow distress signals and showed a red flare, finally sighted by the large freighter *Richard Trimble* which had been buffeted so hard by the storm that she had decided to turn around and head back for shelter at the Soo. The *Trimble* came alongside the *Hamonic* shortly after midnight but was unable to offer any assistance other than the comfort of her company throughout the troubled darkness. At dawn her captain reported that in fighting the storm thus far he had gone sleepless for forty-eight hours and without food for the past thirty hours. Conditions aboard the *Hamonic* were no better.

At dawn the *Trimble* managed to pick up a three-quarter-inch line tied to a life belt floated from the *Hamonic,* and in this way a heavy ten-inch towline was fished aboard and fastened between the two boats, while the crews braved the assault of icy seas that lashed the decks. Then the *Trimble* plowed toward sheltered waters with the *Hamonic* in tow, fetching her into the comparative quiet off Point Iroquois above the Soo where the passenger liner cast off the line and let go her hook. Once again she had survived near-fatal danger and come to safe anchor.

The third time was the charm. On her regular weekly cruise the floating palace started out about midnight from Detroit on what proved to be her final trip. Captain Horace L. Beaton took her up the St. Clair River, passed under the Blue Water Bridge, and brought her into dock at Point Edward a few miles above Sarnia. The lines were made fast about 4:30 Tuesday morning, July 17, 1945. Captain Beaton had taken pains to bring her in gently so as not to disturb the sleeping passengers — many of whom no doubt were dreaming of the next day's trip up into Lake

Superior — and then he retired to his own cabin and fell asleep.

The *Hamonic* was berthed at a long dock paralleled by a frame warehouse. A pile of coal had been heaped high just astern and a steam shovel with a clam bucket stood ready to pour fuel into ship bunkers. At the other end of the dock there were boxcars loaded with inflammable merchandise, and along the entire length of the oily floor of the tinder-dry warehouse there were piled highly combustible packing cases and cartons stuffed against breakage with straw and excelsior paper. To top off this incendiary ambush, a fresh offshore breeze began to blow.

When the stevedores and dock wallopers came to work in the morning, the gas engine that powered their conveyor equipment turned cranky and while a mechanic was working on it to locate the trouble, a burst of flames shot out of the motor. The warehouse caught fire and started going up in smoke. Sparks flew everywhere. The boxcars were quickly ablaze. Raging out of control, flames, fanned by the offshore breeze, leaped across the dock onto the decks of the *Hamonic*.

Captain Beaton, still in his pajamas, raced out of his cabin and onto the bridge. With his ship ablaze from stem to stern, he sized up the situation and made a split-second judgment. The *Hamonic* was doomed and her passengers could not be saved where she was berthed because the flaming dock barred every escape in that direction.

He decided that the only chance to save lives was to reverse his engines and back the *Hamonic* along the dock away from the tongues of fire and suffocating clouds of smoke. He had his eye on the huge coal pile and the steam shovel beside it as he gave orders to clear the lines and grabbed the engine-room telegraph to ring below. Fearful that the flames might already have driven the engine crew away, his heart was in his throat until the propeller began to churn and the big boat started to back up.

Down in the engine room alone was the Chief himself,

139

James D. Neilson. He stood at the throttle of the *Hamonic* and carried out Captain Beaton's signals while the fire licked at him from the walls and dropped down on him from the ceiling. The storage room for processed foods was located just overhead the engine room and the cans, their contents expanded by the intense heat, were dropping through the fire-eaten floor above and bursting all around the chief like hand grenades packed with red-hot fruit and vegetables for shrapnel. Never perhaps has any hero stuck to his post in the face of such a strange and deadly bombardment.

Last man to step off the mass of solid flame which was the *Hamonic,* Chief Neilson, hemmed in on all sides by fire, saw a bare opening opposite the dock and when he appeared at that opening, he saw Captain Beaton who had come around in a small boat to get him.

Meanwhile, rescue operations were in full swing from both the Canadian and the American shores. Coast Guard men and firemen from Port Huron raced across the St. Clair River to the scene. Private speedboats and cruisers picked up survivors in the water as many passengers and crew members leaped for life from the flames.

A remarkable aspect of this wholesale rescue was the part played by the steam shovel on the coal dock. The *Hamonic* had been backed up to where her bow came within reach of the boom on the crane. Elmer Kleinsmith, operator of the steam shovel, shouted to the crowd trapped in the bow:

"When I lower my clam bucket to the deck, ten of you climb in. Take it easy. I'll be back for more until you're all clear."

He steered the crane of the steam shovel until it pointed over the bow of the *Hamonic,* then lowered the boom to pick up ten people and hoisted them to the safety of the dock. Time and again he repeated this operation until all at the bow were saved.

Eventually towed away to be cut up into scrap metal, the *Hamonic* smouldered along the waterfront for several days, but she was no funeral pyre. Thanks to stout hearts and cool heads, not a life was lost in the conflagration except her own.

But for every *Hamonic* there are a haunted number of Flying Dutchmen on Lake Huron who sailed away with all their passengers and crews. Such a disappearance is less common today but no less final than it was in the past century when hazards existed unknown to Lake traffic now.

At the height of the lumber trade, billions of feet of timber were rafted from Cheboygan and from Saginaw Bay down to Detroit. Enormous rafts of logs towed by barges were taken the length of Lake Huron and through the connecting waters into Lake Erie, bound for Toledo, Cleveland, Buffalo, and the Tonawandas. Often a single logging company, the Alger-Smith outfit, had four rafts, totaling eight million board feet of lumber, on Lake Huron at the same time. They put together so many of these floating menaces to navigation that they had $40,000 invested in rafting chains alone.

An enormous raft headed up the Lake and bound for Chicago never reached the Straits of Mackinac. A little way out of Alpena it broke up in a storm on Thunder Bay, scattering four million feet of deadly driftwood along the shore and across Huron, making the waters dangerous for many seasons. A heavy log, half of its length submerged and lost to view, could tear the bottom out of any wooden schooner or steamboat. These monsters formed floating reefs and pinnacles of doom, uncharted hazards lurking in the night, battering rams hurled about by heavy seas.

In their era the juggernauts of pine and hardwood also caused shipwrecks by carrying away channel buoys and markers, and when they were finally outlawed, their replacements proved equally perilous in turn. Called "the sow and her pigs" or "the hen and her chickens" by Lake sailors, among other names less complimentary, these outfits were long tows, a steamboat carrying 600,000 feet of lumber often towing four barges, each with a similar load, the

141

whole shebang stretching half a mile, with the taut tow-line between the craft deadlier than any sea serpent. In smoke or fog or storm by day or dead of night, a vessel might sail directly into such a tow and never realize what sent her to the bottom with all hands. There were cases where ships had their upper works raked cleanly off before the lookout had the slightest glimpse of danger.

For two generations, as already observed in the Lake Michigan section, smoke was a unique and dreaded peril on the Lakes. How many Flying Dutchmen were sent sailing forever by the palls of gloom hung over the inland seas by forest fires will never be known but must be guessed at in the account of shipwrecks where survivors lived to tell the story. In 1871, year of the great Chicago fire, the shipping news noted that this fire, on October 8, and forest fires of the same date which ravaged the Lake region, caused a dense smoke to hang over the waters and made navigation extremely hazardous. A shipwreck on Lake Huron ten days later, in which smoke played a part, was pointed out:

Loss of the Coburn. — One of the greatest disasters of the season was the loss of the propeller Coburn, Captain Demond, of E. B. Ward's Lake Superior line, October 18, in Saginaw Bay, whereby sixteen passengers, the captain and fifteen of the crew, including every officer, except the second mate, were lost. There were upward of seventy persons on board, about forty passengers, and a crew of thirty-five. Among the passengers were eight women and five children, and two families in the steerage. The Coburn was bound from Duluth to Buffalo with wheat and flour. Shortly after passing Presque Isle harbor, the wind commenced blowing from the northeast, and there was so much smoke on the lake that the engine was checked down, and the steamer held head to the wind. A few hours later the wind veered to the southwest and blew a terrific gale. The Coburn labored heavily, but shipped no water of consequence until her rudder was torn off when she drifted into the trough of the sea, making her roll heavily, shifting her cargo. Holes were cut in her bulwarks, and the crew set to work throwing her cargo overboard, but the waves washed over her, tore off her smokestacks, and she began settling. Soon the fireman's gang was stove in and the water rushed into the hold in immense volumes. Ten men got into one of the yawls and seven into the other, leaving the lifeboats bottom side up, untouched. When the *Coburn* went down Captain Demont stood just aft of the texas with his hand on the rail. There were quite a number of persons on the hurricane deck when it floated off, but they were seen only a short time. The *Coburn* was a fine, staunch, new propeller of 867 tons burden, well found in every department, having come out in June, 1870.

The cholera that swept up the Lakes during the Black Hawk War and turned stately schooners and palatial steamboats into plague ships during intermittent epidemics spawned in Asia and encargoed to America for generations, may have put its share of Flying Dutchmen in motion. The first harbinger of woe, the steamer *Henry Clay*, left Buffalo with 370 soldiers bound for Chicago in the summer of 1832. When she was driven ashore and abandoned at Port Huron, only half that number had enough life left in them to attempt an escape from the death ship. They scrambled to the dock in terrified flight. Some fled to the woods, some to the fields, while others lay down in the streets where they died as passing traffic gave them wide berth. A few straggled to Detroit where the kindhearted innkeeper who gave them shelter proved responsible for an epidemic that cost hundreds of lives in the city.

From lunatic captains to cholera at the helm, the Flying Dutchmen sail the Lakes.

Small boats by the score have disappeared on Lake Huron in recent years, swallowed no one knows where by the vast engulfing waters. But no large ship has vanished without trace since the whaleback *Clifton,* another of the "unsinkables" and skippered by Emmet Gallagher of Beaver Island, sailed through a crack in Lake Huron on September 22, 1924, taking all hands — a total of 28 — down with her.

143

Lake Huron has its legend of the "two lost tows," barges that cut adrift in the middle of the night during a storm, never to be seen again. The tugboat captain looked back at dawn and rubbed his eyes to see only half his tow in sight. He raced the tug in wide circles on a hopeless rescue search while his mind raced in circles wondering what had happened.

The Lake of the Hurons also has its true stories of mysterious disappearances in broad daylight and balmy weather. Three-masted schooners have been seen with their proud sails flying like summer clouds on Georgian and Thunder and Saginaw Bay, seen one moment and vanished the next. A blink of the eye by the watcher, a turn of the head ashore, and the mirrored water no longer reflected these stately vessels. Somehow, in the twinkling of time, they were swept from view forever by the magic of the great blue Lake.

The Flying Dutchmen will always sail on Lake Huron in clouds that take the shape of canvas all a-taunto in the wind and in the mist that marks the timeless passage of lost steamboats. Across the years they have gone down with all hands to rise again in ghost patrols that haunt Lake Huron's shores — the steamboats *Keystone State, Water Witch, City of Detroit,* and *Eclipse;* the schooners *Kate L. Bruce* and the *Celtic.* Their names are legion.

They sailed through a crack in the Lake whose every change of mood is watched with deep respect by men who risk their lives to brave her sudden temper. The ultimate measure of that respect is told in this fresh-water proverb: No canny Scot (and there were no better sailors on the Lakes) ever paid in advance for a round-trip ticket on Lake Huron.

STORM THAT BREWED NO GOOD

The preceding Saturday had been a fine day — fine enough for Santa Claus himself to parachute into one northern Michigan community and bring a pre-Christmas treat of candy for youngsters on his sky dive — but the last week of November, 1966, blew off the calendar in a mood reminiscent of the great storm of November, 1913. On Monday the 28th, a howling blizzard gathered power as it swept south, riling up 12-foot waves in Grand Traverse Bay on Lake Michigan. Rocks almost as large as footballs were hurled 300 feet inland by the crashing seas.

The captain and seven crewmen of the steel-laden German freighter *Nordmeer,* aground for nine days on rocky Thunder Bay Shoal off Alpena, braced themselves to weather the blow. Across the state the winds were clocked up to 70 miles per hour, and the Chesapeake and Ohio car ferry *City of Midland No. 41,* with a passenger and crew list of 184 people, was blown onto a sand bar near Ludington, opposite Manitowoc, Wisconsin, with sixty raging miles of Lake Michigan in between. For three days the occupants of the 405-foot *Midland* were marooned within sight of land by the storm.

The brave men aboard the *Nordmeer* were finally forced to abandon their efforts to salvage the ship. Their SOS brought a helicopter to the rescue, plucking them from the dying vessel and whirling them to the waiting Coast Guard cutter *Mackinaw.* Moments later they saw the *Nordmeer* break up, rich prey for divers-of-fortune in better weather.

TEETH OF THE STORM

Down along the Detroit River, early in the morning of the last Monday in November, two sister ships, both owned by the Cambria Steamship Company of Cleveland, a subsidiary of Bethlehem Steel Corporation, were getting ready to resume a long journey up the Lakes and connecting waters. The vessels were the 580-foot steamer *Edward Y. Townsend* and the 603-foot *Daniel J. Morrell,* both of which had put about 60 years of faithful service on fresh water behind them.

The *Townsend* and the *Morrell* had come up from Buffalo over the weekend, clearing Lake Erie in the teeth of the threatening weather, and then casting anchor in Detroit River berths. They were headed north toward Lake Superior, riding with ballast in their holds, destined for Taconite Harbor, Minnesota, to load cargoes of iron ore.

Captain Thomas J. Connelly, 48, of Mentor, Ohio, master of the *Townsend,* was a veteran of 27 years on the water, while the skipper of the *Morrell,* Captain Arthur I. Crawley, Rocky River, Ohio, had 29 years of experience. Although he had earned his master's papers several years in the past, this was Crawley's first season as a captain and his second ship of the year because he had started in the spring with the freighter *Lebanon,* on which he had begun his career the day after graduating from high school. Although the Lakes suited him fine, the 47-year-old bachelor never had wanted his nephews to go on a boat, even in the summer. He had advised them never to become seamen — such a lonesome life. Up early Monday morning, he checked the crew and found the ship still lacked one fireman and three deck hands.

One of the three absent deck hands was Dennis Hale, 26, father of four children, a husky 230-pound six-footer who worked on the Lakes because he made more money there than he could as a chef in the Ashtabula (Ohio) Hotel. When the chance came for him to join the *Morrell's* crew three years before, he jumped at it, and found that he enjoyed life on shipboard, despite a healthy fear of storms. Times when he came home, he and his wife talked about storms, and when they weren't talking about storms they were thinking. She had begged him to quit the boats, and he had promised her finally that this would be his last season.

How many seamen make Hale's promise to their wives, and then go back again the next year for "just one more time"? How many make the promise too late, and never see home again?

Hale had gone home for the weekend, leaving the *Morrell* in Buffalo, intending to drive back there with the family and sign aboard again. But the car broke down on the way so he brought the family back to Ashtabula, then started for Detroit to pick up his ship there, and climbed aboard in the nick of time.

With one of his four missing crewmen back on duty, Captain Crawley started to sail Michigan's mitten, heading for the Thumb area. In his last contact with company headquarters at Cleveland, he radioed that he had weighed anchor from his berth in the Detroit River at 6:55 a.m. because of reports of increasingly bad weather. The *Morrell* passed Windmill Point with Canada on her starboard bow and steamed toward Algonac, Marine City, Harbor Beach, Alpena, and points farther north.

LAST TRIP OF THE SEASON

Aboard the *Morrell's* sister ship *Townsend*, Captain Connelly followed somewhat more leisurely. At 3 p.m. he reported both ships underway, with the *Morrell* ahead. The weather was mean, and getting worse with every gust of wind, as the two old ladies pulled across the Flats and up the St. Clair River into the cold, angry jaws of Lake Huron.

Both ships had undergone the necessary Coast Guard inspections and passed with a clean bill of health. Common to stories told about older vessels, there had been some scuttlebutt about rusty rivets and leakage as in the case of the *Bradley*. In fact, a coal passer aboard the *Morrell* had written his wife a letter several weeks before about the ore carrier's arrival in Escanaba:

"The fog lifted about 7 a.m. this morning so we could get into dock. Two more tubes blew in the boiler. This old boat has just about had it."

On the other side of the story, the *Morrell*, according to one of her former skippers, had the reputation of having passed unscathed through the 1958 storm that sank the *Bradley*, negotiating Lake Superior undamaged in 100-mile-an-hour winds, although it took her 18 hours to make 45 miles.

Entering Lake Huron the two veteran steamers began to feel the full brunt of the storm. Miles ahead of the *Townsend*, the *Morrell* plunged through a heaving jungle of sea. She twisted and groaned under mountainous waves. But there was no indication that the maritime sexagenarian, refitted with new side ballast tanks in 1942, new boilers in 1945, and a new engine in 1956, was in trouble.

Dennis Hale, watchman in the wheelhouse, kept a sharp

lookout across the black wilderness of water. He went off duty at 8 p.m., and went to bed at 9:30, wearing only his undershorts. He kept trying to go to sleep, but he could hear the anchors bouncing around, and books fell from a shelf in his room. In time, however, the big man dozed off, into a twilight zone between sleeping and waking.

With Harbor Beach off the port bow, the *Morrell* and the *Townsend* plunged through the roaring night. Like many another long ship on the Lakes that Monday, they were making the proverbial "last trip of the season," a phrase that always sounded an ominous double meaning and sometimes came true.

CAUGHT IN A CONFUSED SEA

Miles apart and unable to see each other in the blinding snowstorm, the *Townsend* and the *Morrell* kept in touch through radio-telephone, communicating positions, state of the weather, nature of the seas. At 10 p.m. Connelly of the *Townsend* reported winds had reached 50 miles per hour and the seas were 12 feet and building. At the time the *Townsend* was about 8 miles above Harbor Beach. The sea was running from the north-northeast and the north-northwest simultaneously. In effect, both ships were caught in a violent "confused" sea with tides converging on them from two directions at once.

About this same time of night, the freighter *G. A. Tomlinson* passed the *Morrell* and noticed nothing wrong with the other ship.

At one point Captain Connelly considered turning his boat back to the shelter of the St. Clair River, but he felt there was considerable danger of being caught broadside in the swarming seas and unable to get out of the trough.

Captain James A. Van Buskirk, 38, master of the 612-foot *Benson Ford*, overheard the other two skippers talking back and forth. He heard them discussing taking refuge in Thunder Bay, near Alpena, but although he stayed on duty all night, he never heard a distress call of any kind at any time. The *Ford* was downbound from Escanaba, carrying 10,200 tons of iron ore pellets.

148

SKIPPERS TALK WHILE HURON ROARS

Captain Connelly also remained in his pilothouse all night and heard no distress signals. He did pick up a conversation from the Coast Guard cutter *Acacia,* also out in the swirling roar of Lake Huron. The *Acacia* had run into trouble. Rolling heavily and with a boat loose on deck, she turned back.

As the storm developed and the winds reached 65 miles per hour, with the waves cresting at 25 feet or more, the *Townsend* began to roll 15 to 20 degrees. The bow would pitch into the seas and, as it came back, it took solid water over the decks. The water came aboard forward and went off aft. As the bow pitched into the towering seas, the wheel (propeller) was thrown out of the water.

Attempting to adjust to the gale, the *Townsend's* skipper abandoned the regular northbound channel, heading northeast out into the Lake, holding her bow almost head-on into the waves and wind. The *Morrell's* skipper kept steering north-northwest, following the steamer channel, a course that put his ship's starboard side against the wind and waves.

The seas were building so high and fast that Captain Connelly restricted the forward-end crew from going back aft from 10 p.m. to 10 a.m., except for one man who was allowed to get sandwiches.

SISTER SHIPS PART FOREVER

The two skippers kept talking through the storm. When Captain Crawley of the *Morrell* called Connelly at 11:50 p.m., the *Townsend's* master picked up the phone and said he would call back. His ship had started to blow around in the seas and he was too busy to talk. He returned Crawley's call at 12:15 a.m., a quarter of an hour into a new day that threatened to be much worse than the old.

The *Morrell's* master mentioned that his ship had just gone through the same thing as the *Townsend* and that he was working to keep her from being blown around sideways in the waves. The conversation between the two captains was brief. Both were fully occupied with the job of keeping their boats

149

afloat. They wished each other good luck. That was the last word exchanged between them.

The two freighters went their ways, the *Morrell* having reported her position as about 25 miles north of Harbor Beach off the Thumb of Michigan's mitten, an area long feared as a graveyard for Great Lakes ships and seamen. The sister ships had parted forever, each steaming into the unknown through a storm that Captain Connelly called the worst he had ever seen on the Great Lakes.

DEADLIEST DRAMA OF ALL

Since the previous midnight and all day long the turbulent Tuesday of November 29, 1966, the deadliest drama of all was being acted out on the stage of the Upper Lakes. At 9 a.m. the *Townsend* contacted Cleveland, reporting to the chief dispatcher for the Bethlehem Steel fleet. She radioed that her gyroscope was out of order and she was steering north-northeast, "holding into wind at 2 miles per hour in monstrous seas."

At 2 p.m. the *Townsend* was heading for Cove Island toward the top of Lake Huron. She reported her last contact with the *Morrell* had been at 12:15 a.m., when the *Morrell* was 12 to 15 miles ahead.

Another company ship, the *Arthur B. Homer,* had been asked to watch for the *Morrell.* At 6:40 p.m. the *Homer* called in that she was unable to make contact, but noted the storm might have damaged the *Morrell's* antenna.

Nowhere, aship or ashore, had any signal of distress been heard. Central Radio in Rogers City, which handles ship-to-shore radio-telephone traffic for the Upper Lakes, regularly monitored the Standard AM ship distress frequency, but for varying periods Monday and Tuesday night, and into early Wednesday, frequency was not received because of static from heavy snow. Central Radio also monitored the FM but had no record of any call for help on that frequency. The *Morrell,* among other long ships passing up and down the Lakes during the blow, carried both AM and FM equipment.

150

So another long, bitter-cold night of sound and fury swallowed Lake Huron in darkness that beat like the legendary Indian drum, counting the number of shipwreck victims over and over again.

UNREPORTED AT THE SOO

Meanwhile in Cleveland, Arthur Dobson, chief dispatcher for the Bethlehem Steel fleet, had become increasingly concerned about two of his ships. When the reporting station at the Soo failed to mention the arrival of either the *Townsend* or the *Morrell* at the canal Wednesday morning, he put in an urgent call for information. The Coast Guard located the *Townsend* anchored in the St. Mary's River. The *Morrell* was nowhere to be found.

Between the last word from the *Morrell* at 12:15 a.m. Tuesday, and the first evidence of what had happened to the ship thereafter, there was a gap of 37 hours. At 1:12 p.m. Wednesday, the motor vessel *G. G. Post* reported sighting a body, which the Coast Guard at Harbor Beach recovered. The dead man had ice in his hair and wore an orange life jacket identified with the name and markings of the *Morrell*.

The Coast Guard sent out an immediate alert from the Rescue Coordination Center in Cleveland, in the form of a mariner's notice to all shipping on the Great Lakes.

Less than an hour later, the freighter *G. A. Tomlinson* spotted wreckage from a ship. "We came to the aid of a Coast Guard patrol vessel about four miles north-northeast of Harbor Beach," reported Captain Fitch. "Sea conditions were five-to-six-foot waves out of the north-northwest, with the winds about 25 knots (29 miles). We spotted three ring buoys, a two-gallon oil can from a lifeboat, with the name of the *Morrell* on them. This was approximately 2 p.m. We recovered three bodies, all bobbing face-down in life jackets within the space of a mile, and turned them over to a Coast Guard vessel."

Coast Guard planes, helicopters, and ships swarmed into the area. Later in the afternoon, when search parties hunting along the snow-covered shoreline and across the still menacing Lake had virtually abandoned hope of finding any survivors, a helicopter crew from the Traverse City Coast Guard Air Station spotted what they took to be four dead men on a pontoon raft near shore, until one of them "raised his right arm and his head."

Dennis Hale, the burly deck watchman from Ashtabula, greeted his rescuers with three words that he never tired of repeating: "I love ya!" When they told him to rest and promised not to try to interview him about the sinking, he said: "No, no, that's all right, I want someone to talk to me."

WHY AM I ALIVE?

A Coast Guard officer in the helicopter observed Hale to be "in minor shock but in amazingly good condition considering his ordeal. He had no trousers or shoes on, yet his bulk and the protection given him by his shipmates' bodies appeared to have made his survival possible."

One of the rescue pilots remarked, shaking his head in disbelief: "I frankly don't see how one guy lived. I wouldn't think a guy could survive more than two hours in that cold water."

The ambulance man who took Dennis Hale from the helicopter to Harbor Beach Hospital could feel the ice on his neck. The Coast Guard physician who examined him (and found his body temperature 95 degrees, 3.6 below normal) said: "I can tell you why he's alive. It's a miracle. He's 26 and he didn't panic, but it's still a miracle."

While hardened seamen and police asked the same questions, Dennis Hale put the mystery to a priest who visited his bedside after blessing 11 bodies plucked from Lake Huron by boat and helicopter.

"Father, why am I alive?"

"Because God wants you to be alive, my son."

"I know why I'm alive," Hale told the priest. "One, because God wants me to be alive. Two, because God wants me to suffer before I die."

While the solitary survivor recuperated from his ordeal, the rescue work continued. Through Wednesday night helicopters and Coast Guard surface craft criss-crossed over predetermined search areas in a fruitless hunt for other survivors.

By dawn, on Thursday, December 1st, the weather had cleared and the winds had died down. Just off Forestville on the Thumb, rescue boats rendezvoused, then shut off their motors to drift for two hours, figuring the rate and direction of drift would provide a clue on where to concentrate the search.

As a result, nine more bodies were recovered south of Harbor Beach, but as the day wore on, the weather began closing in again. Snow began to fall and temperatures dropped. The search continued doggedly but the last faint hope — that if one man could make it on an open raft, then perhaps other men found safety in a protected lifeboat — went glimmering.

The *Morrell* carried 29 men into Lake Huron Monday night. One returned alive. Twenty bodies had been fished from the water that killed them. Eight men were still missing, and now given up for dead. The maritime world waited to find out how the *Morrell* met her doom as Coast Guard officials held a long session with the only man living who could tell.

SAILOR'S NIGHTMARE COME TRUE

As Dennis Hale told his story the final minutes of the *Morrell* were made as clear as a sailor's nightmare come true. When the pilothouse watchman had gone to bed at 9:30 in the forward crew's quarters, he had tried to go to sleep there in the noisy bow. He had no idea of how severe the weather would become as the seas and winds reached a crescendo in the almost four hours that he tossed and turned on his bunk. Lake Michigan was being lashed by gale force winds of almost 70 miles per hour when the *Morrell* shook in her death tremors like a house cat pounced on by a mountain lion, her spine broken in a blow.

Several times Hale was jarred from the edge of dreams as the *Morrell* lurched through the storm. He tossed and turned in his bunk, somewhere between sleeping and waking. The waves outside were giant bowling balls roaring down Huron

153

alley to make a solid strike and sweep the kingpin into the gutter.

"A loud thump woke me up," Hale said, thinking they might have dropped anchor. "Then there was another hard thump. The lights blinked out. My bunk light wouldn't turn on. I figured it was time to get up. Before I was completely out of bed, the emergency bell began ringing the ship's general alarm."

Hale answered the call promptly. He rushed topside in just his undershorts. As he got to the companionway, a man stared at him and shouted six words that helped save his life. "Oh, my God, get your jacket!"

Hale dashed back to his cabin. In the darkness he couldn't find his shoes or his pants, but he put on his life jacket and peacoat, a sailor's thick, loose, woolen, double-breasted jacket that later protected his upper body from the elements.

He ran out into the howling storm. His bare feet stepped in slush ice on the deck. He could see the boat bending in its death agonies. Amidships was higher than the stern, quite a bit higher, and he saw steam escaping there. The *Morrell* was buckling at No. 8 Hold, and about to crack in two.

In the frantic and confused action, Hale thought he saw at least one of the two lifeboats launched from the stern section. Moments after he reached deck, the bow and stern separated.

The *Morrell's* power for lights and distress signals evidently was lost in the initial stage of the breakup. When the lights blinked and went out, that was it. The first thud must have snapped power cables running from the stern engine room to the forward bridge where the radio went dead, with no emergency power system in the bow to send an SOS or Mayday.

Many of the *Morrell's* crewmen apparently went into the 34-degree waters with their orange life jackets on, perhaps unaware that no one knew they were in trouble and no help was on the way.

GET IN THE RAFT AND HOLD TIGHT

Hale estimated that the elapsed time between the general alarm and the moment the *Morrell's* bow went down was about

15 minutes (about 2:15 a.m. Tuesday). He first had seen a crack that "twisted and ripped at the same time," starting on the starboard side; then he had seen the severing of stern from bow.

"Everybody said get in the raft and hold on tight," so along with a dozen shipmates Hale crowded into one of the two pontoon rafts carried on the forward section, just behind the wheelhouse. Captain Crawley came aboard the raft at first and cheered everybody by pointing out what he identified as another ship off the port bow.

As the bow sank, the seamen on the raft waited for the water to reach their level and wash them into Lake Huron. In one of the most bizarre incidents in the history of shipwrecks, they found themselves abreast of the stern.

"The stern, still powered by its engines, was facing us and it started to run into the bow section, ramming us in the side."

The impact of one of these rammings, perhaps combined with the force of a wave smashing over the submerging bow, hurled the raft and all its occupants into the sea. Cries for help, last calls to friends, were lost between the hills and valleys of the waves and the furious voices of the wind. Orange life jackets bobbed farther and farther apart in the confused tides of the storm. In scant hours, perhaps less than two, these lonesome men, without aid of raft or lifeboat, would say their prayers in the darkness, think wistfully of home and loved ones, then drop their heads from weariness and lack of hope and cruel exposure, to drown in the smother of spray whipped from the waves by the wind. A few might never be found, but most of their bodies would be recovered the next day, or the next, from the frigid Huron or its snow-covered shores, with their boots frozen to their feet and the ice growing in their hair. Many would be identified by FBI agents through their fingerprints, and at least one would carry marks of having tangled with the wild propeller of the *Morrell's* stern section.

Only four men made it back to the pontoon raft catapulted from the *Morrell's* bow: Arthur Sojek, 33, deck hand from Buffalo; Charles Fosbender, 42, wheelsman from St. Clair,

Michigan; John Cleary, Jr., 20, Cleveland; and Hale. They clung to the grating of the raft, unable to speak. The shock of the cold water had snatched their breath away.

BEAST WITH ITS HEAD SHOT OFF

The four men watched a weird drama on the Lake. They saw no signs of life in the water but they stared in awe at the berserk stern of the *Morrell* running all over the Huron, long after the bow had sunk. They never saw the stern go down. Hale said the last time he saw the aft section, it was moving under power, lights shining, and thrashing around in the Lake like a great wounded beast with its head shot off.

Hale lost no time in firing a parachute flare, "because the skipper had said he saw a boat and we were signalling to it." He lost one flare overboard, then he fired two more early Tuesday that went unnoticed except by the desperately hopeful eyes on the raft. Hale saved one flare for a last resort.

The pontoon rollercoasted the waves through the bitter-cold darkness. Half-frozen, the four survivors huddled together for bodily warmth and human company. They talked to keep up their spirits, but "nobody said what they thought caused the ship to crack. We didn't try to reason why. We were just interested in our survival.

"Jack Cleary — he was a nice kid, we called him Butch — asked what chance we had, and I said a lot better than the guys who weren't here on the raft with us now."

The sound of their voices encouraged the four remaining shipmates. "Cleary asked me how many kids I had. Charlie (Fosbender) and I talked about going home."

But the specter of death already had joined the men on the raft. Young Cleary, making his first trip on the Lakes, was the first to go. "Shortly after daybreak I began poking Butch, but he wasn't moving. Sojek also quit moving. We were less than six hours adrift on the Lake and they were dead."

Hale never forgot the glazed expression in the eyes of the two deck watchmen, and he noticed the wheelsman, Fosbender, weakening as the day wore on. He could not help but compare the open raft with its two-inch railings outside to the new life-raft gear that came equipped with coverings that could be zipped over survivors to help keep them warm, plus emergency radio equipment, rations, etc.

The 42-year-old Fosbender began coughing hard. He complained that his lungs were filling with water. "I told him to crawl near me. As he did, he raised himself in the raft and said he saw land. We were heartened but still saw no signs of activity.

"Charlie then moved up and put his arms around me. I couldn't move on the raft. My bare feet were frozen. Now and then Charlie would raise himself to look for life."

Malignant seas were still running and the sun failed to shine all day, not one ray of warmth for men who were freezing within sight of rescue, but it would not be until early afternoon of the next day that an alert sent searching parties out to hunt for the men of the *Morrell*.

"That afternoon I asked Charlie what time it was and he said 5 after 2. I asked him when the ship went down and he said 12 hours ago."

TALKING TO DEAD SHIPMATES

Dennis Hale still had 24 hours of ordeal ahead of him. For Fosbender time was running out. At about sundown he collapsed while looking toward land. "We both could see the land and we had oars and Charlie was still alive, but neither of us had the strength to row. We were frozen stiff."

Fosbender told Hale: "I'm going to throw in the sponge"; and then, as the solitary survivor noted, "He just passed on."

Alone with three bodies on a raft in a man-killing tempest, Hale continued his macabre 36-hour ride on the Huron. He burrowed under the dead men, and their stiff bodies became his blankets. He had no expectations of lasting out the night. Ice began to form on the raft.

"I was unconscious off and on. I had dreams, all kinds of dreams about the ship and other sorts of things. I thought I was on the *Morrell* talking to the wheelsman. I asked him if they had launched the lifeboats."

When conscious, Hale realized his predicament. "I figured maybe through the night I would freeze to death." He suffered weird hallucinations, fantasied he was being attacked by sea gulls, imagined he was back in safe harbor feeding sandwiches to his pals. He talked to his dead shipmates, he shouted into the sky for help, he wanted to know why the others had died so fast and he was still alive.

PRAYING TO LIVE BUT HOPING TO DIE

Somehow he survived Tuesday night on the raft, but when dawn came up Wednesday, Hale thought it was all over. "I had no hope at all. I was praying to live but hoping to die."

He knew the raft had run aground, drifting and bouncing between huge boulders. He could see farmhouse lights in the distance.

"I could have waded ashore but my body was paralyzed with cold and pain. I couldn't move but I began yelling. Then it began to snow hard. I picked ice off my peacoat to eat, but then I saw this figure appear out of nowhere.

"A moustached, milky-complexioned man, dressed in white, stood on my raft warning me not to eat ice. He told me I would get pneumonia if I did. When he disappeared I took more ice. He popped into view again with the same warning. I didn't touch the peacoat after that."

Sometime during the day Hale struggled to shoot off the parachute flare he had saved for a last resort, but his eyes were playing tricks on him and the "boat" he thought he saw turned out to be a buoy. The husky six-footer had drained all of his endurance by mid-afternoon. Ice was forming on his body; the end was near.

But Hale still had the strength and the courage, when he heard the helicopter at four o'clock, to raise his head and wave an arm from the fortress of dead bodies after an incredible odyssey in Arctic weather across tumultuous seas in bare feet, undershorts, and a peacoat.

"I love ya, I love ya, I love ya!"

158

PSYCHOLOGY OF SURVIVAL

The question on everyone's lips following the rescue, the question that haunted Hale himself, concerned why he alone had survived while all 28 of his shipmates had perished. One newsman wondered: "Was it luck, courage, or grace that carried him through?"

Another newsman, less philosophical, decided that Hale had survived, thanks to four factors: the warmth of three dead men, a husky physique, several fortifying hours of sleep, and blind luck.

Weighing 220 pounds at the start of the *Morrell's* fateful trip, Hale dropped to 195 pounds during his siege on the raft. Doctors indicated he may have been protected by the fat on his body.

Asked how he had survived wearing only undershorts and a peacoat, Hale said that for one thing he had to keep moving to relieve the pain in parts of his body. "Not having more clothes on helped too," he added surprisingly. "Pants and shoes might have frozen to me."

Bertha Hale, standing beside the hospital cot, holding her husband's hand, smiled softly as he climaxed the reasons why he lay there alive:

"And I *did* want to get home. I wanted to be with my wife and four children for Christmas."

An indomitable will to survive, to return home, shines like a lighthouse in the saga of Dennis Hale. Gazing at the cuts on his face, the bandage on his little finger, aware of the frost-bitten feet under the covers, his wife said:

"I guess we're the luckiest family in the world."

But there were 28 families that did not fare so well. At St. Clair, Michigan, where the long ships pass up and down the river on their voyages around the Upper Great Lakes, Janice Fosbender waited for her husband to return.

"I know he isn't dead," she said, crying at the very thought of the possibility. "I'll never give up hope, never."

The phone rang, informing Mrs. Fosbender that one of the

159

three dead bodies on the raft had been identified as that of her husband Charles. She sank to the couch, in shock.

"I didn't give up hope," she said, choking on her tears. "Every time the phone rang, I jumped about halfway out of my skin.

"It didn't have to happen. Why Chuck? . . . Why Chuck?"

Many waited, many hoped, many prayed in vain. There were 28 men besides Hale who wanted to return and spend Christmas with their loved ones.

There is a psychology about shipwrecks that never operates in favor of the survivor (see pp. 315-318).

AFTERMATH OF DISASTER

On Friday, December 2nd, the weather turned so cold the Coast Guard was unable to launch two 40-foot motor launches that had been used earlier in the search. They were covered with nine inches of ice. No hope was held for finding any crewmen of the *Morrell* alive, but the search continued. No bodies were found, of the eight bodies still missing. They would bob up here and there along Lake Huron's shore in the days and months to come.

One of the quirks of fate that attend every shipwreck came to light at Sault Ste. Marie where a weather-wrinkled veteran of 25 years on the Great Lakes looked up from his hospital bed and remarked: "If I hadn't gotten off at the Soo on Thanksgiving Day, I'd have had it." A porter in the ship's galley on the *Morrell*, he had come down with a bad cold on the southbound run, a cold that saved his life.

Also in the Soo, Coast Guard inspectors revoked the sailing papers of the *Morrell's* sister ship, the *Edward Y. Townsend*, after examining a crack in her midsection deck, which the skipper, Captain Connelly, had discovered after the storm. The Coast Guard ordered the *Townsend* docked at the Soo and ruled that she could not be moved under her own power and must be towed, unmanned, to a port for repairs.

Down below, a lawyer for Dennis Hale called the *Morrell* unseaworthy and claimed that Bethlehem Steel failed to provide adequate inspection, repairs, or emergency equipment.

A suit for $150,000 was filed, the petition charging that Hale had suffered permanent emotional damage.

HYDROGEN BOMB DIVERS

Sonar-equipped Navy aircraft went out to help the Coast Guard located the *Morrell's* sunken hull, to get a better idea of where to seek the still-missing crewmen and to find out if the wreckage posed any menace to navigation. Preliminary findings were followed up by Ocean Systems, a firm headed by John Lindbergh, son of the famed aviator, and prime contractor in the search for a missing hydrogen bomb in the Mediterranean Ocean near Spain in 1965. Under contract with the Coast Guard, Ocean Systems operated underwater TV gear off the Coast Guard cutter *Bramble,* which positioned marker buoys over the grave of the ill-fated ore carrier. Pictures were taken, in 200 feet of water, of the ship's stern, with the name *MORRELL* visible.

The Coast Guard fixed the scene as 16¼ miles almost due north of Pointe Aux Barques, located south of the top of Michigan's Thumb, which juts into Lake Huron to form stormy Saginaw Bay.

AGING SHIPS AND BRITTLE STEEL

The storm that killed the *Morrell* also confirmed the theory that the Great Lakes are rougher than the sea. During the storm Inland Steel's *Edward L. Ryerson,* a comparatively new (1960), maximum size (730-foot) freighter, battled Lake Michigan. The *Ryerson's* equipment included strain gauges, now installed on a number of fresh-water steamers. Her gauges recorded a stress of 23,000 pounds per square inch, much more than has ever been recorded on an ocean freighter.

The news came as no surprise to Lakemen. They had known it all along — in their bones.

To investigate loss of the *Morrell,* the Coast Guard instituted a five-man Board of Inquiry, thus establishing the shipwreck as a major marine disaster. Meanwhile, lawsuits piled up to $5 million and bid fair to reach double or triple this amount.

161

Conflicting testimony came from both sides: the *Morrell* had been sound, the *Morrell* leaked like a sieve.

One thing seemed sure — that steps should be taken to reduce hazards aboard the aging Great Lakes fleet. An ocean ship that has been in service 20 years is considered old. On fresh water, where corrosion is not a problem, the U.S. lake fleet included 65 vessels 50 years old, 30 ships of at least 60 years of age, and one, the *Samuel Mitchell,* built in 1892, that would never see 75 again. There is no cutoff date for retirement of a Great Lakes ship.

In March, 1968, the National Transportation Safety Board recommended that older cargo ships of the Great Lakes fleet be strengthened structurally or be barred from operating during severe autumn weather. Earlier, Admiral Willard J. Smith, Commandant of the Coast Guard, had pointed out the magnitude of the problem, in that the average Great Lakes bulk carrier ship is about 45 years old, with more vessels in the 50-to-60-year age group than in any other 10-year period. These older ships were made of a type of steel abandoned for large vessel construction in 1948. This steel becomes brittle and subject to fractures at temperatures near freezing such as existed during the Lake Huron storm.

The Safety Board found that failure of the main hull girder amidships caused the *S. S. Daniel J. Morrell* to split in two. The Board also noted that a sister ship, the *Edward Y. Townsend,* about 20 miles away in the same storm, sustained structural fractures similar to those that sank the *Morrell;* and it further noted that the *Carl D. Bradley* had broken up eight years before, apparently because of structural weaknesses. The Board specifically asked the Coast Guard to require strengthening of deck and other structures in the midships area in pre-1948 vessels over 400 feet long, or to curtail their operations.

A number of other safety recommendations and regulations were to memorialize the *Morrell,* but the keynote had been sounded: No longer would iron men be sent out to engage the elements with aging ships and brittle steel.

162

PHILOSOPHY OF SHIPWRECKS

Those who sail the Lakes are men of iron — men of iron nerve, iron will, and ironclad faith. Despite stories of scattered rivets and water in the hold, Dennis Hale said he assumed the *Morrell* was in sound condition:

"I thought if it wasn't safe, the Coast Guard wouldn't have passed it, and the Company wouldn't have let it sail."

A former crewman, voicing his doubts about the boat's seaworthiness, had the question put to him: "Were you ever worried?" "I sure was," he answered, "but I had great respect for the captain's judgment."

The chief dispatcher for Bethlehem Steel's fleet added a final dimension to the philosophy of iron courage that unites the Coast Guard, the shipping magnates, the skippers, and the crews:

"The Company *does* have the authority to order a ship to stop or turn back," he admitted; "but *nobody*," he emphasized, "*nobody* in our office could tell a master when to stop or proceed en route."

That sums up the situation every time a great storm thunders across the Lakes. If every skipper waited for perfect weather to continue his voyage and if every crewman saw disaster in jagged skies and troubled seas, the amount of traffic on fresh water would start few ripples in the world of commerce.

Perhaps the entire philosophy of Lakemen regarding possible shipwreck or survival can be capsuled into the true story about an American skipper who took on a French Canadian pilot to help him chart his course between Quebec and Montreal on the St. Lawrence Seaway.

A savage storm blew up and the ship began to take such a beating that the pilot gave up hope. "No use, Cap'n," he cried. "This boat's done for. She's not gonna make it."

The skipper fought the wheel. "She's gotta make it, Mister," he said decisively. "She's the only boat we got."

On the Great Lakes, the name of the game is Captains Courageous, and crews to match.

163

BOOK THREE

GONE WITH LAKE ERIE WINDS

We leaves Detroit behind us,
We sets our canvas tight;
The tug slows up and casts us off,
Old Erie heaves in sight!

So we watch our tiller closer,
We keeps our sheet ropes clear;
There's no sich thing as stiddy wind
Along Lake Erie here.

    (Schooner tow song, 1890)

The song on the preceding page recalls one of the vanished glories of the Lakes — a line of stately schooners following the huff and puff of a tiny steam tug through the channel until they can lift their wings again and come alive on the open Lake. The date given is approximate, not exact.

1. Lake Erie Takes a Bow

Fourth largest of the Great Lakes, Lake Erie holds the record for being the shallowest of the five and consequently has a history of kicking up the biggest fuss in the least time. A breath of wind is enough to make her start doing somersaults and turning handsprings.

The busiest of all the Lakes today, Erie was the last of the upper Lakes to be discovered by white men, who took a short cut across the country that lay above Lake Ontario and the larger yellow Lake with the green rush shore. They followed a navigator's straight line west along the 46th parallel, historic paddle-and-portage route of Champlain and Nicolet, via the Ottawa River and across Lake Nipissing to Georgian Bay.

Across Erie's quick-tempered waters sailed the first ship to travel the upper Lakes, LaSalle's *Griffin,* and later the first steamboat, the Indian-named *Walk-in-the-Water,* both destined to early ends. Aboard the *Griffin* on her first, and last, trip up the Lakes was Father Hennepin, the Baron Munchausen of the priesthood, whose love of exaggeration could hardly begin to keep up with the sights he described.

"The great River of St. Lawrence derives its Source from the Lake Ontario, which is likewise call'd in the Iroquese Language, Skandaris; that is to say, a very pretty lake.

"Lake Erie, or Erie-Tejocharontiong, as the Iroquese call it, encloses in its Southern Bank a Tract of Land as large as the Kingdom of France. Betwixt the Lake Erie and Huron there is a Streight thirty Leagues long, which is of equal breadth almost all over, except in the middle, that it enlarges itself by help of another Lake, which we gave the Name of Ste. Claire, though the Iroquese, who pass

167

over it frequently when they are upon Warlike Expeditions, call it Otsi Keta.

"The Lake Huron was so call'd by the People of Canada, because the savage Hurons, who inhabited the adjacent country, us'd to have their Hair so burn't that their Heads resembled the Heads of Wild Boars. The savages themselves call'd it Lake Karegnondy.

"There is yet another Streight or narrow canal towards the Upper Lake (that runs into this of Huron) about Five Leagues broad and Fifteen Leagues long, which is interrupted by several Islands, and becomes narrower by degrees, till it comes at the Fall of St. Mary's. This Fall is call'd the Fall of St. Mary Missilimakinak.

"The Lake Illinois, in the Native's Language, signifies the Lake of Men; for the word Illinois signifies a Man of full Age in the vigour of his years. It is call'd by the Miami's Mischigonong, that is The Great Lake.

"The Upper Lake runs from East to West, and may have more than a Hundred and Fifty Leagues in length, Sixty in Breadth, and Five Hundred in circuit. We never quite went over it as we did over all the others I've hitherto mention'd; but we sounded some of its greatest Depths, and it resembles the Ocean, having neither Bottom nor Banks.

"I shall not mention the infinite numbers of Rivers that discharge themselves into this prodigious Lake. It were easie to build on the sides of these great Lakes an infinite Number of Considerable Towns which might have Communication one with another by Navigation for Five Hundred Leagues together, and by an inconceivable Commerce which would establish itself among 'em."

Called a cheerful liar, and worse, by stay-at-homes who preferred exact figures to his grandiose round numbers, the gadabout priest acquired the reputation of America's Munchausen but the verdict of history has proven him to be a prophet. Aboard a vessel doomed to become the first shipwreck on the Great Lakes, he sailed across vast reaches of lonesome waters surrounded by wilderness and he saw along their trackless shores a dream of great cities — "an infinite Number of Considerable Towns, . . . and an inconceivable Commerce . . . among 'em" — that came true in a bustle of navigation between Toronto, Buffalo, Cleveland, Detroit, Milwaukee, Chicago — on the aboriginal waterways from below Erie-Tejocharontiong to Mischigonong and the "Ocean" beyond Missilimakinak.

Two generations in the wake of Father Hennepin, Thomas McKenney, an agent of the Indian Department, embarked on a trip up the Lakes in the summer of 1826 to negotiate a treaty with the Chippewas at Fond du Lac on Lake Superior. Arriving at Detroit, he lost no time in writing a letter back home about the Lake he had just crossed:

"A word about Lake Erie. I knew its length, its breadth, and depth, and yet I must confess I had no more correct conceptions of the lake as it appeared to me than if I had never had the slightest acquaintance with its dimensions. All my previous conception of a lake fell so far short of its actual vastness and ocean-like appearance, as to be wholly absorbed in the view of it. I could but wonder what my opinion of lakes will be, after I shall have seen and navigated Huron and Superior. Lake Erie, though considerably smaller than either, is a vast sea, and often more stormy, and even dangerous, than the ocean itself."

After completing his errand in Lake Superior, McKenney came down Lake Huron and back to Lake Erie aboard a revenue cutter, Captain Knapp, which furnished him another item to write home about from Detroit:

"The deck of this little cutter is made of the masts of the *Lawrence,* Perry's ship. In one of the planks immediately under the tiller is the bruise of a shot. Whatever can be made into convenience and fitness for the duties of a cutter for the lake service, Captain Knapp has most ingeniously effected in this, now ten-year-old boat. But, after all, the thing is too small. These lakes and their commerce demand a vessel of other dimensions."

2. Real Battle of Lake Erie

Thirteen years before Indian Agent McKenney rode down Lake Huron on a boat whose deck was made of the masts ·of Perry's flagship, on the morning of September 10, 1813, the cry of "Sail ho!" rang out from lookouts in the mastheads of the American squadron riding *Put-in-Bay* on Lake Erie. With dawn making a brave show on the British fleet several miles distant, Perry cleared the island and stood out on the open Lake to meet the enemy and, ultimately, to provide another chapter in *Heroic Deeds of American Sailors.*

The sound of cannon had hardly died away nor the smoke cleared on Lake Erie when a ballad called "Perry's Victory" was printed in thousands of broadsides, sung by wayside peddlers, and sold for a penny on street corners throughout the Northwest. Towns in Ohio went wild with excitement. Patriots roared in chorus:

Columbian tars are the true sons of Mars
Who rake fore and aft when they fight on the deep;
On the bed of Lake Erie commanded by Perrey
They caused many Britons to take their last sleep.

On the tenth of September let us all remember
As long as the globe on its axis reels round;
Soon our tars and marines on Lake Erie were seen
To make the red flag of proud Britton come down.

The van of our fleet was brought up complete;
Commanded by Perrey the Lawrence bore down;
Our guns they did roar with such terrifick power
That savages trembled at the dreadful sound.

The sound of the guns as the two fleets engaged at close quarters was actually heard 160 miles from the scene, at Erie, Pennsylvania, in a low rumbling that echoed like distant thunder. Anxious towns along the shore, on both the American and Canadian sides, waited for news of the final outcome. At Cleveland was enacted one of those scenes that typify the intimate relationship between the Lakes and the land:

A Mr. Levi Johnson and his hired hands were building a house, according to the *Cleveland Chronicle,* when they heard a noise in the west which at first they supposed to be faraway thunder. But there were no clouds on the horizon.

All at once Johnson exclaimed, "Boys, it's Perry's guns; he's fighting the British."

With one accord all the workmen threw down their hammers and nails and raced for the water front, but their employer beat them to it. In a few minutes everybody in Cleveland had joined them on the beach, listening to the sounds of battle. Although seventy miles away, they not only could hear the roll of the broadsides, but when the fire slackened from time to time, they could distinguish between the heavier and the lighter guns. Finally, in the *Cleveland Chronicle's* report:

> At length, there was only a dropping fire; one fleet had evidently succumbed to the other. Heavy shots were heard at very end, then all was silence. "Perry has the heaviest guns," exclaimed Johnson; "those are Perry's shots — he has won the day — three cheers for Perry!" "Hip, hip, hurrah!" promptly responded the crowd, willing to believe the assertion; but yet separating with anxious hearts, uncertain what might be the result. In fact, the English had some as heavy guns as the Americans, but not so many of that class.

Earlier in the season, Perry had named his flagship after Captain Lawrence, commander of the *Chesapeake,* then recently captured by the *Shannon* on the Atlantic in still another well-thumbed chapter to be recorded in *Heroic Deeds of American Sailors.* Bringing the *Lawrence, Niagara, Caledonia, Ariel, Scorpion, Somers, Porcupine, Tigris,* and *Trippe* into line against the British line of *Detroit, Queen*

171

Charlotte, Lady Prevost, Hunter, Chippewa, and *Little Bell,* Perry took the brunt of the battle by engaging the *Detroit,* the enemy ship with the heaviest fire power, thus fighting broad pennant against broad pennant, commodore against commodore.

Going into action, the twenty-seven-year-old leader had hoisted the burgee or battle flag, inscribed with large white letters on a blue background which could be read throughout the fleet: DON'T GIVE UP THE SHIP. They were the last words of the dying Lawrence.

Perry's squadron numbered nine vessels against the British six, but they had been so hastily built from trees along the Erie shore that it might well be said that the wood was still growing, and the enemy had a preponderance of sixty-three guns to fifty-four which concentrated on the flagship with the bold motto.

> *The Lawrence sustained a most dreadful fire;*
> *She fought three to one for two glasses or more;*
> *Whilst Perrey undaunted did firmly stand by her*
> *And on the proud foe heavy broadsides did pore.*
>
> *Her masts being shattered, her rigging all tattered,*
> *Her sails all in ribbands, her wheel shot away,*
> *And few left on deck to manage the wreck,*
> *Our heroes on board her no longer could stay.*

According to *Heroic Deeds of American Sailors* Perry's last words to the officer left in charge as the young commodore lowered himself away to be rowed over to the *Niagara* were:

"Lieutenant Yarnall, sir, I leave it to your discretion to strike or not, but the American colors must not be pulled down over my head today."

> *There was one gallant act of our noble commander,*
> *Whilst writing my song I shall notice with pride;*
> *When launching the smack that carried his standard,*
> *A ball whistled through her quite close by his side.*

Says Perrey those villians intend shure to dround us,
But push on, my brave boys, you need never fear;
And then with his coat he plugged up the boat,
And through sulphour and fire away he did steer.

The prose version of this historic transfer from one vessel to another in the midst of battle is somewhat as follows:

> When Commodore Perry left the *Lawrence*, there were but himself, his little brother, and fourteen men alive and unhurt on board. He jumped into the boat with eight stout seamen at the oars, and put off at thirty minutes after two. He stood erect in the stern of the boat, and the British saw it as, with the zealous men at the oars, the little craft sprang away like a race horse. A shower of grape, cannister and bullets flew about him, but he heeded them not till, at the entreating tears of his crew, he finally sat down, and quickly the boat reached the *Niagara*.

The famed Niagara, now proud of her Perrey,
Displayed all her banners in gallant array;
Full twenty-five guns on her deck she did carry,
Which soon put an end to the sad, bloody fray.

Perry ran up his pennant and hoisted the signal for close action. Loud cheers resounded from every vessel in the squadron, as, under full press of sail, he bore down upon the British line and broke through between the *Hunter* and the *Detroit* at half pistol shot, taking the *Lady Prevost* with his broadside port and the entangled *Detroit* and *Queen Charlotte* with his full starboard broadside.

In the vernacular of *Heroic Deeds of American Sailors*, British Commodore Barclay went down with a desperate wound aboard the *Detroit* and many shrieks told of the destruction the guns had wrought. The decks of the *Lady Prevost* were swept, and Perry luffed athwart the bows of the *Detroit* and *Lady Charlotte*.

The bold British Lion now roared his last thunder,
When Perrey attacked him cloas on his rear;

The American Eagle soon made him coush under
And roar out for quarters as you soon shall hear.

O had you been there I vow and declare
That such a grand sight you had nere saw before,
When six bloody flags that no longer could wag
Were laid at the feet of our brave Commodore.

Lives there an American boy who has not thrilled to the report Perry sent to William Henry Harrison over on the mainland? "Dear General: We have met the enemy and they are ours; two ships, two brigs, one schooner and one sloop." Then the postscript: "Send us some soldiers to help take care of the prisoners, who are more numerous than ourselves."

The whole British fleet was captured complete;
Not one single vessel from us got away;
And prisoners some hundreds, Columbians wondered
To see them all ankerd and moored in the bay.

Students of history have noted dissension between the beardless Commodore and his first captain; but boys, including the grown-up kind, and ballads are hero-worshippers and not defamers of character:

Brave Elliott whose vallour must now be recorded,
On board the brave Somers so well played his part;
His gallant assistance, to Perrey afforded,
Will place him the second on Lake Erie chart.

'Twas delightful to see those noble commanders
Imbracing each other when the battle was ore,
And vewin with pride those invincible standards
That never had yealded to any before.

Says Perrey, Brave Elliott, give me your hand, sir,
This day you have gained immortal renown;
And as long as Columbia Lake Erie commands, sirs,
Let brave Elliott with Laurels be crowned.

174

The last two lines in the middle stanza were correct.
The Battle of Lake Erie marked the only occasion in history
when an entire British fleet, commanded by a veteran of
Trafalgar, surrendered to any enemy's flotilla. No wonder
the ballad crowed until the whole backwoods echoed:

> *Great Britton may boast of her conquering heroes,*
> *Her Rodneys, her Nelsuns, and all the old crewe;*
> *But Rome in her glory nere teald such a storey,*
> *Nor boasted such feats as Columbians can do.*

Considering the ratio of population, the ballad of
Perry's victory outsold any popular recording of today. It
was still a prime favorite at county fairs and other festivals
half a century later. Patriots took the song to heart because the naval engagement on Lake Erie represented a
decisive triumph for them. It meant that the Northwest
Territory and the Mississippi Valley should be American,
not British, and that the United States should extend from
the Great Lakes to the Gulf of Mexico instead of being
fenced in perhaps on the borders of Ohio. It nullified
the victories of the Canadians and their great Algonquin
ally Tecumseh at Detroit, Fort Dearborn, and Mackinac,
and restored control of the Lakes to Uncle Sam, thus insur-
ing that the hundreds of thousands of immigrants about to
people the heartland of the continent would largely sail and
settle under the Stars and Stripes:

> *May heaven still smile on the shades of those heroes*
> *Who fought with brave Perrey, whose cannons did roar,*
> *And checked the proud spirit of those murdering*
>   *Neroes*
> *Who wanted to make us base slaves evermore.*

> *Then everyone sing till we make the woods ring!*
> *Let us toast our brave heroes by land and by sea:*
> *While Britons drink sherry, Columbians drink Perrey*
> *To the land of the brave and the home of the free.*

175

Another far-reaching outcome of the Lake Erie triumph was the agreement suggested by President Monroe in the peace terms, an agreement that might well be called the Monroe Doctrine of fresh water:

"The naval force to be maintained upon the American lakes by his Majesty and the Government of the United States shall henceforth be confined to the following vessels on each side; that is —

"On Lake Ontario to one vessel, not exceeding 100 tons burden, and armed with one eighteen-pound cannon. On the upper lakes to two vessels, not exceeding like burden each, and armed with like force.

"All other armed vessels on those lakes shall be forthwith dismantled and no other vessel of war shall be there built or armed."

Today no armed vessels patrol the waters of Lakes split down the middle with two thousand miles of international boundary line. The only war-making forces on the Great Lakes are the elements, and they continue to be more destructive than any battle ever fought on fresh water. The total loss suffered by Commodore Perry's flotilla was thirty killed, three less victims than the *Carl D. Bradley* claimed a century and a half later. The British losses were 41 killed, not even half enough to rank with the least of Lake Erie's major disasters.

The war of men against the sea has no peace terms but unconditional surrender, no armistice save death.

The real Battle of Lake Erie goes on, day and night, around the clock.

3. Over the Falls

One of the ships that struck her colors to Perry's fleet on Lake Erie, Commodore Barclay's flagship, the *Detroit,* years later played the star role in one of the greatest and most spectacular shipwrecks ever staged.

But first, to set the wild scene of action, here are pictures evoked by the European Baron Munchausen and his American counterpart, Father Hennepin.

"Pray, my dear Baron Munchausen," said the lovely Fragrantia, "were you ever at the Falls of Niagara?"

"Yes, my lady," replied I. "I have been, many years ago, at the Falls of Niagara, and found no more difficulty in swimming up and down the cataracts than I should to move a minuet."

Father Hennepin, whose tall tales were no match for the magnitude of the reality, stood at the Falls and reported: "I could not conceive how it came to pass that four great Lakes, the least of which is 400 Leagues in compass, should empty themselves one into another, and then all centre and discharge themselves at this Great Fall, and yet not drown a good part of America.

"Betwixt the Lake Ontario and Erie, there is a vast and prodigious Cadence of Water which falls down after a surprising and astonishing manner insomuch that the Universe does not afford its parallel. It is so rapid above this Descent that it violently hurls down the wild Beasts while endeavoring to pass it so as to feed on the other side, they not being able to withstand the force of its Current, which inevitably casts them headlong above Six Hundred feet.

"The Waters which fall from this vast Height do foam and boil after the most hideous manner imaginable, making an outrageous Noise, more terrible than that of Thunder;

for when the Wind blows from off the South their dismal roaring may be heard above fifteen Leagues off.

"The rebounding of these Waters is so great that a sort of Cloud arises from the Foam of it, which are seen hanging over the Abyss even at Noon-day, when the Sun is at its heighth. In the midst of Summer, when the Weather is hottest, they arise above the tallest Firrs, and other great Trees, which grow in the slooping Island which makes two other great Out-lets, or Falls of Water.

"When one stands near the Fall, which makes the most Beautiful and at the same time Frightful Cascade in the World, and looks down into this dreadful Gulph, one is seized with Horror, and the Head turns round, so that one cannot look long or steadfastly upon it."

American travelers and sight-seers who followed the trail-blazing priest had firmer heads for the spectacle and demanded entertainment to keep them at the scene. Enterprising landlords who had begun to build hotels and boardinghouses on both sides of the Niagara River no doubt saw a typical picnic family throwing sticks and other items into the rapids to watch the debris sail over the Falls. Thereby was born a commercial idea, originally promoted in sensational handbills as follows:

"The huge pirate ship *Michigan,* with a cargo of furious animals, will pass over the Falls of Niagara on the 8th of September, 1827. Plenty of refreshments and comfortable quarters are available, and entertainment is promised for all who may visit the Falls on this remarkable occasion, guaranteed for its novelty and the remarkable spectacle which it will present to be unequalled in the annals of infernal navigation."

The *Michigan,* a double topsail schooner that had been condemned as unseaworthy after eleven years of service in the Lake trade, was bought by a party of speculators, including Niagara landlords, beverage dispensers, carnival operators, and the like. Several thousand excited spectators lined the shores of the Rapids and the rim of the Falls, anticipating the big event from dawn onward on the scheduled day.

Fitted out in Buffalo with a menagerie consisting of a variety of dogs and more or less wild cats which prowled her decks, an Arabian camel, an elk, several hawks and geese, a swan, and a bear, the *Michigan* was sailed down the Niagara River by her Scotch master, Captain Rough, who took her gingerly through the white water toward the growing thunder of the Falls and at last abandoned ship to dive with his crew into a small boat and row in haste for the Canadian shore just above the cataract.

The crowd that had been yelling, hushed and then gave a long sigh as the schooner hurried to her doom out in midstream, her rigging strained and the wheel spinning madly on her afterdeck. Sails set for oblivion, over she tumbled, this barbaric American version of Noah's Ark in reverse.

There is no record of any wreckage coming ashore below the whirlpools in the Niagara gorge. In her book of travels called *Domestic Manners of the Americans,* a best seller for the past century, the lady globe-trotter Mrs. Trollope told of her trip to Niagara where she picked up local gossip to the effect that, after the War of 1812, three of the British ships stationed on Lake Erie were condemned as unfit for service and some of their officers obtained permission to send them over the Falls. The first was torn to shivers by the rapids, and went over in fragments; the second filled with water before she reached the cataract; but the third, which was in better condition, took the leap gallantly and retained her form till it was hid in the cloud of mist below.

To let Mrs. Trollope continue in her own words: "A reward of ten dollars was offered for the largest fragment of wood that should be found from either wreck, five for the second, and so on. One morsel only was ever seen, and that about a foot in length, was smashed as by a vice, and its edges notched like the teeth of a saw. What had become of the immense quantity of wood which had been precipitated? What unknown whirlpool had engulfed it, so that, contrary to the very laws of nature, no vestige of the floating material could find its way to the surface?"

Two years after the so-called pirate ship *Michigan* sailed over Niagara Falls with its helpless cargo of animals, the local tradesmen put on another show, on October 6, 1829. It was an all-day extravaganza featuring a number of explosions as well as a vessel hurtled to destruction. A negative-minded spectator surmised that the landlords on both sides of the river were trying to drum up trade by getting a lot of people together. From the hardened traveler's viewpoint:

"For this purpose several rocks were blasted off at various points of the rocks overhanging the gulf. But it was a sorry affair. The gunpowder explosions, in comparison with the majestic roar of the waters, might be likened to the report of so many pop-guns mingling with the thunders of Jove — the tumbling fragments like pebbles cast into the valley from the brow of Olympus — the smoke, like a capful of fog compared with the volumes rolling up from the crater of Vesuvius. Indeed the whole affair was as contemptible as it would be to attempt to add to the majesty of the cataract the pouring of a bucket of water by its side from a teakettle. Several thousands of people, however, collected on both sides, many of whom probably had never before had curiosity enough to see the falls themselves — if even they saw them now. The descent and wreck of the vessel among the rapids was an interesting spectacle, however."

The latter spectacle become quite the habit at Niagara, so it must have put money in certain pockets. Two years later, the shipping news noted the following as an event of the season of navigation:

> *Superior Goes Over the Falls.* — A rather unusual event transpired in September, 1831, by the fitting out and sending over Niagara Falls of an old hulk called the *Superior*, which had served well her time on the lakes. A large con-

course of people were attracted from all parts. She struck an island a short distance above the precipice and there remained for one month, when high water floated her to smithereens.

During the Patriot War or Canadian Rebellion, on a mild December night in 1837, a party of Canadians boarded the steamer *Caroline* at her dock and, after an exchange of shots, won control. They took her out in the middle of the stream, removed everyone aboard, and set her loose down the rapids. Both shores watched her go blazing along and, as she went over the Falls, the *Caroline,* first steamer to take the plunge, must have looked like a pinwheel fired to celebrate Independence night. In fact, the short-lived war won for Canada the independence she enjoys to-day. The *Caroline* was not a useless sacrifice.

Back in 1813, another struggle for independence had resulted in serious damage to the British commodore's flagship during the Battle of Lake Erie. The *Detroit* was sunk in Misery Bay near Perry's flagship *Lawrence,* but in 1835 Captain Miles raised and rigged her as a bark, whereupon she navigated the Lakes for a number of years. Finally she was purchased by a hotel keeper at Niagara Falls with the view of furnishing a circus for visitors there on a summer day. A live bear was placed on board, together with some other animals, and she was set adrift above the rapids, this noble relic whose decks had once run red with heroes' blood. A great crowd watched her from the banks of the Niagara River, expecting to see her go over the Falls, but she caught on the rocks and went to pieces. So perished the *Detroit,* a brave ship that deserved a better end; perhaps public sentiment prevailed against such shipwrecks, the most violent in the history of the Great Lakes, because that is the last record of such a fresh-water Roman holiday.

4. Smoke on the Water

A happier kind of Noah's Ark, American style, helped celebrate the opening of the Erie Canal on October 26, 1825, as relays of signal cannon boomed out the news from the shores of Lake Erie to the banks of the Hudson and on down to New York City, sending the glad tidings five hundred miles in ninety minutes. While the cannon roared, the swift packet boat *Seneca Chief,* made of stout Lake Erie red cedar and carrying top-hatted celebrities including De Witt Clinton himself, started out on her historic voyage from Buffalo to Sandy Hook.

At Rochester, New York, while thousands cheered from the canal banks, the *Young Lion of the West,* fitted out like a circus parade, swung in behind the *Seneca Chief.* The decks of the *Young Lion* showed a menagerie calculated to set her up in business as a floating zoo; a fox, a fawn, a brace of eagles, a pair of wolves, and four raccoons.

The packet *Niagara* then joined the procession and behind her came a boat actually named the *Noah's Ark* and carrying among her passengers an uneasy black bear. While the cannon boomed and bands played at every landing, while flags waved and multitudes cheered themselves hoarse and church bells rang out night and day, these trail-blazing ships went out the Erie Canal and down the rolling Hudson River into New York Harbor. There, after all the fancy speeches were over, a brass-bound cask of Lake Erie water aboard the *Seneca Chief* was emptied into the salty Atlantic Ocean. At the same time, bottles of water from the great rivers abroad, the Thames, the Seine, the Elbe, the Rhine, the Orinoco, the Ganges, and the Nile, were poured, thus symbolizing the union of all the waters on earth.

Then back went the *Seneca Chief,* the *Young Lion of the West,* the *Niagara,* and the *Noah's Ark,* to pour a cask of salt water into Lake Erie. Fireworks went off along the route to celebrate the wedding of the Great Lakes to the

Seven Seas, and the Erie Canal prepared to do a land-office business in transporting immigrants to the docks at Buffalo where steamboats were ready to carry them up into virgin territory and boundless reaches of fortune.

The smoke of the *Walk-in-the-Water* had pointed the way on September 1, 1818, and the description has been handed down to posterity by the *Cleveland Chronicle*:

> Residents along the shore saw upon the lake a curious kind of a vessel, making what was then considered very rapid progress westward, without the aid of sails, while from a pipe near its middle rolled forth a dark cloud of smoke, which trailed its gloomy length far into the rear of the swift-gliding mysterious traveler over the deep. They watched its westward course until it turned its prow toward the harbor of Cleveland, and then returned to their labors. Many of them doubtless knew what it was, but some shook their heads in sad surmise as to whether some evil powers were not at work in producing such a strange phenomenon as that, on the bosom of their beloved Lake Erie. Meanwhile the citizens of Cleveland perceived the approaching monster, and hastened to the lake shore to examine it.
>
> "What is it?" "What is it?" "Where did it come from?" "What makes it go?" queried one and another of the excited throng. "It's the steamboat, that's what it is," cried others in reply.
>
> "Yes, yes, it's the steamboat, it's the steamboat," was the general shout, and with ringing cheers the people welcomed the first vessel propelled by steam which had ever traversed the waters of Lake Erie.

During her years on the upper Lakes (and they numbered only three), the *Walk-in-the-Water* was known simply as "The Steamboat." Patriarch of the smoke-puffing clan, she became the first steamer to ride Huron, the first to dip her paddles into Michigan. Actually named after a Wyandotte chieftain but walking in the water like a thing alive — perhaps, as the Indians whispered, towed by sturgeon which the white men had trained — she opened an era in which proud steamers visiting the upper Lakes could come home

183

decked out with evergreens, tied to flagstaff, masthead, and bowsprit, as an indication of the far-off regions they had seen.

Harbinger of thousands of steamboats to come, the smoke of the little *Walk-in-the-Water* passed from the Lakes on the last trip of her third season. Plowing along at her eight miles an hour in late afternoon on October 31, 1821, the quaint teakettle on a raft, as sailors dubbed her, was hit by one of the sudden Erie squalls and wrecked on the beach near Buffalo. No lives were lost but a citizen of Detroit, writing to Henry Rowe Schoolcraft, the Indian Agent at Mackinac and the Soo who supplied Longfellow with the legends of *Hiawatha*, said:

"This accident may be considered as one of the greatest misfortunes which have ever befallen Michigan, for in addition to its having deprived us of all certain and speedy communication with the civilized world, I am fearful it will greatly check the progress of emigration and improvement."

Instead of being checked, progress was accelerated. New steamboats were built to take care of multiplying traffic. During the season of navigation in 1835, a total of 1,900 vessels docked at Cleveland. In May of the following season, ninety steamers arrived at Detroit, and at least 50,000 passengers were taken up the Lakes that year.

Boats were overloaded, chances were taken, carelessness prevailed, steerages were packed, deck litter was appalling, but the settlers bound for the new lands were as impatient and as reckless as the captains and crews. Fatal fires were caused by Old Country passengers who knocked out their pipes on the soft wood below decks as they retired for the night.

Rivalry between captains and competition between steamboat lines were sharp. A new era had arrived — steam locomotive by land and steam leviathan by Lake. The whole country was going up in smoke. As was done on the Mississippi, rival Lake captains challenged one another to races, and record crossings between ports were hailed with more enthusiasm than victory in the World Series today. The first arrival of the navigation season was greeted with much the same spirit as a modern college campus might welcome home the team that has just won an invitation to the Rose Bowl. On June 11, 1839, the *Chicago Daily American* let off steam headlining:

THE ARRIVAL OF THE ILLINOIS:

Our City was all life and animation this morning, and the docks crowded to witness the arrival of this magnificent boat on her first trip up for the season. She had a little difficulty this morning on account of her great size [about 180 feet long], and stood off the pier a short time; but she soon came up in gallant style. She left Buffalo on the morning of the second — remained in Detroit a day and a half, and left there last Saturday morning. She came well freighted and brought about a hundred passengers and one or two hundred steerage. We understand she had a rough and stormy time in Saginaw Bay, but that she rode the waves "like a thing of life," with admirable ease, quietness, and beauty, and won for herself the reputation with her other superior qualities of being a first-rate sea boat.

When the *Illinois* steamed into Milwaukee sometime later, the *Milwaukee Commercial Herald* broke out into seven stanzas of poetry, the first being a fair sample of the rest:

> Ho, all ye travelers to the west,
> If you are bound across the lake,
> And wish to take the boat that's best,
> Go on the Illinois with Blake.

When steamboats were the rage, Lake captains had all the color and popularity of today's baseball star and All American selection. Newspaper editors were fiercely partisan. In describing the record run of one steamer into Detroit, the *Detroit Daily Advertiser* defied any comparison: "That will do, we don't know the boat that can beat it."

185

Top hats, gold-mounted walking sticks, ruby-set watches, and other treasured souvenirs were presented by main-street merchants to the captains who cleared port with the first boat, arrived in port with the first boat, or came home with the last boat of the season of navigation. As a result, smoke rolled across Erie — long trails of smoke that stretched across the Lake to indicate fast passages; a sudden puff of smoke as a record-breaking steamboat fired a deck-cannon salute before rounding into harbor; and ominous black billows of smoke rising straight up from the water out over the Lake, to mark the place of a floating funeral pyre, the blazing death of a ship that never again would come triumphantly home to the tune of sawmill whistles and church bells while every able-bodied person in town came hurrying down to cheer her into dock.

5. Explosion and Fire

The shipping notice of 1830 carried the shadow of coming events in a brief item of the season:

> *First Steamboat Explosions.* — In September, the boilers of the *Peacock* exploded soon after her departure from Buffalo, which resulted in the loss of fifteen lives, mostly emigrants. Captain John Fleeharty was in command. This is recorded as the first explosion on the American side of the Lakes. The steamer *Adelaide,* Captain Christie, which was also running this year between Chippewa and Amherstburg, exploded in June, killing three persons. She was 230 tons burden, and low pressure.

Another grim prelude to the two Lake Erie shipboard fires that are ranked among the thirteen worst disasters in Great Lakes history was enacted about thirty-five miles from Buffalo, in June of 1838, when the steamer *Washing-*

ton caught fire beneath her boilers and went up in smoke during the night. Many passengers were aroused from sleep to find their cabins already in flames. The captain made the decision to shut off the engine so that a lifeboat could be lowered. About twenty-five were brought safely ashore in this way, but the launching of the boat had given the fire so much headway that the machinery could not be started again. An estimated forty people were burned to death or drowned. Boats from shore rescued many who had jumped into the water, their clothing ablaze. One of the passengers thus picked up listed the toll:

"Mr. Shudds is the only survivor of his family of seven. A lady passenger lost three children, a sister, and a mother. Mr. Michael Parker lost his wife and parents, sister, and her child. But I will not further continue the cases of individual bereavement."

Three years later, in almost the exact place on the chart, off Silver Creek, Lake Erie, on the night of August 9, 1841, the sixth worst disaster in fresh-water annals occurred when the side-wheel steamboat *Erie* caught fire after an explosion presumably caused by paint and turpentine in her deck litter.

Only a few short months before this tragic event, the editor of the *Buffalonian* had breezily announced:

> Charles M. Reed has done the handsome thing, and sent us his advertisements for the season and engaged us to advertise the starting notices of all his magnificent steamboats, the grand steamships *Jefferson* and *Madison,* the beautiful *Buffalo,* and the elegant *Erie.* Mr. Reed understands how to do business. A few months ago he married a beautiful wife, and now look at all his steamboats. This is real enterprise, and he will in a few years be the richest man on the lakes.

The elegant *Erie,* decked out with a fresh coat of paint destined to be her doom, cleared Buffalo late in the afternoon, bound up the Lakes for Cleveland, Detroit, and Chicago. There was a fresh breeze blowing and the waves were kicking up their heels, but the *Erie* made a brave show with her white hull, churning paddle wheels, and her two tall smokestacks. She took the choppy waters in stride and was about forty miles out of Buffalo at nine o'clock that night. Then came a noise no louder than as if someone had dropped a bottle on deck. Moments later the steamboat was ablaze from stem to stern, her fresh white paint crackling into black death.

There were upwards of two hundred passengers aboard, including 140 Swiss and German immigrants. They had piled the *Erie's* decks with the possessions they were taking into new lands: wagon wheels, family beds, cradles, chests of clothing, kitchen goods, farm implements, and barrels of provisions. Along with them, too, they carried their life savings, $180,000 in gold and silver coins earned and hoarded across the years to give them a fresh start in America.

On the course of the *Erie* but twenty miles ahead, the steamer *DeWitt Clinton* saw the red glow in the evening sky astern and turned about in a race to pick up any survivors. The steamers *Lady* and *Chatauque,* still further away, also hurried toward the scene. Hours distant but on the track of the *Erie,* the steamer *Fulton* drove toward the wreck. As these rescue ships approached, they came across floating debris that told its own story — a basket, a chest of tea, a box of lemons, hats, caps, cloaks, bonnets, and small pieces of burnt wood.

By the time the *Fulton* arrived only such relics as these remained to indicate the area where perhaps 175 people lay at the bottom. As the steamboat came into this vicinity, the captain checked her speed in token of respect while she passed over the unmade graves in solemn motion which was more fitting than any common tribute to the memory of the dead.

At the instant of disaster aboard the *Erie,* Captain Titus had rushed from the upper deck to the cabin where the life preservers were kept. Flames drove him back. Only one person managed to get a life preserver, Mrs. Lynde of Milwaukee, and she was the only woman saved in the disaster.

188

Captain Titus next tried to stop the engine because the brisk wind and the vessel's passage were fanning the blaze. But flames drove off the engineer. Then the wheelsman was ordered to put the helm hard-a-starboard, and the steamboat swung slowly around toward shore. This crew member stayed at his post until the machinery quit, making his duty useless, and, although rescued from the water, he died later of his burns, the one proven hero among the sailors.

There were three small boats aboard. Captain Titus ordered them lowered away, but only two of them were launched and, due to the heavy seas and the headway of the vessel, they both swamped immediately.

A colored gentleman named Edward Johnson, a ship's cook, has left the best eyewitness account of the shipwreck and the survival of twenty-nine including all the chief officers and the lone lady. A finger-count number of immigrants, all badly burned, were saved from the more than one hundred who had crowded into the steerage on the final lap of their voyage to the New World.

When the fire broke out amidships, according to Johnson, there was no attempt to fight it. People rushed for the boats, all of which he saw in the water, afterwards, bottom up.

"The people hallooed and screamed, and commenced jumping overboard. A tall gentleman came aft where I stood, followed by three ladies, who were screaming for mercy. He said, 'Don't be alarmed, we shall all be saved,' and then sang out, 'Man, run your boat ashore!' and in the next minute he jumped into the water from the taffrail, and was followed by the three ladies, neither of whom had made the least preparations to save themselves. This was the case with most of the people, who seemed to have lost all their senses. They would scream as they jumped from the vessel, strike the water, and nothing more could be heard.

"While the boat was leaving the harbor at Buffalo, I noticed a young lady, who was very gay, and who talked quite loud. She told a gentleman who was in conversation with her that she expected to be seasick, and that if he would get her things from the cabin, she would stay on deck. After the boat was on fire, the lady came to the same gentleman who was then standing in the corner by the taff-rail, and asked him to go and look for her father, to which the gentleman replied that it was of no use. He said he would try to save her, and having picked up a settee, he held it over the stern, and directed her to get over and take hold of it that he might thus let her down into the water. In attempting to do this, she let go her hold too soon, and fell into the water, and as she did not come up again, I supposed her head had struck on the rudder-blade. The gentleman then went overboard with the settee."

The Negro cook found a board fastened to the deck by an iron leg, and he wrenched it loose to help him in the water. Carrying the board somehow, he climbed over the stern and let himself down by means of the tiller chains.

"When in the water I could see lights all along the shore, and around the burning vessel the most appalling sight was displayed. Human bodies were plainly to be seen floating around by the glare which the fire threw out, and cries for help were heard in every direction."

Johnson called himself a good swimmer, and he had gotten about a mile and a half from the flaming steamboat when he saw two men in the water nearby. It must be remembered that the year was 1841. Detroit had organized its Anti-Slavery Society in 1837 and was a key station on the Underground Railway to Canada along with various Ohio towns, but Negroes on the Great Lakes still had reason to be wary of their brothers under the skin. When the two men adrift on the water called out to Johnson and asked what was keeping him up, he replied:

" 'Nothing.' I thought they were as good swimmers as myself, and I did not feel willing to share my board with them. Then said one of the men, 'O Lord! I do not think I can stand it to get ashore.' Hearing this, my sympathy

190

was awakened, and I hallooed to them and said, 'Come to me, I have a board.'"

The two men swam up and clutched one end of Johnson's board while he clung to the other end by the iron leg. After a while they saw the captain's yawl bottom side up, with ten or twelve people clinging to it. Dog-paddling alongside the board, they reached this boat. A short distance away could be heard a woman's voice calling for help. Captain Titus remarked that she was Mrs. Lynde and had a life preserver. Another person, also trying to keep a grip on the yawl, called out to her:

"My dear woman, you are doing better than we are!"

But the kind-hearted Negro could not bear to hear the cries for help echoing across the choppy night.

"I proposed to Captain Titus that if he would take hold of the end of my board, and agree to give it to me when I should come back, I would go for Mrs. Lynde and bring her up; to which he assented, and I swam towards her.

"When I reached her, she was lying nearly on her back. She had a life preserver on, reaching around her body under one arm and over the other shoulder. An oar was in the water near her, which I caught hold of to assist myself, and as I came up to Mrs. Lynde, she laid hold of it. I then seized her arm and swam with her towards the yawl, during which she complained much of the cold. When I had brought her to the yawl, I requested her to lay hold of the boat, but she declined to do so, and said, 'Let go, I shall do now.' I did so, and Captain Titus gave me my place again."

The steamboat *DeWitt Clinton* reached the scene about an hour after disaster had struck the side-wheeler *Erie*. No longer elegant, all her upper works had burned away. Her hull was a mass of dull red flame. A few crew members and passengers were still fighting for life in the lurid glow, some screaming in agony, half burned to death, half drowning.

The *Clinton* launched boats and, including those still

clinging to the captain's yawl despite its having flipped several times in the choppy waves, picked up twenty-seven survivors. The little steamboat *Lady* arrived in time to pick up two others, making a total of twenty-nine saved from the hundreds who had embarked from Buffalo only five hours before, apparently with the best years of their lives ahead of them.

In the final estimates, minimum loss of life was put at one hundred, with a possible maximum of 250. Consensus placed the toll at 175, a figure surpassed in shipboard fires on the Great Lakes only by the *Phoenix* in Lake Michigan six years later and the *G. P. Griffith* in Lake Erie nine years later.

An hour past midnight all was still at the scene of disaster, all except the dead crackling of fire. With no hope of further rescues, the *Lady* and the *Clinton* fastened lines to the remains of the *Erie's* rudder and attempted to tow the hulk ashore, but she sank about four miles from land, gasping out the last of her life in fiery steam as she went down in eleven fathoms.

There the charred ruins of the *Erie* lay for the next fourteen years, another mystery ship with a supposed cargo of sunken treasure in gold and silver coin, her secrets buried under sixty feet of water. Like any wreck haunted with the rumor of the wealth lying below, such as the *Pewabic* in Lake Huron, the *Erie* stole attention from even greater tragedies.

6. Death and Treasure

It is a commentary on human nature and a confirmation of the hope that springs eternal in man's breast that no story of shipwreck, however large the loss of life involved, can hold people fascinated as long as a story of sunken treasure. After a certain amount of horror, the mind rebels but it never shies away from great expectations or the vaguest possibility of sudden fortune. Along the Great Lakes the person who owns not even the leakiest rowboat is the one most likely to be waiting for his ship to come in.

"I'll buy that for you," a husband promises his wife; "We'll get that for the family," parents promise children; "just as soon as our ship comes in."

All of us, one way or another, are waiting for our ships to come in. Who knows what a ship may bring? The mystery is universal. In the present century we use the expression figuratively. In the past century people dropped whatever they were doing to run down to the dock and see for themselves, whenever a steamboat blew for a landing or a flying cloud of canvas hove in sight.

In the years following the conflagration of the once elegant side-wheeler *Erie,* crowds gathered at the shore to stare out across the water. In conversation they paid their routine tributes to the death toll, but in their hearts they wondered how much gold and silver lay out there, eleven fathoms under.

The years dreamed along with the wishful treasure hunters. Lake Erie kept adding minor disasters to her number, swallowing her full quota of steamboats and schooners, passengers and crews, but in 1850 she became an arena of wholesale destruction. The navigation season went into the maritime books as the most disastrous that had yet been recorded, in terms of lives lost; and Lake Erie claimed,

193

almost to a man, the grim total estimated from 431 to 450. In no season have all the Great Lakes combined taken such a toll as Erie alone took in 1850, except for the one shipwreck that dwarfs all others, the capsizing of the *Eastland* at the foot of Lake Michigan in 1915.

The season of navigation on Lake Erie for the year 1850 opened at Cleveland on March 2. On March 23 the steamer *Troy,* en route to Black Rock near Buffalo, exploded her boiler. A number were killed outright, others jumped overboard and were drowned, several died of injuries. A total of twenty-two perished.

Little more than a month later, the steamer *Anthony Wayne* left Toledo with twenty-five passengers on April 27 and picked up forty more at Sandusky that afternoon. She cleared port at ten that night and was standing out on the Lake less than three hours later when her two starboard boilers exploded, tearing away the steerage cabin above and shattering the hull. The captain's stateroom, next to the steerage, was blown to pieces and his bed flipped upside down, but by a freak of the accident he escaped injury.

Frightened passengers jumped overboard to take their chances on drowning rather than being burned alive. Many were scalded and kept moaning for help and water as they clung to the floating hurricane deck. A yawl was launched in which twelve persons reached shore. The captain and five others managed to get in a half-sinking lifeboat and after six hours of constant bailing reached the beach near Vermilion. The *Anthony Wayne* sank fifteen minutes after the explosion, going down in flames and carrying away the foremast to which six passengers were clinging. Estimated loss of life ran from thirty-eight to sixty-nine, and the havoc on Lake Erie had just begun.

On another midnight less than three weeks later, the steamer *Commerce* put out from Port Maitland on the north shore of the Lake. Aboard was a detachment of the 23rd

FT. WILLIAM

ISLE
ROYALE

LAKE SUPERIOR

COPPER
HARBOR

KEWEENAW
PENINSULA

SOO CANAL

DULUTH

SAINT IGNACE

BEAVER
ISLAND

PETOSKEY

CHE

CHARLEVO

MANITOU
IS.

PREVAILING
WINDS
SOUTH WEST

WISCONSIN

LUDINGTON

PENTWATER

MICH.

SHEBOYGAN

PORT WASHINGTON

MUSKEGON

GRAND HAVEN

MILWAUKEE

LAKE
MICHIGAN

SOUTH HAVEN

N

WAUKEGAN

ST. JOSEPH

ILLINOIS

CHICAGO

INDIANA

CANADA

ULT STE. MARIE

MANITOULIN IS.

GEORGIAN BAY

ALPENA

LAKE
HURON

SAGINAW
BAY

POINT AUX BARQUES

PORT HURON

SARNIA

TORONTO

LAKE   ONTARIO

OSWEGO

ROCHESTER

NIAGARA
FALLS

BUFFALO

NEW
YORK

DETROIT

LAKE
ERIE

AMHERSTBURG

ERIE

PENNSYLVANIA

TOLEDO

CLEVELAND

OHIO

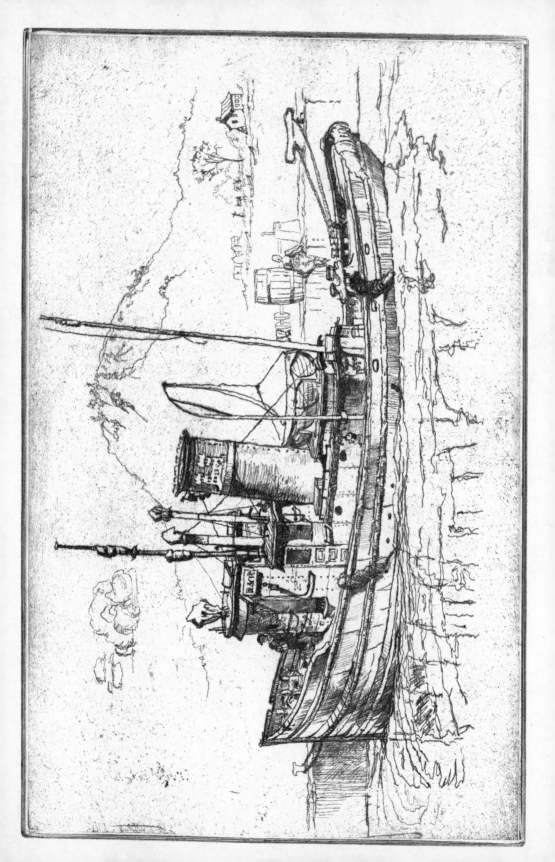

Welsh Fusiliers, one of England's historic regiments, bound from Montreal to garrison duty in London, Ontario. There were 150 in the regimental party and some of the men were accompanied by their wives and children.

A short way out of harbor the *Commerce* collided with the in-bound steamer *Despatch*. She sank in forty feet of water, every foot claiming a life. The weather was clear, both steamboats showed lights, and to this day no satisfactory explanation of the accident has been offered. An officer, twenty-two privates, and thirteen women and children connected with the regiment were drowned. Two non-military people lost their lives.

Ironically, a number of the soldiers who survived the shipwreck were living on borrowed time which came due at the Battle of the Alma during the Crimean War. One of the officers who conducted himself gallantly in the hour of collision, Lieutenant F. P. R. Delme Radcliffe, fell shot through the heart only thirty yards from his goal while leading the attack on a Russian battery in the face of a shower of grape and shell.

Lake Erie's third shipwreck of the 1850 season claimed forty-one lives, but the very worst was yet to come, the worst fire in Great Lakes history, the third worst disaster in the annals of the inland seas, but one that, for the curious reason already mentioned, always has received small notice in proportion to its size.

On a fine Sunday morning, June 26, the large steamboat *G. P. Griffith* took her departure from Buffalo. There were 256 in the steerage, forty-five in the cabins, and a crew of twenty-five. Many of the passengers were hopeful immigrants from England, Ireland, and Germany.

A ballad printed in an old newspaper, originally penned by the hand of Kate Weaver, seems to have taken several shipwrecks by fire, including that of the *Erie* and of the *Griffith,* and woven them into one. To a certain point it tells the story:

195

'Twas on Lake Erie's broad expanse
One bright midsummer day,
The gallant steamer Ocean Queen
Swept proudly on her way.

There is no record of any *Ocean Queen,* and the name *Griffith* would fit the metrical line just as well. In general, the majority of other details in the ballad could fit the *Griffith:*

Ah! who beneath that cloudless sky,
That smiling bends serene,
Could dream that danger, awful, vast,
Impended o'er the scene?
Could dream that ere an hour had sped,
That frame of sturdy oak
Would sink beneath the lake's blue waves,
Blackened with fire and smoke?

Actually the *Griffith* had come across the Lake in fine style that Sunday and was steaming along three miles offshore and about twenty miles from Cleveland at four o'clock Monday morning when fire was discovered. The ballad continues with accurate details:

A seaman sought the captain's side,
A moment whispered low,
The captain's swarthy face grew pale,
He hurried down below.
Alas! too late! Though quick and sharp
And clear his orders came,
No human efforts could avail
To quench the insidious flame.

Aboard the *Griffith* the mate had reported smoke coming from the hold. When the first alarm was given, the passengers, half-clothed, tumbled up on deck. The circumstances were frightening but they behaved remarkably calm. Not one scream was heard. Nobody made a motion to leap overboard. They seemed to have faith in the captain.

> *The bad news quickly reached the deck,*
> *It sped from lip to lip;*
> *And ghastly faces everywhere*
> *Looked from the doomed ship.*
> *"Is there no hope, no chance of life?"*
> *A hundred lips implore;*
> *"But one," the captain made reply,*
> *"To run the ship ashore."*

We have no record of the wheelsman's name aboard the *Griffith*, so the choice of the ballad-maker is as good as any. Again the details are accurate, even to the steering directions. The nearest shore lay to the southeast of the *Griffith*.

> *A sailor whose heroic soul*
> *That hour should yet reveal —*
> *By name John Maynard, Eastern born —*
> *Stood calmly at the wheel.*
> *"Head her southeast!" the captain shouts*
> *Above the smothered roar;*
> *"Head her southeast without delay!*
> *Make for the nearest shore!"*

> *No terror pales the helmsman's cheek*
> *Or clouds his dauntless eye,*
> *As in a sailor's measured tone*
> *His voice responds, "Aye, Aye!"*
> *Three hundred souls — the steamer's freight —*
> *Crowd forward, wild with fear,*
> *While at the stern the dreadful flames*
> *Above the deck appear.*

At this moment the shore was less than two miles away from the *Griffith*. The captain ordered full steam ahead, which increased the draft and fanned the flames, but it seemed a chance worth taking, with the beach and safety only five minutes distant.

John Maynard watched the nearing flames,
But still with steady hand
He grasped the wheel, and steadfastly
He steered the ship to land.
"John Maynard," with an anxious voice,
The captain cries once more,
"Stand by the wheel five minutes yet,
And we will reach the shore!"

Here the ballad departs from the facts of the ill-fated *Griffith.* The heroic wheelsman of the *Ocean Queen* burns to death but brings the steamboat onto shore, saving all three hundred souls on board.

Half a mile from safe haven, the wheelsman of the *Griffith* struck a sand bar out in the Lake. Captain Roby himself led the panic. He threw his wife, his two children, and his mother overboard, and followed them into the water, never to be seen again. With that example as a guide, the passengers went frantic. They ran in circles around the blazing deck and burned to death. They jumped into the water without throwing a stick of furniture or loose board to help buoy themselves up. They beat at the waves with their fists and drowned. Only the strongest swimmers survived and one of them, the barber's wife, was the solitary woman saved of all the wives and mothers and daughters who had gone aboard the *Griffith* at Buffalo, bound around the Lakes to raise families in a prosperous land. The mate swam to shore and brought help in small boats. In all, thirty men and the lone woman survived from the original passenger and crew list of 326. Estimates vary, but at least 250 and perhaps 296 perished in that red hour on Lake Erie.

In a short time the waves washed a hundred drowned bodies onto the beach. The shipping news noted that people had gone down so close together that eight bodies were recovered by drawing one to the surface with a hook. A trench was dug along the Lake shore and whole families of unidentified immigrants were buried without coffins in this common grave.

Many bodies never came ashore, for a reason peculiar to shipwrecks by fire, even on shallow Lake Erie. When men go down in a disaster on the Great Lakes, the bodies, as on any ordinary lake, may become inflated, rise to the surface, and float ashore. But quite often, depending on the season of the year and other conditions, when men drown on the great cold upper reaches of Huron, Michigan, and Superior, the bodies descend to such a depth in the icy water that they are preserved almost as if in a deep freeze. Decomposition is slowed considerably and, before the gases have a chance to start inflation, these bodies are decently covered and weighted down with a shroud of silt and plankton, entombed on the Lake bed until Judgment Day.

The reason why burned bodies are not so often recovered was explained by an old Lake captain when he described an explosion and fire aboard a steamboat. Everyone had jumped overboard except a man named Sam. He clung to the wreck until his clothing caught fire. Then he went down like a torch snuffed out in the water.

"They'll never find Sam," the old Lake captain said. "They'll find the drownded bodies, come spring, certainly see, but they'll never find Sam. A balloon that's been pricked ain't a balloon any more, is it? Won't hold gas. Neither will a burned body. Burned bodies sink. Never found, certainly."

In the decade of the greatest ship burnings on the Great Lakes — the holocausts of the *Erie* and the *Griffith* on Lake Erie and of the *Phoenix* on Lake Michigan — in the period from 1840 through 1850, it is estimated that one thousand lives were lost in explosions and fires aboard Lake steamboats, and Lake Erie claimed almost half that number in a single year. Even after the *Griffith* disaster in 1850, another one followed before the end of the season of navigation. The boilers of the steamer *American* exploded on the Lake in July at a cost of eleven more lives.

Meanwhile, the steamer *Delaware* pulled the wreck of the *Griffith* off the fatal sand bar. There it fell apart in deep water, out of sight and out of mind, while the side-wheeler *Erie* remained very much alive in the public fancy. Colored lithographs of the blazing *Erie* sold briskly but none of the *Griffith* received wide circulation. The two steamboats had much in common. They counted among the thirteen worst disasters in Great Lakes history and they each featured the survival of a lone woman. But the one carried down with her a rumor of sunken treasure, and that made all the difference in popularity.

People looked out from the Lake shore or stared at the lithograph on their walls and wondered: "Was there $180,000 or $200,000 aboard when she went down?"

No one knows the exact answer because treasure hunters are understandably vague about such matters. But finally in 1855 a salvage party raised the hulk of the *Erie* and towed her into Buffalo Harbor. The shipping news of that year was content to remark that large amounts of specie were recovered, paying the operators well for their enterprise. There were more definite reports that almost $200,000 in gold and silver, in sovereigns and rubles and marks and kronen and five-franc pieces, had been found.

The hard-earned cash that had crossed the Atlantic to buy land in Illinois and Wisconsin had been waylaid and transferred to other pockets by Lake Erie.

7. Charting Courses by Shipwrecks

In little more than a century Lake Erie has taken so many wrecks to her shallow bosom that a number of landmarks on government charts are relics of disaster. Modern ships are enabled to steer safe courses thanks to the remnants of those who went wrong. As an example:

> For Detroit River, departing from a position 1 mile south of Southeast Shoal Light steer 302 degrees for 10 miles to a position 7/8 mile 32 degrees from Armenia Wreck Lighted Buoy, etc., etc.

Today's wheelsman keeps in the deep channel marked by lights and buoys set on the ships that went down in bygone days. There is a whole philosophy of life in that fact, as well as another revelation of the ties that bind the Lakes to the land.

The intimacy between Lake and land remains, but the whole era that marked many a boyhood in the past half-century is shipwrecked now, gone like a puff of smoke in the Lake Erie wind, a Flying Dutchman that sails only in the memory of the thousands who then took it for granted, as a way of life that would last forever.

In those days people could step from the floor of a house to the deck of a steamboat — and never leave home. Water was as much their natural element as air. Every pleasant weekend countless parents drove the family car aboard one of the Windsor ferries that hustled across the Detroit River into Canada for a picnic or an overnight stay at some place like Oxley Beach where the youngsters could walk along the Erie shore from Amherstburg to Leamington and dream up wild stories of shipwrecks from the driftwood they came across.

Every hot summer day mothers packed picnic baskets

for their families and they all went for a ride out the river into Lake Erie, to catch the breeze aboard one of the passenger boats that ran almost as often as streetcars. A boy could stand on deck and look out at Put-in-Bay and hear the roar of Perry's guns in the cannonading of a summer thunderstorm. On holidays, when men could get off work and come along, engineer fathers would take their children down into the engine room to watch the great silver arms of the pistons exercising up and down in a setting of shiny brass, and the youngsters would stare in awe at men natty as cooks in a working area as spotless as their mothers' kitchens. Or the fathers might take the children up to the observation windows and call out, "The up-bound freighter is the *John M. Nichol* and the down-bound freighter is the *William H. Stevens*," when the names at the bow and the stern were only a blur to the sharp young eyes of their offspring. This was a private little joke shared by many fathers and it was some time before the youngsters grew smart enough to realize that, long before they could read the letters, their fathers could tell the name of the long ship by some trait which identified her from the rest of the crowd, a sign as distinctive to Lake dwellers as a baby's birthmark.

Now and again parents would drive the family car aboard a D & C boat for an overnight to Cleveland, and more rarely a maiden aunt or two might take the children on a trip to Niagara Falls across the Lake, and, provided they were lucky enough to run into a storm, the grown-ups would get so seasick that the youngsters had all the titbits on the dining-room menus to themselves. At the Falls they watched the great curtains of water descend with a sound like the ruffle of ten thousand drums and they itched to throw something in and see it take the plunge.

They paddled and rowed and putt-putted and sailed on the Detroit and up the St. Clair, swarming like water bugs in the busy strait where even now a big boat passes Windmill Point every twelve minutes during the season of navigation. They played baseball and football on Belle Isle so near to the down-bound channel in the Detroit River that a home run or even a long forward pass might land aboard a freighter lying low in the water with a cargo of iron ore consigned from Duluth to Cleveland.

Their lives were filled with white spray, blue depths, green shallows, churning paddle wheels, and towering sails. They were amphibious. The whole region lived up to the name of its first steamboat — *Walk-in-the-Water*. Land-lubbers and Lake-goers, they went from shore to boat and from boat to shore with no more feeling of transition than have people today who step from curb to car and back again.

Being constantly around the water never imbued them with the familiarity that breeds contempt, but it made them carefree of danger. Their greatest fear in boyhood was not of getting into accidents but of being discovered badly hurt or drowned in soiled underclothes. They went on trips with stern admonishments to put on clean things *beneath* their holiday attire. Somehow these boys got the idea that it would be perfectly all right if they fell into the paddle wheel or the propeller, just as long as they were picked up in spotless linen. They never dreamed of the boat catching fire or getting rammed in a fog or being keelhauled by a submerged rock. They were always too worried about the state of their B.V.D's.

As a person grows older, he realizes how basic this idea is in human nature. Everybody wants to die in a decent way, with as little embarrassment to himself and to others as possible.

There is no better illustration of this than the case of Leathem D. Smith, president of a shipbuilding firm and trustee of the Great Lakes Historical Society, who purchased the thirty-eight-foot racing sloop *Half Moon* from James Roosevelt, son of F. D. R. He was caught in a squall on Green Bay on June 23, 1946, with a party of five, including two of his executives, his daughter Patricia, 18, and her college friend Mary Loomis, also 18. Only one life preserver bobbed free when the *Half Moon* overturned, and the craft was sinking. Smith gave the life preserver to the girls and shook hands with his daughter before they started to swim ashore. She was the only one who made it, after six hours in the water. Miss Loomis, exhausted, slipped from the preserver near the beach.

Another case in point occurred on Lake Michigan in 1957 near Charlevoix. Three young Coast Guard men took off for a spin in a small boat powered by a heavy outboard motor. They flipped in choppy water off the South Point. It was April, the ice had just cleared the bay, survival time was at a minimum. The three boys clung to the bow, unable to kick the boat toward shore because the weight of the motor dragged the stern under. One boy, weaker than the others, fought against shock and exposure but realized that he could not hang on by himself and did not want to endanger the chances of his two mates by having them try to hold him up. He said his prayers aloud, made an act of contrition, took his hands off the boat to cross himself, and slipped down. The other boys were rescued by the Coast Guard minutes later just as they, too, were losing their holds from exposure and exhaustion.

A shake of the hand, a short prayer, a quiet leave-taking from life so that others might have a chance to survive — this is what many parents meant to teach their children in the tradition of the Great Lakes, where boys might be called upon to prove themselves men at any moment.

How many times boys brushed death on those carefree excursions out the Detroit River and into Lake Erie nobody knows. A dramatic illustration of the narrow margin between disaster and survival was given on the night of June 18, 1936, when more than 1,500 excursionists on the huge steamboat *Tashmoo* were poised on the brink of drowning without knowing a thing about it. Homeward-bound in the Sugar Island Channel of the Detroit River, busiest waterway in the world, the *Tashmoo* hit an obstruction. Down below in the engine room the water quickly swirled to the stokers' waists, while up above the band played on for hundreds of dancing passengers. Captain McAlpine gave orders that sent the *Tashmoo,* a proud sight with all her lights ablaze on the water, full steam toward the nearest dock in a race against complete disaster which could easily have claimed more lives than the *Eastland* disaster. Thanks to the engine-room personnel who stuck to their posts and the gallantry of the rest of the crew, the *Tashmoo* reached Amherstburg inside ten minutes. No sooner had she discharged her passengers than down she went beside the dock in twenty-five feet of water.

8. Introducing Herself in Person

Lake Erie has always had more personal relationship with the land than all the other Lakes, simply because more people have come to dwell around her shores and more boats have trafficked her waters. Lake Erie sailors are no more colorful than the sailors on the other Lakes, but there have been more of them, and they have oftener appeared upon the stage of dramatic events.

Erie is the Lake of short hauls, quick trips, stops and starts, hello-goodbys. If a nineteenth-century steamboat captain didn't pause along the way for a bite between meals at Toledo or Sandusky or Lorain or Ashtabula or Conneaut, Ohio, or Erie, Pennsylvania, or Dunkirk, New York, he could enjoy an early breakfast in Detroit, a late lunch in Cleveland, and a midnight supper in Buffalo, where he could take a cat nap while freight and passengers came aboard, and then resume his Lake Erie menu in reverse.

Steamboats on Erie were as familiar a sight in each port, and as welcome, and almost as regular, as today's mailman. They carried the mail, of course; they brought the latest news. They served the purpose of today's interurban and commuter trains; they were Greyhound buses running on fresh water.

Better known in their day than television celebrities, the captains of crack steamboats strutted in port, promenading the water front while admiring eyes took in their blue coats, brass buttons, nankeen trousers, white vests, low shoes, white silk stockings, ruffled shirts, high hats, jingling gold watch chains and seals. In the era of the Civil War they sported Prince Alberts and stovepipe lids and General Grant beards that gave them the appearance of Barnum's trained walruses.

They called anything that floated a boat, and on occasion they even used the word ship, but the term had no relation to size on the Great Lakes. A boat was a boat, from a lumber hooker to a battlewagon. The day would come when fresh-water boats grew large enough to serve as aircraft carriers, but boats they remained to the Lake people who in general steered clear of salt-water parlance to measure speed in miles rather than knots and to keep time by the Big Ben alarm clock rather than ships' bells.

A captain had a whole list of pet names for his boat; she was his darling, his sweet business, his plaything, his huckleberry. There were steamboat engineers who petted and stroked their machinery and talked baby talk to the various parts in an effort to coax more speed out of them: "It's a sweet little engine; it's the prettiest little piston; it's a cute little valve; it's the nicest little bearing. . . ."

The captains were always roaring for more speed so the engineers had plenty of practice on baby talk. Coming out of Cleveland in a heavy fog, Captain Wight of the *William Penn* once observed what he figured to be the smokestack of another steamer between his boat and the shore. He ordered full speed ahead, opining that he would never allow anything on Lake Erie to pass him, not if he knew it! The race went on, sparks flying and paddles churning, until the fog cleared to reveal that the supposed rival smokestack was nothing but a fire-blasted tree along the shore.

This same Captain Wight was coming out of the Buffalo harbor one day when the steamer *Illinois* hove in sight abaft the *William Penn* and gained rapidly on her. Whereupon an anxious passenger said:

"Captain, she is after us, isn't she?"

"Never mind," said Captain Wight, shaking his fist. "We will be *after her* directly!"

Spokesman for all steamboat captains on Lake Erie, it was Wight who bragged that the *William Penn* could "run anywhere where the ground was moist."

By Lake Erie custom when a captain made a record run, he hoisted a broom atop the smokestack or foremast and kept it there until beaten. The shipping news of 1839 made this note:

> During the season there was considerable rivalry in regard to speed, and not infrequently in company a high pressure of steam was carried. The steamer *Cleveland* claimed to be the fastest boat, without the necessity of racing, which was inserted in her bills. She claimed to make the run between Cleveland and Buffalo in fourteen hours, and from Detroit to Buffalo on one occasion, with a fair freight and one hundred passengers, in twenty-one hours and thirty-eight minutes, the distance being three hundred miles. Not long after this, however, the steamer *Buffalo,* Captain Levi Allen, made the distance between Detroit and Buffalo in nineteen hours, and carried the broom for the remainder of the season.

The year 1853 marked another famous racing season on Lake Erie. Captain McBride's *Queen of the West* challenged Captain Hazard's *Mississippi* on the run from Buffalo to Cleveland, and lived up to her name. Among other contests that same year, the steamboat *Queen City* raced the *Alabama* over the identical course, a distance of 173 miles, and had a winning time of twelve hours and ten minutes, giving her an average speed of almost 15 miles an hour.

These contests continued across the years on Lake Erie with the most famous of all reserved for the year 1901 when Detroit's crack excursion boat *Tashmoo* raced Cleveland's *City of Erie* on June 4 over a course laid out from Cleveland's breakwater to the lighthouse off Erie, Pennsylvania, almost one hundred miles.

A historic event never to be repeated because of the disaster inherent in such trials of speed, the two floating palaces of the Lake approached the starting point at about 9:30 in the morning. For more than a hundred miles the south shore of Lake Erie was lined with holiday crowds. Business shut down; school was closed; passenger steamers were charted from Detroit and other ports to bring spectators to the scene; thousands of dollars had been wagered on the outcome of the race.

A cannon boomed and the race was on with the *Tashmoo* and the *City of Erie* almost abreast, their paddle wheels kicking up huge swells and clouds of spray flying back from their sharp bows.

At Fairport, Ohio, the *Tashmoo* forged ahead; at Ashtabula Harbor, the *City of Erie* pulled abreast again; at Conneaut she was two lengths ahead; twenty miles from the finish line she had increased her lead to three lengths. On the last stretch the *Tashmoo* desperately tried to close the gap, and the wake she and her rival kicked up almost swamped the timekeepers and the judges in their boats, but the watches showed that the *Tashmoo* had come in a heartbreaking forty-five seconds behind the *City of Erie,* both steamboats averaged just a fraction less than twenty-two miles an hour for ninety-four miles, a record still to be envied by most modern steamers and respected even by the ultramodern 520-foot *Aquarama* in her heyday on the Detroit-Cleveland run, whose cruising speed across Lake Erie was set at that same figure.

Although the *Tashmoo* lost her race against the *City of*

Erie in June of 1901, she went on to win the greatest victory any steamboat could boast, on another June day thirty-five years later, when, mortally wounded herself, she carried 1,500 passengers to safety, and then died alongside the dock.

From the year 1818 when the *Walk-in-the-Water* started posting records for other steamboats on Lake Erie to shoot at, until 1901 when the *Tashmoo* and the *City of Erie* ended such debates, rival captains on the short hauls across the shallow inland sea took desperate chances to beat one another into Cleveland, Detroit, Buffalo, and all points.

These captains also took big chances to extend the season of navigation. One winter Captain Whitaker of the steamer *United States* took his boat out of Buffalo and plowed through drift ice until he came to a large field of ice that barred passage into the open Lake. Instead of returning to port, he herded all the passengers on the upper deck and told them to run from one side of the steamer to the other all together. This gave the boat a rolling motion that helped break down the ice while Captain Whitaker backed up and drove ahead until he had rammed his way through into navigable water.

The desperate chances taken by captains in overloading their boats was matched by the nonchalance of the passengers who regarded this as a sign of a boat's popularity and thought no more about it, except perhaps for taking a kind of pride in the matter. One traveler, hearing about the shipwreck of such a steamboat named the *Mayflower,* reminisced casually:

"I have often waited for her, in company with others, at Buffalo, twenty-four hours at a time, and when the hour for her departure arrived, she would appear to be in an almost sinking condition, loaded as she was with passengers, their baggage, and her usual freight."

Then this traveler would hop aboard, with cheerful disregard for possible consequences, and add his weight to the steamer's sinking condition, which was in the true spirit of Lake transportation.

Despite the chances the Lake Erie captains took, both in sail and in steam, and despite the shipwrecks that resulted, they also should be credited, on the other side of the ledger, with bringing many a boat into safe harbor, thanks to a brand of seamanship never excelled on salt water.

Late in the nineteenth century a large ocean-going ship put out from port to cross the Lake at about the same time an old fresh-water captain started out in his little boat. A storm blew up, wrecking the former vessel, but the veteran skipper weathered the gale and brought his boat safe to the far shore. A company official was rushed to the scene to investigate the disaster and question the survivor of the storm.

"We can't understand it," he said. "Our ship was built to cross the Atlantic."

"Yup," the old Lake captain agreed, and he added, meaning no offense, "but she wasn't built to cross the Great Lakes, certainly see."

"We want to get to the bottom of this," the company man said, anxious to find a technical reason for the small boat's survival. "How did you make it through a storm that sent a western ocean ship down?"

The old Lake captain had survived gales in which he could see the Muskegon clay banks or Sleeping Bear dune through the centerboard slot when his Mackinac boat heeled over in the wind. He had been out on the Lakes when a hurricane turned mountainous seas into hills by blowing their tops off into white squalls of spindrift. Now he reflected on the company man's question. "Well," he said finally, "I did a lot of bailing that day."

Not at all satisfied, the company official kept insisting that there had to be a more scientific explanation of why an ocean-going vessel had been shipwrecked in a storm that a fresh-water cockleshell had survived.

Eager to oblige, the old Lake captain considered the subject further and then came up with his ultimate answer:

"I had to favor her something awful to keep her on top," he said. "A boat's like a woman, you have to favor a boat sometimes, certainly see." He paused and nodded for emphasis. "If I hadn't favored some of them, I wouldn't be here, certainly."

There were hundreds of such captains on the Lakes. They went out in weather that literally scared fish in frightened schools from one depth to another. They made gallant rescues under impossible conditions, and now and then a wild spark of humor would show in their ice-blue eyes:

"Was they anxious to leave the wreck? Didn't say. One hit me with his suitcase and the other knocked me down jumping aboard."

Their golden era is gone in smoke, but the memory of the old Lake captains may be seen in the long sunset ladders of pure molten gold that climb the high wall of Lake Erie from the Canadian shore. Each flowing step in the ladder, every rising wave, is a tribute to one of them.

9. Collision in the Fog

With her short hauls and heavy traffic, Lake Erie always has been a cozier body of water than the other Lakes, especially when compared with the cold and aloof reaches of upper Huron, Michigan, and Superior. Sometimes this closeness between Lake and shore could become grimly intimate, leading to such a notice as appeared in the shipping news of the 1854 season of navigation:

> The schooner *K. R. Johnson*, laden with wheat, foundered with all hands off Fairport, Ohio. Captain Snell, who commanded her, was seen in the rigging by his wife on

shore, waving his coat, but finally fell off in sight of home and friends, and was drowned.

With boats shuttling back and forth, crisscrossing along the way, Lake Erie could become too cozy for comfort even in a slight haze or fog. In the small hours of Friday, August 20, 1852, the steamboats *Atlantic* and *Ogdensburg* were approaching each other under such conditions off Long Point along the south shore, and the fifth worst disaster in Great Lakes history was in the making.

Due to her close association with Niagara Falls, Lake Erie very early became a favorite with newlyweds. At least one of the crack vacation liners of the past was nick-named the "Honeymoon Special." By mid-nineteenth century, steamboat lines already were advertising such features as the following:

> The bridal chamber, situated in the upper cabin, in point of splendor puts anything we have seen to the blush. The sheets are of linen cambric, the quilt of straw-colored moire-antique; the sheets and pillowcases are edged with point lace and the beds are of elaborately carved rosewood. The floor is covered with a heavy pile of tapestry while golden mirrors reflect the gorgeous furniture of the entire room, which is commodious and gilded throughout. We advise every young man to take a look at it.

There were honeymooners returning from Niagara Falls and happy in such a bridal chamber as the luxurious side-wheeler *Atlantic* clipped along toward Detroit through the ill-omened night. One of the fastest boats on the Lakes, she had made the trip from Buffalo to Detroit in 1849 in sixteen and a half hours, the quickest passage up to that time.

Large for her era, the *Atlantic*, 267 feet long and 1,155 tons, had eighty-five staterooms. She could carry three hundred cabin passengers and a still greater number of deck or steerage passengers. The clerk lost his trip sheet when the boat went down, but he judged that there had been between five and six hundred passengers aboard, about 150 cabin passengers and some 426 deck passengers, most of whom

212

were immigrants, including two hundred Norwegians from the steep farms of Stavenger and Christiansund who would never see the broad prairies of the Midwest for which they had left their native fjords.

The other boat in the accident was another palatial liner, but the brand-new *Ogdensburg* had a propeller instead of paddle wheels. Powered from the stern, she drove across the water toward Buffalo, her bows carving the Lake into white slices.

Reports about visibility differ, as do most reports on any disaster. The later accounts all speak of a dense fog, but the more contemporary accounts mention the weather as slightly hazy, with almost a dead calm prevailing, and the stars visible. At any rate, without a cry of warning from a lookout, the steamboats came together with thunderbolt impact in the night and then a grinding of wooden timbers as the *Ogdensburg* backed water and took herself out of the hole she had driven into the *Atlantic's* port side, so deep that her liberty cap had extended over the deck of the mortally wounded paddle-wheel steamer.

At first there was no great alarm aboard the *Atlantic*. Believing that no grave damage had been done, the *Ogdensburg* continued on her course for about two miles, her crewmen hacking away at the wreckage on her bows until screams across the night hurried her back to the scene of collision.

Meanwhile the *Atlantic* had kept on her own westward course without losing a stroke of her engine. Neither the captain nor the chief engineer seem to have realized the extent of damages, because the doomed steamboat drove ahead until her fires were extinguished by the rapidly rising water.

Then, at the moment of vital decision, when a voice of real command might have saved the situation with minimum loss of life, the captain apparently lost his head. He bungled in attempts to launch a small boat and then injured himself by falling into a yawl, which made him completely useless. In the wake of the disaster, the survivors held a meeting and

213

censured him for not providing sufficient life perservers and small boats to save those who drowned, and they asserted that there was an entire lack of authority to prevent passengers, especially women, from throwing themselves wildly into the Lake.

Panic swept the sinking steamer. Following the grim pattern in such disasters, many of the passengers and crew jumped overboard without making any preparation. Others threw chairs, benches, settees, bedding — anything that would float — into the water before they leaped for life.

The last cries for help and the first cries of hope mingled in the night as the lights of the *Ogdensburg* were seen hurrying to the rescue. Fortunately the *Atlantic* continued to float some distance, and when she sank, her stern, buoyed up by air in the after hold, remained above the surface. Hundreds got death grips on this wreckage and all who clung to it were saved by the gallant crew of the *Ogdensburg*.

When the survivors were brought into Erie, Pennsylvania, the early estimates of loss were about 325. After the first shock and hysteria wore away, the toll was scaled down to a minimum of 150 and a maximum of 250.

The name of Captain Pettys is not among the proud names in history, but there have been more than enough brave deeds inscribed on the honor roll of steamboat men to make up for his lack of command on the night the *Atlantic* was bringing back the honeymooners from Niagara and the immigrants from Norway, only to sink them, along with the seven proud pennants on her staffs, in thirty fathoms of Erie water, six miles off the south shore.

214

10. Messages in Bottles

The shipping news for the navigation season of 1845 carried the following notice:

Boisterous Weather. — The extremely boisterous weather was very destructive to lives and vessels, amounting to, as nearly as a careful account can make it, thirty-six vessels driven ashore. Twenty of these became total wrecks, four foundered at sea.

The boisterous weather struck again in November of 1869, visiting all five of the Great Lakes with the worst toll of shipwrecks in recorded history. A catastrophic storm rode a gale out of Lake Superior to hurricane down Lake Michigan and Lake Huron, and blast across the lower Lakes to blow Lake Erie and Lake Ontario spray into clouds that dropped snow on the St. Lawrence River.

From the Apostle Islands in Lake Superior to the Thousand Islands at the foot of Lake Ontario, the Lake shores were littered with masts and spars, hulls and sails, lifeboats and life belts, the latter ironically named because they contained nothing but dead men. In Buffalo and Chicago, in Detroit and Cleveland, in Saginaw and Toronto, in Duluth and Milwaukee, owners waited for ships that would never come in, and women yearned in vain for the sailors they had kissed good-bye.

Through four November days, eighty years ago, the storm king raged over the Lakes, striking icy fists at six propellers, a paddle-wheel steamer, one tug, eight barks, four brigs, fifty-six schooners, three barges, and eighteen scows — a total of seventy-seven vessels wrecked or swept from sight forever.

There are some who claim that this storm marked the turning point between sail and steam on the Lakes. Shipping men examined the statistics and decided that sailing vessels were too vulnerable to fresh-water's boisterous winds and lee

215

shores, whereas steamboats could fight for the sea room that meant survival.

This point has nothing to do with the fight for supremacy between sail and steam, but to offer in evidence a last-minute message corked in a bottle that washed ashore on one of Lake Erie's so-called Wine Islands the next spring:

"Nov. '69. Mast gone. Sinking fast. Good-bye all. *Gold Hunter.*"

There were at least half a dozen *Gold Hunters* on the Lakes in this era, three of them schooners and all lost or wrecked, but only one left a farewell note that was found, and she remains unidentified.

Earlier in the same decade, on August 18, 1861, Mrs. E. Bowen was walking along the docks of the bustling Cuyahoga River in Cleveland when she spied a corked bottle floating toward shore. The message read:

"On board schooner *Amelia,* August 12, off Grand River, schooner lost foremast, also mainsail, leaking badly, cargo iron. Must go down. All hands must be lost. C. S. Brace, captain."

There were at least three *Amelias* on the Lakes in this era, starting with the one in Perry's squadron, and all of them schooners, but only this one delivered a message written by a dead man's hand and both the sailing vessel and the captain remain unidentified.

No great mystery is inferred. The large, shallow Lake has swallowed many an unlisted ship and unlicensed master. Sailing in those days was a haphazard business. Even so, the authenticity of some farewell notes found in bottles could provide an interesting subject for speculation. A number of them have a studied calm, or a theatrical flair, or a gossipy newsiness that may not be inconsistent with their having been written while death looked over the writer's shoulder, but they either bear a resemblance to the crank letters that follow a tabloid crime or they give the impression of having been planted, as a hoax, after the shipwreck, in a place of easy finding.

216

Dropping notes in bottles during pleasant weather long has been a popular hobby among Great Lakes sailors. Such notes generally contain the writer's name and address, along with the request that any finder drop him a line as to where it was picked up. The vast majority of these hobbyists are still waiting for their bottles to be discovered.

A professor studying Great Lakes currents at the Duluth Branch of the University of Minnesota has reported that out of a thousand bottles dropped in Lake Superior to test currents, only 350 have been found.

These bottles were dropped under average circumstances, not in the height of a storm whose heavy seas could plunge them to depths where they would explode under pressure, or smash them against rocks, or coat them with ice, or hurl them high onto uninhabited shores, or a thousand other mishaps which glass is heir to.

This raises a much more interesting and dramatic question than the genuineness of farewell notes found in bottles. How many have been written at death's elbow on a sinking ship during a man's last few precious moments of life, never to be found?

One of the most genuine instances of a farewell note at the moment of shipwreck, and certainly one of the most poignant, was written by Captain Hugh M. Williams to his wife during Lake Huron's great storm of November, 1913, that also created havoc on Lake Erie. Captain Williams commanded the government *Lightship No.* 82, anchored at the entrance to Buffalo Harbor. After the storm, the lightship was no more to be seen than if she had been swept clear of Erie by a giant's broom. The only clue to her fate was found on one of her boards which came ashore. On this board the captain had written these few last words to his wife:

"Good-bye, Nellie, ship is breaking up fast — Williams."

11. Black Friday

Among old-time Lake dwellers, Black Friday long has been a household phrase, rivalled only by Dark Sunday, somber nickname for the November, 1913, Lake Huron storm, when the clouds were so dark and the blizzard so thick that midday differed not at all from midnight.

October 20, 1916, marked the grimmest modern date in Lake Erie's shipwreck-studded history. The storm king who visited her differed from other storm kings in that he concentrated all his force against her instead of wasting any strength on her big sisters.

On Black Friday there were four boats caught out on the open Lake: the schooner *D. L. Filer,* the lumber hooker *Marshall F. Butters*, the Canadian steamer *Merida,* and the whaleback freighter *James B. Colgate.* They all went down in the storm. Four brave captains stayed with their ships to the last. Three of them lived to tell the story. Two of the three were the only ones left to tell what happened, because they survived the bitter experience of watching their entire crews perish.

The Canadian steamer *Merida* was sighted once on Black Friday, about ten miles off the Southeast Shoals in Lake Erie, by Captain Massey of the steamer *Briton.* He observed her to be making bad weather of her passage, and he considered himself lucky to be able to make shelter off Cedar Point. The doomed *Merida* was never seen again. Several days after the storm blew itself out, bodies of men were found floating in the middle of the Lake, their heads bowed in life preservers bearing the name *Merida.* All hands were lost, twenty-three.

The steamer with the most ominous number aboard on Black Friday proved to be the most fortunate as far as human survival was concerned. The lumber carrier *Marshall F. Butters* carried thirteen men, counting captain and crew, out the mouth of the Detroit River into the storm. She was loaded with shingles and boards for Cleveland, and her cargo started to shift as she rolled wildly in the sharp seas. The *Butters* developed a list.

"Trim cargo!" roared Captain McClure. "For your lives!"

Fear of death put wings on the feet of the men, and eyes in their hands, but they were unable to keep the ship from sinking under them. Water crashed aboard. Captain McClure grabbed the steamer's whistle and sounded the distress signal, but it had no more chance of being heard above the storm than a pin dropping in a boiler factory.

As the *Butters* settled lower in the water and the fires in her boilers went out, she lost headway and drifted at the mercy of Black Friday. Ten of the crew launched lifeboats and took their chances that way. Captain McClure stayed with his ship. Two of the crew kept him company while he yanked in desperation at the steamboat's whistle while the decks began going awash.

Two large freighters, the *Frank R. Billings* and the *F. G. Hartwell*, were approaching the scene. The *Hartwell* picked up the men in the half-swamped lifeboats. Captain Cody of the *Billings* could not hear the distress signals of the *Butters*, but he read the message conveyed by the puffs of white steam from the doomed ship's whistle.

Despite mountainous seas he drove his big freighter all the way around the *Butters*, dropping storm oil as he went in order to calm the waters and get close enough to send a line aboard. This he managed in a display of great seamanship, and the remaining men were pulled to safety aboard the *Billings* in the nick of time before the lumber hooker went to the bottom of Lake Erie.

"That wind blew seventy miles an hour," Captain McClure said after his rescue. "Worst storm I ever experienced."

With perverse disregard for "unlucky" numbers, Black Friday had spared thirteen men at a point thirteen miles from the Southeast Shoals, but the storm hurried across Erie toward other victims.

The wooden schooner *D. L. Filer,* with a cargo of coal from Buffalo bound around the horseshoe to Saugatuck on Lake Michigan, was caught by Black Friday just on the verge of safety as she neared Bar Point at the mouth of the Detroit River. Crashing mountains of water opened her at the seams; the pumps, manned by a veteran crew of six Norwegian sailors, could not begin to take care of the inflood; and the schooner settled in the shoals, eighteen feet below.

As the *Filer* went down, all six members of her crew scrambled up into the foremast which poked out high above the water, while the captain climbed into the aftermast and clung there by himself. Under the strain of the storm and the weight of the six crew members, the forty-five-year-old foremast cracked and came smashing down into the waves where five of the men drowned. The sixth swam to the aftermast and clung to it with Captain Mattison throughout a night of terror and tragic disappointment.

Once a steamer passed so close that they could almost reach out and touch her sides. They shouted until their voices cracked, but the big ship plowed on her way, their cries unheard in the Black Friday night.

Dawn brought a new day to Lake Erie, and the D & C passenger boat *Western States* came steaming out of Detroit bound for Cleveland. Captain Salem Robinson sighted the telltale mast and the two survivors clinging to it. He ordered a boat lowered, which sped to the scene. Passengers crowded the rails of the *Western States* to watch the rescue. At the last moment, a horrified gasp came from the steamer's decks. On the brink of being hauled aboard the lifeboat, one of the men had lost his grip on the mast and tumbled to death, his body never reappearing above the surface.

Captain Mattison alone survived. Black Friday had made him a skipper without a ship or a crew.

But Black Friday had another, and an even more incredible, drama to enact on the troubled waters of Lake Erie.

Shortly after midnight on the fatal date of October 20, 1916, the stout whaleback steamer *James B. Colgate* pulled out of Buffalo with a load of coal for Fort William, Ontario, up in Lake Superior.

Captain Walter J. Grashaw noted the rising wind and the waves hammering at the breakwater as he took the whaleback out into the open Lake, but he never gave a thought to turning back. The *Colgate* was a seasoned veteran of many storms. In her twenty-four years she had ridden out everything the Lakes could throw at her, and she was still a strong-growing girl as Lake freighters go.

Captain Grashaw had served as the *Colgate's* first mate for ten years before he had been given this, his first, command only two weeks before. He had complete confidence in her; he knew every strong point and weakness she had. He could keep her on top by *favoring* her through the storm.

Bucking tremendous seas, the whaleback made slow work of it during the night and at dawn she was only coming up to Long Point on the Canadian shore, not quite opposite Erie, Pennsylvania, with the broadest and roughest part of the Lake still ahead. Although tired from an all-night vigil, Captain Grashaw still put trust in the *Colgate's* survival. He counted on the blows she had weathered in the past, but now she was driving into the teeth of a storm whose likes Lake Erie had never seen.

At dawn the gale had begun to freshen into a hurricane. Black Friday went berserk across the water, turning Erie on her beam-ends. Giant waves crashed aboard the *Colgate* all day long and by nightfall she was taking so much punishment that the pumps were no match for the tons of Erie water piling into the hold and threatening to shift the cargo.

When eight o'clock struck, the whaleback began to list. The crew of twenty-six recognized the ominous sign. Veteran sailors gave up hope of the boat's survival. They went down on their knees, unashamed, and prayed that help might come.

But the *Colgate* had no radio, and ship-to-shore phones

belonged to the future, the future in which the *Colgate* had no part.

A slashing rain drove over the Lake. Captain Grashaw, his oilskins almost blown from his body, fought his way up to the bridge and turned on the searchlight at the risk of being blown overboard. The weird beam searched the night in vain for another ship and then swept the deck to reveal the hatch covers popping under the twofold pressure of waves driving from above and the water and coal shifting in the hold from below.

Twenty years a sailor, Captain Grashaw knew that no ship could last under such a pounding. What thoughts passed through his mind may be conjectured. He was riding a doomed whaleback on his first command.

At ten o'clock Black Friday night, the *Colgate* went sliding down, bow first, to the bottom of Lake Erie. No wreckage remained on the surface to offer makeshift rafts for the crew. Anything that a man might cling to, anything not firmly attached to the boat, had been torn loose by the storm hours ago.

All twenty-six of the crew wore life preservers. So did the captain. But no life preserver could keep a man alive on Black Friday. It would keep his body floating on the surface after the storm, that was all. Meanwhile, without something to hold onto, to raise his head above the smothering waves, every last man of the *Colgate* must drown.

Captain Grashaw struggled in the noisy seas. Then out of the wild night came something that bumped into him. He turned and grabbed a hold. It was a real raft, five feet by nine, that had been aboard the *Colgate*. Two of the crew were on it, and they helped their captain to join them.

In the roaring darkness the three men, a stoker, an engineer, and a ship's master, fought to survive on a raft tossed about by Black Friday until it flipped over completely and broke their holds. Only two men got back aboard. The stoker never returned.

At dawn the raft flipped again. This time the exhausted

engineer did not quite make it back. Alone on the raft the captain stared out across the empty water that had swallowed his whole crew. He wanted to die; he should have died of exhaustion and exposure and shock; but an indomitable will to survive kept him on the raft all day Saturday and then all through the dark hours for the second night. He pounded his fists and kicked his feet against the raft to keep circulation in his body.

During the night a passenger ship headed over the Lake from Buffalo to Detroit came close enough for Captain Grashaw to wave his hands and shout. But no one saw or heard the man on the raft and he watched the bright lights of the liner disappear down Erie's waters.

At dawn on Sunday morning, lying half dead on the boards that had beaten him alive but kept him from drowning, he heard the hoarse voice of a ship's whistle. He raised himself to wave feebly at the car ferry *Marquette* & *Bessemer No. 2*. The men in the pilothouse saw him.

Captain Grashaw had survived Black Friday and two of the darkest midnights imaginable, a total of thirty-five unbelievable hours on a storm-tossed raft in Lake Erie. He lived twelve years more on borrowed time, this Captain Courageous of fresh water who kept his broken heart from giving up, even after his ship went down, his proud first command, and his men were lost, the entire crew, one by one, to leave him alone on a handful of boards at the mercy of Black Friday, the Storm King who rules supreme in the history of Lake Erie.

12. Dead Reckoning by Modern Disasters

We already have pointed out old wrecks as guiding lights on Lake Erie's chart, but modern shipwrecks are also quickly utilized as aids to navigation.

Even today, with 698 lights on the American side of the Lakes alone, and every safety device that science can provide, from radar to radio phone, the wrecks pile up.

In late April of 1944, hustling to meet wartime needs, the long ships raced through a soupy fog on Erie, with foghorns throwing out three blasts every sixty seconds, signal bells jangling, and lighthouses sending their hoarse blasts from shore landmarks.

Loaded with 7,500 tons of ore from Lake Superior, the 448-foot *James H. Reed* was feeling her way through the pea soup at 5:30 in the morning about forty-five miles off Long Point along the Canadian shore. So was the Canadian steamer *Ashcroft,* bound from Buffalo to Toledo for a load of coal. Their courses crossed.

The *Ashcroft* smashed into the *Reed* and down went the latter ship almost at once. Ten of her crew died in late April's forty-two-degree water, when survival time is narrowed to icy minutes.

To indicate the traffic on Lake Erie in that fog, the *Ashcroft* delivered twenty-three survivors and five bodies to Ashtabula.

The *Sherwin* picked up another body and transferred it to the Coast Guard tender *Crocus.*

The *Clarence B. Randall* picked up two bodies and delivered them ashore at Conneaut.

And the *Simaloa,* bound across the Lake for the north shore, brought another two bodies into Port Colborne.

The Coast Guard promptly performed its necessary chores and then notified all shipping that the *James H. Reed* was

224

lying in sixty-six feet of water, forty-two miles and 247 degrees from Long Point Light station, with spars showing above water, and that she was marked with lighted buoys showing uninterrupted quick-flashing white lights, and that a buoy had been set five hundred feet bearing sixty-eight degrees from the wreck.

A few minutes after the *Ashcroft* rammed the *Reed,* over on another part of the fog-bound Lake the 412-foot *Frank E. Vigor* was feeling her way through the Pelee Channel with six thousand tons of sulphur for Buffalo. Bound up in the same channel, the *Phillip Minch,* high in the water with no cargo, came ramming into the *Vigor's* starboard so hard that the two boats stuck together long enough for some of the *Vigor's* crew to step aboard the *Minch* before their ship parted, keeled over, and sank.

All hands were rescued and taken to Lorain aboard the *Minch.* The Coast Guard went to work and then announced to all shipping that the *Frank E. Vigor* was sunk in seventy-five feet of water, twenty-eight and a half miles, seventy-seven degrees from Southeast Shoal Light, and that a Coast Guard vessel was anchored 1,800 feet due west to mark the location until lighted buoys could be placed.

There are a thousand and one tales on the Lakes, but sailing by wrecks might indeed have come straight from the opening pages of the *Arabian Nights,* which, of course, had their own great sailor Sinbad:

> Verily the works and words of those gone before us have become instances and examples to men of our modern day, that folk may view what admonishing chances befell other folk and may therefore take warning; and that they may peruse the annals of antique peoples and all that hath betied them, and be thereby ruled and restrained. Praise, therefore, be to Him who hath made the histories of the Past an admonition unto the Present!

Or, to put it as does Coast Guard Chart No. 34, Fairport to Cleveland, Ohio:

225

WRECKS. — The barge *L. L. Lamb,* loaded with large rip-rap stone, foundered August 16, 1902, one mile NNW of Fairport East Pier Light, in twenty-six feet of water. In 1904 the scattered rock which formed the cargo was leveled off so as to leave a least depth of twenty-three feet over it.

The barge *Cleveco* sank in December 1942 in about fifty-six feet of water at a position approximately nine miles eight degrees (N. 3/4 E.) from Cleveland East Entrance Light. The least depth over the wreck is 25.6 feet, and a horizontally banded red and black light buoy showing a quick flashing white light is moored off its lakeward side.

Dead wrecks keep today's shipping alive.

13. Hail, Erie, and Farewell

As we have noted, Lake Erie is the Lake of quick exchanges, greetings, and good-byes: Good morning, Detroit; Good night, Buffalo; So long, Amherstburg; Hello, Sandusky.

Lake Erie also is the Lake of the lone females, the unfortunate or black-hearted vessels, the Flying Dutchmen of the shoals, and of much more that the heart understands beyond words.

LAKE ERIE'S LONE FEMALES

For an unknown reason, the Lake that goes directly to Niagara Falls has shown a partiality toward lone females. There was the case of the barber's wife, only woman to survive the *Griffith* disaster; there was the cool Mrs. Lynde of Milwaukee, solitary female survivor of the Erie holocaust; and then there is the fantastic case of a lady from Buffalo, which sailors regard as without parallel in the annals of survival on fresh water or salt.

This lady, an aunt of the famous Captain Gilman Appleby, had gone for a visit up the Lake and was coming back home to Buffalo aboard the schooner *New Connecticut* in the autumn of 1833. Off Erie, Pennsylvania, a white squall struck and rolled the sailing vessel over on her side. Water came aboard so fast that the crew figured anyone in the cabin must be drowned, so they lowered the yawl, jumped in, and pulled for shore, leaving the boat in a sinking condition but still wallowing above the surface.

When Captain Appleby heard about this tragic event, he wanted at least to recover the body of his aunt and give her a decent burial. Three days after the accident he asked Captain Wilkins, who was coming down from Detroit on the steamboat *William Peacock* to board the wreck, if he saw it and, if possible, to get the body of his aunt and take it to Buffalo.

Captain Wilkins did come across the disabled vessel, drifting down the Lake. The schooner lay on her side and, to all appearances, was full of water. A boarding party from the steamboat used a searching pole, and it was supposed that every part of the cabin had been touched without making any human contact. Captain Wilkins concluded that the body had floated out of the cabin into the Lake, so he abandoned further search.

Told of the hopelessness of the situation, Captain Appleby was still determined to overlook no possibility of finding his aunt's body so that he might give her a funeral service ashore and interment in the family grave plot. With the aunt's son aboard, he sailed out to the wreck with a working boat that had facilities to right the schooner and tow her into port. He directed the grappling and pumping and buoying operations until slowly the schooner began to roll upright.

When the vessel had nearly reached a level position, his aunt came walking through the water up the stairs to the deck.

The shipping news for that season of navigation, which we quote verbatim, recorded the event under the subtitle:

A Remarkable Deliverance. — Captain Appleby caught his aunt in his arms and supported her while her son wept and the sailors screamed. Five days and nights she had been in the water, a portion of the time up to her armpits. She could not lie down, and what sleep she obtained was while standing. All the food she had was a solitary cracker and an onion which floated on the water. She stated that after the vessel capsized, and was abandoned by the crew, she found herself alone in water waist deep. The cabin floor was open, but the water was two feet above it, and the sea made constant changes in her position. When Captain Wilkins arrived with his steamboat, she could hear the boarding party talk and walk on the vessel but, although she used her voice to the utmost to attract attention, she could not make them hear. She saw the pole thrust into the cabin door and asked if she should hold on to it and be pulled out, but no answer came.

MOTHER BECKER, LIFESAVER

Still another case involving a lone female on Lake Erie resulted from a shipwreck in late November, 1854, when the schooner *Conductor,* loaded with grain from Buffalo, and driving through a blinding snowstorm, failed to see Long Point Light, and went crashing aground.

The sailing vessel had struck off one of the most lonesome places along the Canadian shore. Only one family lived in the area and the husband was already gone for the day, when his wife saw a smashed yawl on the beach. She went down to investigate and then looked out toward the sand bar half a mile from shore. There she saw the wrecked schooner with torn sails and decks awash. A number of men were clinging to her rigging as the masts whipped savagely in the gale.

Only a lone woman stood between those sailors and certain death by drowning or freezing. She cupped her hands and called encouragement across the water. Then she raced back to the house up the beach to let her youngsters know that they would have to get along without her for a while, as later celebrated in verse by Amanda T. Jones:

> Sped Mother Becker, "Children, wake;
> A ship's gone down, they're needing me;
> Your father's off on shore; the lake
> Is just a raging sea."

A strapping woman, Mother Becker stood six feet without her shoes on, and generally she wore none, because the family was too poor to afford them. Now she went back to the shore through the overnight snow, barefooted.

She made a bonfire of driftwood, as a sign of hope to the sailors who held death grips on the schooner's rigging. She tried to fix the yawl, but it was beyond repair. She tried to build a raft but there were not enough materials. She thought of going for help, but the nearest place was fourteen miles away and, if the men saw her leave, they might lose heart.

Mother Becker saw only one way for the survivors to be rescued. She cupped her hands and called: "Swim! You've got to jump overboard and swim. I'll help you get to land. *Swim!*"

One man finally braved the attempt. Mother Becker saw him take off a heavy coat and climb down from the mast. In the water he struggled for headway while she did her best to keep up his courage. A few strokes from safety, he lost strength and started to go down. Out she went in her flimsy dress through the icy water and hauled him in to shore. She put warm blankets around him beside the fire and gave him hot tea from a big tin pot. Restored to life, he proved to be the schooner's captain, Robert Hackett. He said that he had told his mate Jerome to come next if he made it, but otherwise for all six men to stay in the rigging another night.

"Another night," said Mother Becker with her bare feet in the snow and her dress frozen on her, "another night and they'd be naught but statues carved out of Lake Erie ice." She cupped her hands. "Swim! I'll fetch you to shore. But *swim!*"

The mate Jerome tried the long pull next and when he began to flounder, Captain Hacket plunged to the rescue of his first officer. Mother Beckett watched the struggle, saw both men disappear, and again went into action:

She sought the men, she sought them far;
Three fathoms down she gripped them tight;
With both together up the bar
She staggered into sight.

The great-hearted Amazon repeated her performance until every last man of the seven who had clung to the schooner's rigging was safe on shore. She had made them a promise and she kept it.

Today, 105 years later, the portrait of the woman called the Guardian Angel of Long Point Bay hangs in the Abigail Becker Ward of Simcoe Town Hospital, with a large gold lifesaving medal on her breast and a gift Bible resting on her ample lap. Her exploit was told for the *Atlantic Monthly* by the poet John Greenleaf Whittier. But her heroism received more practical recognition in the form of a hundred-acre farm voted her by the Canadian Parliament and in a purse holding one thousand dollars in gold from the Lifesaving Association of New York because two of the men she rescued were U.S. sailors.

Mother Becker never went without shoes again. The owner of the shipwrecked schooner paid her a visit, noticed the total absence of footgear, measured the feet of the lifesaver and her children, and within a few weeks sent a huge chest containing shoes in all varieties for the family of the lone woman who had stood on the gale-swept Erie shore, barefooted in the snow, to call across heavy seas: "Swim! I'll fetch you to shore. But *swim!*"

"BAD LUCK" BOATS

Old-time sailors were superstitious about a schooner or a steamboat that ran into trouble. They blamed her personally for it. In their minds a boat was not so much unfortunate as black-hearted. With human perverseness and cruelty, she did away with men.

If a boat capsized and sank with all hands, other sailors regarded it as a crime, an act of premeditation or criminal negligence on the part of the vessel. They said, accusingly: "She drownded her crew."

In a sailor's vocabulary, men never drowned. They were *drownded,* deliberately, in cold blood, by a murderous ship.

Lake Erie had two classic examples of black-hearted boats. One was the Canadian schooner *Erie Wave.* On her first trip out she capsized, and two of her crew were lost. On the next trip she capsized again, and two of her passengers went down. On her last trip she ran into a squall between Port Rowan and Clear Creek, Ontario, and only two of those aboard survived.

Perhaps the outstanding case among "bad-luck" ships is recorded in the shipping news of the 1888 season of navigation:

> *Loss of an Unlucky Vessel. —* The schooner *Walter H. Oades* collided, August 20, with the schooner *R. Halloran,* two miles from the Dummy, Lake Erie, and sank in half an hour. The *Oades* was built in Detroit and was one of the most unlucky vessels on the lakes. While she was under construction a fire broke out on her, and one side was almost consumed. When nearly ready to launch the ways settled and she fell three feet, necessitating heavy expense in getting her into the water. Then she ran ashore at Rondeau point, after which she was sold by her builders. Later, while she was at anchor in the St. Clair River, she was run into by a big steamboat. She went on the bank in shallow water, and while the wreckers were at work she slipped off into deep water. She was repaired and while waiting settlement with the insurance companies she was run into and lost her jib-boom. At one time she was thrown upon the Buffalo breakwater by a heavy sea, and her minor mishaps would fill a book. When she was lost there was no insurance on her as the agents refused to take the risk because she was "unlucky."

ERIE'S FLYING DUTCHMEN

The busiest of the Lakes, with all her heavy traffic, is broad enough to have had stretches of solitudes on which schooners and steamboats have sailed away to join the other Flying Dutchmen of fresh water.

On December 9, 1909, the big car ferry *Bessemer & Marquette No. 2* took off from Conneaut, Ohio, to steam across Lake Erie to Port Stanley, Ontario, with a load of railroad cars. Only four years old and considered as seaworthy as anything afloat, she cleared the breakwater and was never seen again. Somewhere out on the horizon she vanished forever with her crew of thirty-six men.

The tug *Silver Spray* sailed through a crack in the Lake somewhere off Cleveland on April 15, 1911, taking all nine hands along.

As recently as December 18, 1950, the stout tug *Sachem* disappeared on Lake Erie with her entire crew of twelve to join the ghost patrol of Flying Dutchmen that haunt the American and Canadian shores.

Even the shallowest of the Great Lakes is plenty deep enough to hide tall-masted secrets and lose a railroad train or two in a crinkle of her flowing sleeve.

GALLANT PARTING

For old-time Lakemen, taking leave of Lake Erie, even in the pages of a book, is much the same as parting from friends and family, from scenes of birth and boyhood, from generations of auld lang syne that came into the world within sight and sound of western Erie water on lower Huron, the perpetual five-o'clock-rush-hour highway on the inland seas.

Parting can be hard, but good examples have been set on Lake Erie. When the paddle-wheel steamer *Chesapeake* collided with the schooner *John A. Porter* on a June midnight in 1846, she filled rapidly and started down. In the wake of the tragedy, the shipping news described the death of Daniel A. Folsom as a touching incident during this season of navigation:

When the engine ceased to work, the yawl boat was manned and sent ashore. Ten men were put on board and four women, among the latter being Mrs. Folsom. She at first refused to go without her husband. He knew it was no use to debate the question and seizing their child put it on board. She immediately followed, and the husband took an affectionate leave from her at the gangplank as the boat departed. He was never heard of afterward.

BOOK FOUR

DOOMED ON LAKE SUPERIOR

Our deck was coated tons with ice,
But not a sailor knew,
Some would be froze and some be drowned
Of our big freighter's crew.

The huge seas raked her fore and aft,
The cold wind loud did roar,
We struck stern on and swung broadside
To our doom on Superior.
  (Lake song, 1894)

In its original form the ballad on the preceding page celebrated the loss of the vessel *Antelope*, presumably in Lake Michigan. Guesswork also fixes her as a schooner and the odds are in favor of the guess. There were thirteen *Antelopes* on the Lakes: seven schooners, two propellers, one brig, one scow, one barge, and one tug. They capsized and burned and foundered and were lost all over the various Lakes. But two of the schooners were wrecked on Lake Michigan in the year 1894, and therefore this date is applied to the song, which later became popular in the recital of other disasters, as shown in the adapted stanzas above.

1. Pretty Tall Water Here

To say that Lake Superior is the greatest of the Great Lakes is to say much, but it draws no picture of the vastness of this haughty queen of fresh water who has a copper crown, the iron hills for a footstool and the coldest blue eyes in creation.

To say that Lake Superior, even today, remains the most aloof and remote of the Great upper Lakes is merely to echo the century-old outcry of Statesman Henry Clay against the congressional proposal to dig a shipping passage between her and her sisters below.

"Dig a canal up there?" he scoffed in effect. "Why not propose to build one on the moon?"

To say that Lake Superior could drown Massachusetts, Connecticut, Vermont, New Hampshire, Rhode Island — all the New England states — with room to spare; to say that a boat bound from Sault Ste. Marie to Duluth could travel a couple of days without sighting the mainland — these also belong to the overworked common stock of examples.

To say that Lake Superior is 383 miles long, 160 miles wide, 602 feet above sea level, and 1,008 feet deep at her lowest sounding, is to recite the bare details of her majestic size.

But facts and figures are poor measures of true greatness, which goes beyond reason and must be judged by impressions. One of the old-time commercial fishermen once told about taking an Ottawa Indian helper up into Lake Superior on his Mackinaw boat. The Ottawa, a stalwart brave, was accustomed to set nets at a depth of a hundred feet or so on Lake Huron or Lake Michigan, but the commercial fisherman chose a bank on Lake Superior where the nets were set at a hundred fathoms. The Ottawa never blinked or said a word as they went down to a depth un-dreamed about in his experience. When the time came to haul them up, the process seemed to last forever — hand over dripping hand in the icy water. The Ottawa's fingers turned black and blue from the cold and the bruising strain of lifting from a depth of six hundred feet. His nails were torn and bleeding. Finally, he and the commercial fisherman brought their catch to the surface. Many of the fish were hauled up from such a depth that the difference in pressure caused them to swell and burst like overpuffed balloons when they reached the surface.

At last the Ottawa spoke the only words exchanged between the men all day, and they seemed to cover the subject. He stared at his wrecked hands and at the exploded fish in the nets, and then he looked out across Lake Superior.

"Pretty tall water here," he said.

Depending on the season, Lake Superior has two temperatures — solid ice and melted ice. Handsome and imperious, domineering and cruel as a great court beauty in the heyday of royalty's arrogance, she is the hardest to know, and the most respected, of all the Lakes. There were five sisters, but only one was born queen. Loyal sailors love her for the very reasons that others cannot abide her.

There is the honest-to-goodness story of the Lake Superior captain who had been forced to sail the lower waters for a while. He came back from balmy airs and sunny climes to his native habitat. As his ship was locked up through the Soo Canal, he beamed at the dark clouds as if he were greeting old friends. He buttoned his jacket up to the throat against a wind that carried alternating gusts of rain and snow. He took long gulps of Lake Superior air and blew out the frost on his breath, as if he were relishing the smoke of a choice cigar.

"This is what I call living," he said. "None of your monotonous blue skies around here!"

2. Look Out Below!

Across the years Lake Superior has held imperial sway over the other Great Lakes, beginning with the commercial influence of her fur trade and fisheries, and continuing to the present day with her copper, iron, and uranium deposits. She is the Lake not only of violent storms and wilderness waters but of violent men who tore metal out of the bowels of the earth to build the big steel ships that carried enough ore down from Lake Superior to supply the arsenals of democracy with the necessary raw materials for making the weapons to win two world wars.

But beyond such powerful obvious reasons, there are deeper implications to Superior's influences on the lower Lakes. Not one of the thirteen worst disasters in fresh water is charged against her, yet she has been linked with several of them in a strange chain of command involving visitations of doom by remote control.

This record dates back to the era before the opening of the Soo Canal when the propeller *Independence,* built on Lake Michigan, was hauled around the rapids at Sault Ste. Marie on greased ways up the main street and slid into the Big Lake. First steamboat to leave a trail of smoke on Superior, she plowed past the Pictured Rocks for eight seasons, delivering men and machinery to the mining camps at Iron Bay and Copper Harbor, and returning with deck-loads of ore in barrels that were transferred onto mule-powered railroad cars and hauled to other boats waiting below the falls and rapids of the St. Marys River at what then represented the headwaters of navigation on the inland seas.

On November 22, 1853, the *Independence,* trying for one of those notorious last trips of the season, and bound for the copper country, blew up on her way into the open Lake. There is a story that her purser, hurled 150 feet high by the explosion, grabbed hold of a flying bundle of hay

239

and came down unharmed on it. Four lives were lost. The captain and his fourteen-year-old son, George Perry McKay, were standing watch aboard when the boilers gave way. The boy survived to become a captain himself and to command the ill-fated *Pewabic* on the night she went down on Lake Huron with 125 lives and a legend of sunken treasure.

The *Pewabic,* it will be remembered, had other ties with the great Lake up above. She belonged to the pioneer transport line founded by John Tallman Whiting, one of the prime movers in promoting and constructing the canal that opened up Lake Superior, and her loss drove him bankrupt.

Another finger of doom touched Captain Jack Wilson when he took the first boat through the Soo Canal into Lake Superior in June of 1855. On an unforgettable September night on Lake Michigan, five years later, he was in command of the *Lady Elgin* when she went to the bottom with a hole in her side that let out the lives of 297 persons.

While running errands and doing chores for Lake Superior, ships came to violent ends on other Lakes. There was, for instance, the case of the propeller *Goliah.* She left the St. Clair River on September 13, 1848, with an extremely heavy cargo including 20,000 bricks, 30,000 feet of lumber, forty tons of hay, two thousands barrels of provisions and merchandise, and two hundred kegs of blasting powder, bound for the Lake Superior mining companies. Soon after daylight the next morning she was sighted about eight miles off the Canadian shore, her mast and smokestack overboard, drifting toward the beach which was being lashed with a high surf. Clouds of black smoke billowed from her decks, and a short time later she exploded, throwing fire and fragments to a tremendous height. No bodies ever were found of the eighteen persons aboard. Three hundred barrels of flour and corn meal, consigned to Copper Harbor to help get the miners through the long Lake Superior winter, washed up at Goderich and Kincardine, on Lake Huron.

The hardest winters in those beginning years of mining,

farming, fishing, trapping, and lumbering on Lake Superior were spent at the Duluth end of the Big Sea Water which the Ojibways called Gitche Gumee. Immigrants arrived by the thousands, and, unable to make a living from the iron-rich rockland, were frozen or starved out. Unknown to them, they had homesteaded mineral properties worth billions of dollars but they moved on because the flinty soil would not grow corn and potatoes.

One winter the entire town of Duluth might have starved if it had not been for the goodhearted act of a popular steamboat captain named E. B. Sweet. He knew that the people were desperate but they could not even afford return passage to civilization, so he posted a sign in the general store:

ALL WHO WANT TO GO BACK EAST
GET IN TOUCH WITH ME
AT THE DOCKS
Ben Sweet

Unable to believe their eyes, the people raced through town, spreading the news as they dashed for the docks toting their carpetbags. Captain Sweet's steamboat was almost in a sinking condition when he took off for Saulte Ste. Marie at the other end of the Lake. Behind, the town of Duluth lay almost depopulated. The captain had taken seven hundred passengers on credit — seven hundred promissory notes for individual transportation were in the ship's safe. The stern code for Lake Superior dwellers is exemplified in the fact that all but one of those notes were ultimately paid, and no doubt the person who signed it came from far below.

But Captain Sweet is seldom remembered for this generous act. His name is too closely associated with the *Phoenix* holocaust on Lake Michigan, where he played the lame role of a disabled master and escaped with his life while from 190 to 250 passengers lost theirs.

Another steamboat that worked her heart out for Lake Superior to carry mining men and machinery through the

241

Soo Canal came to a violent end on another Lake. The stout propeller *Chicora*, often seen on old photographs of the Soo locks, met her doom in a mid-winter storm on Lake Michigan as she tried to navigate the ice fields between Milwaukee and St. Joseph. She left port early in the morning of January 21, 1895. The barometer was unusually low but Captain Stein took off with his crew of twenty-three and a solitary passenger. It later developed that he had been ailing and wanted to see his doctor in Michigan as quickly as possible. The falling barometer alarmed the owner of the boat so much that he hurried down to the dock at St. Joseph and notified the captain of another boat of his, lying in the harbor there, not to leave. Then he wired the same instructions over to Wisconsin, but the *Chicora* had already sailed by the time the message arrived.

The storm burst upon the smooth Lake as the day advanced, and the *Chicora* failed to keep her schedule in St. Joseph that afternoon. Days later her spars and other wreckage drifted into the Michigan shore between South Haven and Saugatuck. Rescue vessels fought their way through ice fields and zero weather in a vain search for survivors. No bodies were ever recovered.

This well-loved relic of Lake Superior's palmy days was celebrated in a ballad that seems to have been modeled on the style of Edgar Allan Poe's "Raven":

> *Oh, the hearts that watched her going, ever smaller,*
> *smaller growing*
> *Out upon the seeming shoreless waste of waters*
> *glad and free,*
> *Growing dimmer, dimmer, dimmer in an irridescent*
> *shimmer,*
> *Until a speck she faded 'tween the blue of sky and sea.*

> *Here's a sigh for the Chicora, for the broken, sad*
> *Chicora;*
> *Here's a tear for those who followed her beneath*
> *the tossing wave.*

242

*Oh, the mystery of the morrow! From its shadows
let us borrow
A star of hope to shine above the gloom of every grave.*

On Dark Sunday, Huron's November storm of 1913, the bulk of vessels lost or stranded were somehow under the spell of the Lake Superior doom, for they were either headed down from the big upper Lake with grain and iron or they were headed up for Superior with coal and water ballast.

On Black Friday, Lake Erie's October storm of 1916, the most dramatic of the shipwrecks involved the whaleback freighter *James B. Colgate,* bound up the Lakes with a cargo of hard coal for Canada's grain port of Fort William on Lake Superior.

During Lake Michigan's so-called Armistice Day storm, the November hurricane of 1940, with its cyclonic winds of 85-126 miles per hour carrying a blizzard, the most dramatic shipwreck, featuring the rescue of survivors by the fish tug *Three Brothers,* again involved a freighter hard at work for Lake Superior — the *Novadoc,* bound from South Chicago up to Fort William with a cargo of powdered coke.

No doubt other examples could be found to illustrate this touch of doom by remote control, but we have listed enough to conclude that, like all absolute monarchs, Lake Superior has the power of life and death over her subjects; and, like all who occupy high places, she has a habit of exacting tribute from those beneath her.

3. Down With Their Boots On

In the November 1913 storm that sent eight big ships down with all hands on Lake Huron, there were two ships wiped off the Lake Superior chart without a trace, three ships whose captains and crews lived to tell incredible stories of wreck and survival, and a number

243

of other ships that had to be dismissed with routine notices in newspaper listings of wholesale disaster:

The *Hamonic* aground off Whitefish Point, Lake Superior. Crew and passengers safe.

The *A. E. Stewart*, also aground in Whitefish Bay.

The *F. G. Hartwell*, in difficulty in Whitefish Bay with ore cargo. Crew taken off.

The *Acadian*, aground on a reef near Sulphur Island in Lake Superior.

The *John T. Hutchinson*, ashore at Point Iroquois in Lake Superior.

The *Thistle*, small steamer, grain-laden, ashore at Calumet Harbor, Lake Superior.

The *Major*, wooden steamer, sprung leak and abandoned thirty miles off Whitefish Point in Lake Superior.

These were the hardly-worth-mentioning difficulties encountered by Lake Superior shipping in Huron's 1913 storm, but the *Turret Chief*, the *William Nottingham*, and the *L. C. Waldo* ran into memorable experiences.

Paying no attention to the hurricane warnings hoisted at Sault Ste. Marie, the four-thousand-ton *Turret Chief* had locked up through the Soo Canal en route to Fort William. Empty of cargo, she rode high on the jagged Lake and took a beating from the sharp waves. The storm tossed her around so badly that when her captain figured he must be off the Canadian shore, the freighter was perilously close to the American.

Driven far off her course and disabled by the gale, the *Turret Chief* drifted wildly for fifty miles before Lake Superior heaved her up on the rugged coast of the Keweenaw Peninsula. As the vessel crashed ashore and was wedged in the rocks, the crew with Captain Paddington came tumbling overboard on the first lines they could grab and hit the beach.

The eighteen survivors had no idea of their whereabouts, and the Keweenaw shore is no place for a picnic even on

244

a summer day. A blizzard was blowing. The marooned sailors were wet to the skin. Their clothing quickly froze until they rattled like windowpanes in the storm's blasts. The matches they carried were sodden. Not a one would strike. And they had no food.

On this bleak coast, in the bitter weather, with a few evergreen boughs and sticks of driftwood for shelter, they crouched without a fire and nothing to eat from Saturday until Monday morning. Death from exposure and starvation stared them in the face. Then, like something out of one of Ernest Hemingway's early stories with a Lake Superior setting, came a file of Indians pigeon-toeing through the snow. In less than two hours, Captain Paddington and his crew were gulping scalded coffee around a pot-bellied stove at Copper Harbor.

Meanwhile the freighter *William Nottingham* had left Fort William with a cargo of grain for the lower Lakes. Caught out on the open Lake at the height of the storm, she had bucked the mountainous seas for more than forty-eight hours and still had not reached any sheltering land. Then her coal bunkers went empty. Her fuel was gone.

The captain faced a desperate decision. Unless he kept steam up in the boilers, the engines would stop, the *William Nottingham* would lose headway and go smashing into Coppermine Point.

There was one chance. At the risk of having the seas wash into the hold, he ordered the crew to open the hatches and shovel grain up on deck and down the coal chutes into the bunkers.

With every gust of wind and roll of the boat threatening to haul them overboard, the crew shoveled wheat in a race with death. Down below, the engine-room gang heaved the wheat into the fire doors and pressure began to rise in the boiler gauges again. With blazing grain for fuel, the *William Nottingham* picked up a little speed and fought her way out of open Lake Superior into Whitefish Bay.

Then, on the verge of making Sault Ste. Marie with a

proud head of steam, the freighter struck a shoal four miles off the steamship lane and the seas began to break her to pieces on Sandy Island. Three of the crew drowned in a desperate attempt to launch a lifeboat and reach help. All the rest were brought safely off the wreck by the Coast Guard within a few hours.

Out of Two Harbors, Minnesota, in the teeth of the storm, the ore carrier *L. C. Waldo* had started across the Lake, bound down for Cleveland. Deep in the water with her heavy cargo of iron, she carried a crew of twenty-four, including two women, over the boiling green seas.

Huge waves broke over the *Waldo's* bows and raked her decks with spray that froze and encased her with tons of ice. At nine o'clock that night, Captain John Duddleson, a real blue-water sailor, born at the Soo, stood in a pilothouse whose windows were blind with frost. It was like being in the solitary cell of a madhouse, with an insane wind screaming murder in the darkness. At visibility zero he steered by compass alone, and prayed for his guardian angel to keep a sharp lookout.

At midnight Captain Duddleson bent over his chart, laying a compass course for Manitou Island, off the Indian-arrow point of Keweenaw Peninsula, hoping to gain the island's shelter before the wind blew the *Waldo* off the map.

He drove the big freighter through the storm. Pounded by thunderous seas, she wallowed and rolled, righted herself and lurched ahead time and again. But Lake Superior had been waiting for the decisive moment to deliver her knockout punch. She cocked a fist masthead high and struck with the solid weight of a hundred tons of water.

The giant wave ripped the pilothouse as if it were no more than a flimsy orange crate. Captain Duddleson and his wheelsman, caught in the backwash of the sea that had hurled their working quarters overboard, leaped for a hatchway, lost their balance for a blurred drowning moment, but clung to a stanchion as the bulkheads parted.

Gallantly the *Waldo* raised her bows and plunged for-

246

ward into the maelstrom of Lake Superior, but her pilot-house was gone, her compass demolished, her electric light plant out of commission, her main steering wheel so damaged that she could not maintain a course against the wind. In the roaring night she began to founder.

Above the storm, Captain Duddleson shouted to the wheelsman: "Get a compass from one of the lifeboats and bring it to the deckhouse for'ard!"

The wheelsman inched his way aft, over the ice-sheathed deck, and completed his slippery round trip. The two Lake-men set the hand compass on a stool and, for four hours, wrestling the spokes of an auxiliary wheel, they steered a course by the ghostly light of a flickering hurricane lantern.

But the storm king was not to be denied his sacrifice. With the wind dead aft, the seas broke over the *Waldo's* stern until in an occasional flare of sparks only her stack could be seen, pouring black smoke into the white smother of spray and snow.

Captain Duddleson came within half a mile of making his desperate passage between Gull Rock and Keweenaw Point, an amazing feat of seamanship in a storm that made other masters miscalculate their ship's positions by as much as a hundred miles. But the slim half-mile margin proved fatal to the *Waldo*. With a smash and a shudder she fetched up on a reef running out from Gull Rock on Manitou Island.

At grey dawn on Lake Superior Captain Duddleson ordered everything lashed fast, but the combination of wind and waves and rocks quickly turned the *Waldo* into a shambles. The life rafts and the lifeboats were swept away before the crew could lay a hand on them. When the forward deckhouse went over the side, the captain ordered all hands on deck and into the battered after deckhouse. The engine-room gang came up just in time and the deck watch came riding the lifeline from bow to stern as the waves broke over them, only bare-survival moments before the *Waldo* broke in two.

For two days and nights twenty-three men and two women huddled in the perilous shelter of the aft house. They rigged a bathtub into a stove and tore every last bit of wood out of the *Waldo* to keep from freezing to death. When the food supply got down to two cans of tomatoes, Captain Duddleson said, "These are for the women," and the rest of the crew nodded in unanimous agreement.

Toward the end of the second day the steamer *Lakeland,* through a rift in the blizzard, caught sight of the *Waldo.* She could not get near enough to help, but she carried a rarity in Great Lakes navigational aids for those days — wireless equipment. Her report of the *Waldo's* plight went sparking across Superior and broadcast the broken vessel's position.

At daybreak next morning, Captain Thomas H. McCormick, of the Portage Coast Guard station, reached the wreck of the *Waldo.* In the beam of the rescue tug's searchlight, she looked like a phantom ship that had sailed herself into a fog of ice.

Captain Charles A. Tucker of the Eagle Harbor Coast Guard brought another tug to the scene and together they fought the seas until lines were strung to the *Waldo* and Captain Duddleson, with his twenty-four sailors, counting the two women in the crew, were hauled to safety by rescuers as coated with ice as were the survivors.

Today there are duplicate letters on proud display in the Coast Guard stations at Portage and Eagle Harbor:

> There is transmitted herewith a gold medal of honor, awarded to you by this Department under Acts of Congress, in recognition of your heroic conduct upon the occasion of the rescue of the crew of the steamer *L. C. Waldo,* which went ashore on Manitou Island, Lake Superior, during the great storm of November 8-11, 1903.
>
> It affords the Department great pleasure to have this opportunity to commend the services rendered by you at that time. Respectfully, Bryon R. Newton, Asst. Sec. Treasury Dept.

To recite all the deeds of heroism in the 1913 storm would be to repeat a hundred times the bravery of the Coast Guard skippers McCormick and Tucker with their never-say-die crews. The lifeboats of the storm were the tugs of the Great Lakes Towing Company. As sturdy and powerful as they were small and compact, they went everywhere, burying their pug noses under tons of raging water but shaking loose like Chesapeake retrievers to drive ahead, pointing slowly but stubbornly into the waves and the blizzard to where giant freighters with their waiting, watching, and praying crews were foundering in the merciless seas.

Only masterful seamanship kept the tugs themselves from breaking against the steel flanks of the ships they drove through howling death to save. But somehow they got lines aboard. Then, with chesty puffs and coughs of exultation and encouragement, their engines would pull away, dragging stricken cargo carriers out of the trough of the seas or the surf of the rock-bound coasts. Wherever any ship whistled for help, the tugs sent an answering whistle that they were on the way, no matter how rough the sea.

But there were two vessels whose whistles for help were never heard, two vessels never seen again after they cleared port to go out into the storm. The large carrier *Henry B. Smith,* in the command of Captain James Owen, bound down from Superior to the lower Lakes with a cargo of iron ore, was lost somewhere between Marquette and the Soo. Not a body, not a trace of wreckage, ever gave a clue to her doom.

The sturdy Canadian grain carrier *Leafield,* built in Scotland to survive any storm on the high seas, went crashing onto the rocks of Angus Island, fourteen miles from Fort William, her entire crew of eighteen perishing in the icy waters.

What happened aboard the *Henry B. Smith* before she took her plunge into oblivion may be guessed at by the tragedy preserved in ice aboard the barge *Plymouth* fifty miles below Superior at the top of Lake Michigan near St. Martin's Island, where Longfellow's ballad of "The Wreck of the Hesperus" had come true:

Lashed to the helm, all stiff and stark,
With his face turned to the skies,
The lantern gleamed, through the gleaming snow,
On his fixed and glassy eyes.

Toward the close of the storm, the Coast Guard sighted the *Plymouth* in distress and hurried to her aid. They stepped on the boat to find themselves in the midst of death. Lashed to their posts, the captain and her crew of seven men had been frozen to statues of ice while the *Plymouth* sailed on to survive the 1913 disaster alone.

4. Solitary Survivals and One Exception

Three men have lived to bring back a tale of solitary survival in the roll call of Lake Superior shipwrecks, and one man is remembered for refusing to lift a finger to save himself in a disaster where all the rest aboard were rescued.

On August 28, 1863, the side-paddle steamboat *Sunbeam*, described as an elegantly furnished passenger liner and a great favorite with the Lake-traveling public, came out from Ontonagon bound for Portage Lake around the Keweenaw Peninsula. She ran into a gale on her way up toward the tip of land but weathered the storm until into the next day when her captain gave up hope of reaching the shelter of Copper Harbor, twenty-four miles distant, and ordered Wheelsman John Frazer to turn the *Sunbeam* about in the face of the wind. When this was done, the steamboat fell into the trough of the waves and rolled crazily. Efforts to hoist a jib and hold her steady with the small sail resulted in no good. The engine, driving full steam, could not move the boat a foot against the storm. Finally she careened, her pilothouse falling flat against the water, and she was held in that position by the gale while the waves thrashed her to bits.

The shipping notice for the season of navigation reported that "the story of the sole survivor is substantially as follows":

> The captain had told Frazer to stick to the wheel and do what he could to turn her if she righted again, but when Frazer saw no hopes of her coming up again, and the mad waves running over her, he broke the window on the upper side of the pilothouse and made his way to the small boats. One of the lifeboats had disappeared. The two remaining boats were filled with passengers and crew. Frazer got into the yawl where he had only standing room, but just then a woman, he thinks the chambermaid, begged to be taken aboard. The self-sacrificing wheelsman lashed himself to the fragment of deck with the signal halyards of the flagstaff, floating near, and soon after picked up a demijohn, which he secured with the ends of the rope.

When Frazer left the wreck, the upper cabin had been swept off and soon afterwards the *Sunbeam* settled and went down, bow foremost. The wheelsman saw the yawl sink and then he saw the lifeboat, upside down and with two men lying crosswise on it, swept out of sight. He stayed on his makeshift raft from eight o'clock Friday evening until two o'clock Saturday afternoon when he drifted into a shore where red sandstone cliffs bulged at the Lake. The waves dashed his raft to pieces against the rocks, ripping open his forehead and crippling his knees and shoulders. He fell back into the water but the next wave threw him up on the rocks again, where he caught hold of a shelving projection and crawled into a small cavern. Here he remained about eight hours waiting for the wind to go down and the sea to calm, when he crawled hand over foot across the rocks to the beach. On Monday afternoon, weak and numb with cold, he signaled to a party coasting along the shore in a small boat from Ontonagon and was rescued. He had survived an ordeal of sixty-seven hours since the shipwreck that had taken twenty-eight lives and spared him alone of all those aboard the *Sunbeam*.

In 1892 another wheelsman became the only survivor of a famous wreck on Superior's historic chart. On Sunday, August 28, of that year the two-year-old all-steel ore carrier *Western Reserve* sailed out of Cleveland on what was meant to be a pleasure trip combined with the ultimate business of picking up a cargo of iron ore at Two Harbors, Minnesota.

In her short career the three-hundred-foot *Western Reserve* had already made several record-breaking hauls. She was the pride of the Lakes and the apple of her owner's eyes, Captain Peter G. Minch. He was so confident of her sea-worthiness and so anxious to show her off that he had arranged a family excursion on this trip. He invited his sister-in-law and her little daughter and took along his own wife and their two youngsters, a seven-year-old girl and a boy of ten named Carl. Another son, Phillip, was left ashore.

As the *Western Reserve* rode out of Cleveland up the Detroit and St. Clair rivers, across Lake Huron and up the St. Marys, through the Soo Canal and out into Whitefish Bay on Lake Superior, it seemed as if no ship could have been entrusted to better hands. Himself an experienced sailing master, the owner had the regular master aboard, Captain Albert Myers, and Chief Engineer W. H. Seaman had long lived up to his name as another veteran officer of the Minch fleet.

Throughout most of the trip the three children, under the watchful eye of working sailors, romped on deck without a care, and the wives sunned themselves and enjoyed the Lake breezes. The *Western Reserve* showed no hurry to get anywhere. She loafed along through the tag-end of August, riding high and empty on the smooth water, and was locked up through the Soo Canal at six o'clock Tuesday evening.

Out on Whitefish Bay the waves began to kick up and, although the wind was moderately fresh for Lake Superior, the two captains decided to take no chances with their precious cargo of human lives. They would stop a while and consider the weather. Perhaps at the back of their minds lay the persistent dock-side scuttlebutt that the *Western Reserve* had been made from steel too brittle for safety, and that once chilled by the waters of Superior and lashed by the critical combination of waves, her plates would crack under the pounding seas. She would break up and go down.

The owner and the captain had long since agreed that this behind-the-hand scuttlebutt was no more than schooner talk, voiced by sailors who believed that only wood could float. But at any rate, the two masters Minch and Myers agreed to put the *Western Reserve* under shelter of land and drop the hook to take observations.

The engines were stopped and the anchor was run down in a cove on Whitefish Bay. But the wind showed no signs of increasing nor did the waves reach alarming proportions. Perhaps the two captains began to feel sheepish about all their precautions. Anyway, they hoisted anchor and steamed out into the open Lake.

At nine o'clock that night, sixty miles above Whitefish Point, the *Western Reserve* ran into a gale. Almost without warning a crash signaled the steel carrier's doom. A crack appeared on her deck, forward of the boiler house. The main mast went by the board. The crack in the deck widened. There was an agonizing wrench of metal, and the ship broke in two.

Inside of ten minutes the pride of the Lakes plunged six hundred feet to the bottom of Superior. Masterly seamanship in the crisis had resulted in the lowering of both the metal and the wooden yawl boats, and they were cast adrift from the wreck, carrying all twenty of the officers and crew as well as the owner, the two women, and the three children.

But just before the great steel hull was swallowed by the mounting seas of Lake Superior, the metal lifeboat capsized, spilling eight crew members and Captain Minch's son Carl into the wilderness of water. The wooden lifeboat, with seventeen people aboard, including all the family passengers, raced toward the scene of struggling bodies, but only the ship's steward and the young boy were rescued.

The nineteen survivors now in the wooden yawl faced the fact that they were sixty miles from the safety of Whitefish Point on storm-bound Lake Superior at night. The two mothers stared into the darkness as they clutched their little girls to their breasts. The men bailed or bent to the oars, and ten-year-old Carl begged his father for a man's turn at rowing the lifeboat.

Wheelsman Harry W. Steward of Algonac, Michigan, had an iron grip on the tiller which Superior was trying to grab away from him. All at once a cry of hope rang out in the blackest hour of the night. "Look!" someone shouted. "There's a boat coming toward us!"

An up-bound freighter came plowing through the storm across Whitefish Bay, but the lifeboat carried no lights or flares. Even in the darkness the survivors waved frantically to attract attention. The high voices of the mothers and their daughters were drowned out by the gale.

At seven o'clock Wednesday morning, a heartbreaking mile from shore, the yawl capsized. There were a few screams, desperate attemps to save one another, then the heavy seas swept the victims apart. Only the wheelsman and the owner's son remained above the surface. The boy bore up manfully for a while but not far from land he wore out his last strength and slipped under.

The stout arms of the wheelsman carried himself ashore where he fell down exhausted. Then he trudged through the wild country to Lifesaving Station No. 12, ten miles distant, where he told of his lone survival, never an easy story to tell.

The only wreckage ever found of the *Western Reserve* was the starboard light, which floated ashore with some boards. The owner's son, Phillip, who had been kept home from that ill-fated pleasure trip, lived to be an old man and passed his latter days in a house that he named *Starboard Light.* And every night of his life the electric light burned

in his window in memory of the loved ones who had gone down with his father's ship.

A short life, and not a merry one, that is the history of the 420-foot ore carrier *Cyprus,* launched on September 17, 1907. She disappeared on Lake Superior twenty-five days later, perhaps because her crew neglected the order that every landlubber learns on reading his first sea novel: "Batten down the hatches!" This safety measure consists of covering every hatch and all the fastenings with heavy tarpaulin tightly belted down to keep water from leaking into the hold during a heavy sea, when enough might seep through to slosh around and shift the cargo, with disastrous results.

The *Cyprus* cleared Superior, Wisconsin, at nine o'clock Wednesday morning, October 9, 1907. The Lake was stormy but no more than average rough, and all other freighters completed their runs without mishap. It is a fair guess that Captain Huyck and his crew may have been careless about battening the hatches after the *Cyprus* took on her cargo of iron ore. The big carrier went out into the blow, the water creaming over her long deck with every dip of her prow into the high seas.

Making slow progress in the storm, the *Cyprus* plowed across Lake Superior all day Wednesday, all that night, all day Thursday, and on into the fatal night. Early in the evening she picked up company, the freighter *George Stephenson,* also down-bound for the Soo Canal and steering the same course toward Whitefish Point. The officers and crew of each ship could see the friendly lights across the way. It gave them a comfortable feeling in the storm.

Suddenly the comfortable feeling was gone. The men in the pilothouse of the *Stephenson* stared and rubbed their eyes. The lights of the *Cyprus* had disappeared. The big steel ship was blotted off the Lake.

Eighteen miles off Deer Park on the south shore of Superior, the Cyprus had gone into a list that could not be

255

straightened out by her frantic captain or crew. Down she went, in a twinkling, three hundred feet to the bottom.

Eighteen men went down with the wreck. Four of the crew clambered onto a life raft and drifted on the raging Lake until two o'clock in the morning when their handful of boards smashed into the breakers and flipped. One man made shore, and he never knew how. Second Mate Charles Petz was found at daylight on the beach by a Coast Guard search patrol, so far gone with shock and exposure that he barely knew the name of his ship, but he gradually recovered to tell his short and grim tale of lone survival.

Then there is the story of Captain William E. Morris, master of the bulk freighter *William F. Sauber,* who cleared Ashland, Wisconsin, on Saturday, October 23, 1903, with a cargo of iron ore for Lake Erie. The *Sauber* headed out across Superior into a late autumn storm, but Captain Morris cleared the dangerous outthrust of Keneenaw Peninsula safely and set a course for Whitefish Point.

But the weather turned sharp cold and what sailors call "the little ice devils" began to attack the *Sauber* as she rolled through the gale. Driving sleet and freezing spray lashed the ore carrier, weighting her down with tons of deadly ice until she wallowed in the water and her bottom spanked the seas.

When his ship sprang a leak and the water started to gain on the pumps, Captain Morris gave quiet orders to his first mate. "Hoist distress signals to the masthead and tell the crew to put on life preservers."

Meanwhile, he drove the freighter through a sixty-mile wind and tried to gain the shelter of Whitefish Point. At nightfall, Sunday, the steel freighter *Yale* sighted the distress signals and stood by the sinking vessel throughout the darkness, until lifeboats could be launched to take the men off the *Sauber.*

Captain Morris watched his crew go one by one safely over the side. The chief engineer offered him the last seat in the lifeboat. His answer was unprintably emphatic. The men threw him a line but it fell from his shoulders because he would make no effort to fasten it around his body. The old girl had been good to him. He could not bear to turn his back and leave her to die alone.

A few minutes later, while the crews of the *Sauber* and the *Yale* doffed their caps in the icy wind, Captain Morris went down with his ship.

So there they are, the stories of the lone survivors and the story that shows the reverse of the medal, the man who could have been saved but chose to die. In whose boots would we rather stand? It is a soul-searching question that perhaps many a solitary survivor has put to himself in the small cold hours of a windy night.

5. Wild Cliffs and Frozen Beaches

Lake Superior is the Lake of the long ships, the long hauls. Every type of vessel, from the Chippewa dugout to the tall-masted schooner to the gaudy passenger liner, has parted her waters, but to most people she will always be the Lake of the red bellies, the whalebacks, the steel ore carriers, the grain ships, the bulk freighters. Numbers of today's fleet are passing the 730-foot mark, which was the maximum length set by the U.S. Corps of Engineers for passage through the Soo Canal, until the new Poe Lock opened in 1968, 113th Soo Locks navigation season, and paved the waterway for the thousand-footers to come, Goliaths of the Lakes, designed to match the world's largest lock (1,200 feet long, 120 feet wide, and 61 feet from the top of the lock wall to the floor). A single long-ship perhaps carries more tonnage than all the scows and barges the Erie Canal carried on the busiest day of that waterway's hard-working history.

In effect, the ore and grain carriers, the bulk freighters, are a tow of many units linked into a single piece, a string of over-water boxcars, the rolling stock of an entire railroad line welded into a train carrying more tonnage than any combination of locomotives ever pulled overland.

The real barge and schooner tows were a feature of Lake Superior transport well into the twentieth century and they have been involved in some of her most spectacular shipwrecks. True, the loss of life in any single one of Superior's disasters cannot be compared with the major collisions and holocausts and founderings on the lower Lakes, but the individual impact is at least as great and the dramatic backdrop stands unequalled. Often, in a Lake Superior disaster, to survive the shipwreck is to perish on the shore. As stern and rockbound as the coast of Maine for the most part, Superior also has stretches of beach lonesomer and more forbidding than that of Robinson Crusoe because his at least showed one footprint and was washed by tropic seas instead of ice water.

On Sunday afternoon, September 29, 1895, the schooner-barge *Elma* broke loose from her tow in a gale off the Pictured Rocks in Lake Superior, five miles of colored sandstone rising in weird formations that have delighted the traveler and menaced the sailor since time began.

Aboard the *Elma* were seven men and the captain's three-year-old son. Her masts and rigging went by the board, her spars crashed into the sea, and her hulk drove straight for the Pictured Rocks. She struck aground one hundred feet in front of the formation named Miners' Castle by travelers, because of its arched portal, turreted entrance, high windows, and other fanciful resemblances in sandstone.

Slowly the schooner began to break up. Between her and the dubious refuge of Miners' Castle raged a maelstrom. The captain buttoned his little son snug against his own heart inside the great peacoat he wore, resolved that whatever happened to them would happen to them together. A sailor named Johnson took one look at the boy's face

258

peeking out from that blue harbor and volunteered to try to get a lifeline ashore. He made his attempt on the schooner's yawl, and the men on the wreck payed out the ropes as he fought a passage toward Miners' Castle. At the last minute, the wind and sea picked up the yawl and smashed it like a box of matches against the cliff. All the lines were tangled and lost in the wreckage, but Johnson caught a grip on holes in the rocks and lifted himself by fingers and toes until he reached a larger opening into which he crawled, safe above Lake Superior.

Aboard the stranded schooner another sailor, named Rudolph Yack, stole a glance at the peek-a-boo face in the captain's coat and offered to swim ashore with lines tied around his body. He fought his way through the surf to Miners' Castle, but before he could find a grip, the waves smashed him unconscious against the rocks and he went down. As the crew in desperate hurry tried to haul him back, the rope broke and his body disappeared forever.

Finally, just before nightfall, the crew succeeded in floating a line across the maelstrom to Johnson who climbed down from his safe perch to grab it. Darkness prevented any rescue attempt. He sat all night in his hole in the rocks, with the rope tied around his waist, thinking about the captain's little boy.

At dawn lifelines were rigged between the doomed schooner and Miners' Castle. Soon every last man, and the precious cargo buttoned inside the captain's coat, had been hauled high and dry into a cavern of the Pictured Rocks where a driftwood fire was built. Two loaves of bread had been saved from the schooner and they were portioned out.

For two days and nights the six men and the boy stayed in their cliff-side haven. The captain's son had the time of his life toasting bread in the fire and playing with toys carved from driftwood while the sailors who kept him amused faced the dread of freezing to death or starvation. They were about to make the desperate attempt of escaping on a raft built from storm wreckage when a lighthouse keeper, who had seen the smoke of their fire, came rowing up the Lake to their rescue.

There are cases on record in Lake Superior's history where shipwrecked crews, after landing their lifeboats on wilderness shores remote from any outpost of civilization, have been saved by coming across a rusty cookstove and dented cans of peaches and beans; cases, too, where half-frozen survivors were rescued on a desolate beach by a homesteader who was looking for his strayed cow.

There are cases not so fortunate. Between Grand Marais and Munising on the south shore of Lake Superior, along the stretch of coast that Longfellow himself named as the setting of his Hiawatha epic, lie the Au Sable banks, dunes of perpetual ice preserved between layers of wind-blown sand across the centuries. This frozen beach was used by the Indians as a natural refrigerator. The natives still preserve fish and game in summer by digging down through the sand a foot or two until the everlasting ice is reached.

Off these shores, on the ominous 18th of November, 1914, Captain J. P. Jennings was towing two schooner barges, the *Annie M. Peterson* and the *Seldon E. Marvin,* with the steamer *C. F. Curtis.* All three vessels were of a respectable size, about two hundred feet each, and they were laden deep with lumber bound for Tonawanda, near Buffalo. The tow carried a combined crew of twenty-six men and two women — a cook and a stewardess.

During the night Captain Jennings ran headlong into a blizzard. What happened thereafter is guesswork. The tow must have parted, the barges crashed, and the steamer foundered. The bodies of six men and the two women were found, all frozen stiff, two days later about eight miles from Grand Marais. Wreckage and eight more bodies came in along the Au Sable banks. Somehow two survivors reached shore. Their tracks could be seen in the snow and sand. But they had not come across an abandoned logging camp with a derelict cookstove and left-behind matches. They had frozen to death on the beach of eternal ice.

6. Navigating Under Northern Lights

Remote Superior has never been much of a Lake to inspire ballads, but the death of young Dr. Douglas Houghton, the 36-year-old geologist who discovered and surveyed much of the copper country on the Keweenaw Range to touch off the first mining rush in the United States, has been preserved in a good rousing chantey by Marie E. Gilchrist. The ballad follows in close detail the affidavit made by the two survivors after the wreck, which is such a pattern of its kind that it has been repeated aboard lifeboats and other small craft a thousand times in the more than hundred years that have passed since the little doctor drowned in the untamed waters off the wilderness shores of Lake Superior.

Houghton left Eagle Harbor on October 13, 1845, in an open boat rowed by four voyageurs: Peter MacFarline, Baptiste Bodrie, Tousin Piquette, and another. The young doctor was a fearless man and accustomed to have his own way:

A land breeze and a heavy sea,
Pull away, boys, pull hard.
Houghton said: "Tonight we must be
At Eagle River. The schooner leaves
Tomorrow, taking Oliver, here."

MacFarline said: "It's going to blow.
Shall we put in?" The Doctor said, "No!
This breeze can't hurt us; there's nothing to fear.
We shall soon be in; pull away!"

Today there may be seen near the water-front town of Eagle River a plaque beneath a small monument, inscribed: "In Memoriam, Douglas Houghton, The Father of U. S. Copper Mining." Appropriately the good doctor met his death along the copper-studded Keweenaw, the peninsula that juts out on Lake Superior's chart like a sea serpent with head poised to strike — and many a time it has struck against shipping.

Douglas Houghton sat in the stern,
Pull away, boys, pull hard.
It began to snow and the wind took a turn
Northeasterly, and the snow came faster.
Meemee, the dog, crouched by his master.
We had better keep on, pull away.

Darkness came and a heavy sea. Spray washed aboard, wetting all the men to the skin. The voyageurs wanted to put ashore at Sand Beach but Dr. Houghton scoffed at their fears and told them they would soon enjoy a good hot meal and a dry bed.

They knocked and they rolled in the waves for an hour.
We shall soon be in, pull away.
MacFarline bailed with all his power.
"Better put on your belt," he spoke
Just before a big wave broke.
The belt washed away from the Doctor.

At last even the plucky geologist, with the boat shipping water in mountainous seas and the snow drifting aboard in white squalls, decided that it might be best to go ashore. But the voyageurs told him it was too late. They were past Sand Beach and coasting a dangerous shelf of rocks. Again insistent on having his own way and despite the protests of the voyageurs, Dr. Houghton steered for land.

Heavily each man leaned on his oar.
Pull away, boys, pull hard.
They were now two hundred yards from shore.

We must get to shore, pull away.
Along came a wave with spray and thunder,
The boat capsized with all hands under.
"Better keep on," said the Doctor.

MacFarline caught the keel and stayed afloat,
He pulled Houghton up by the collar of his coat —
"Take off your gloves and hold on!"
Houghton was a brave and little man,
"Don't mind me, get ashore if you can,
Peter," he said. The sea took them there
And sent the boat straight into the air.
"I'll get along," said the Doctor.

But when MacFarline and Bodrie struggled back to the surface, the pioneer geologist had disappeared along with Piquette and the nameless voyageur. The two survivors heard the breakers roar in the darkness. They were hurled against the rocks by four waves in a row, and on the last bruising surge they were able to get ashore, chilled to the bone.

They searched and called in the freezing blast
But gave up hope of the others at last.
Come away, boy, come away.
"We have lost our brothers," Bodrie said,
"Perhaps one of us will not be dead
Before we reach Eagle River."

The two survivors made the rugged wilderness trek into Eagle River by midnight and search parties immediately went out in hopes of finding Keweenaw's beloved young doctor. But three feet of snow fell before daylight, and Houghton's body was not recovered until spring. His fame, however, in the copper country, and in the ballad's stanzas, remains deathless.

No man need be ashamed of coming out second best in an October battle with Lake Superior, as a grim notice in the shipping news of 1876 bears witness:

Burning of the St. Clair. — The steamer *St. Clair* burned to the water's edge while off Fourteen Mile Point, between Ontonagon and Portage Lake ship canal, about two o'clock Sunday morning, July 9. A total of twenty-six were lost. The fire enveloped all the boats except a large yawl. As it touched the water, there was a rush for the boat, and it immediately capsized. It was righted and capsized six times, and, when finally kept right side up, contained only four of the crew. They ripped up the seats and used them for paddles and cruised about in search of the unfortunate passengers. Only two were picked up, one of whom was dead. Most of the passengers put on life preservers, but the water was extremely cold and they soon perished.

Even on a calm summer night in Lake Superior, five days after the Fourth of July, the big ice-blue body of water gave her victims a choice of two evils — they could burn to death or they could freeze to death under the sweeping search beams of the northern lights.

The law of the white jungle rules supreme on the big cold Lake, the law of blizzard and frozen wastes. Her storms have swept living icicles from wooden schooner decks and modern steelways. She has, on occasion, clamped winter down so quick and tight that whole fleets have been trapped in her blue ice.

In November of 1926, the Chicago grain market was threatened with panic while Cleveland and Pittsburgh iron masters almost had nervous breakdowns because the thermometers aboard ore and grain carriers in the St. Marys River dropped to thirty-five degrees below zero and two hundred and forty-seven long ships were locked in ice outside the Soo Canal — miles of ships, two and three and four abreast, caught in the deep freeze — plated white with frost and belching protests of black smoke from the red and silver stacks.

For ten days this pile-up of twenty dozen freighters gave the North Country a spectacle of the world's strangest city on ice, more busy smokestacks than a factory town, boulevards of lights under the dark winter sky. Enterprising tradesmen hitched up their horses and drove sleds piled high with meat and provisions out to this maritime metropolis where they did a brisk business. A few of the hardier sailors stumbled across the ice to shore where they bought tobacco and courted the girls.

Finally the weather moderated for a spell, and the railroad car ferry *Ste. Marie,* doing double duty as an icebreaker, broke through from the Straits of Mackinac and left an open passage down to Lake Huron and Lake Michigan. With a celebration of 247 whistles, the long ships bucked through drift ice out the St. Marys into open water.

Weathermen predicted that such unusual conditions probably would not be seen again in half a century. The Lake Superior region took the dare. At the end of November, 1937, in the usual last-minute rush to make one more haul for the season, twenty-six grain carriers left Fort William and locked through the Soo Canal only to find their passage blocked by the whaleback *James B. Eads* that had been caught in an ice jam.

While tugs tried to release the whaleback and clear the channel into Lake Huron, the master of one of the held-up grain carriers recorded his ship's thermometer at forty below. At the end of five frosty days the tugs gave up and left the whaleback tight as a cork in the St. Marys River. In the bottleneck behind, and marooned for the winter, were the twenty-six grain carriers loaded with six million bushels of wheat. They delivered their cargoes the next April, an elapsed time of five months for the haul.

Go back or go forward in time and the story of Lake Superior's white jungle differs only in minor details. On June 6, 1917, a spring gale locked seventeen ships in ice at Duluth. After the breakup navigation was menaced by icebergs that bulked underwater to a depth of seventy feet.

Forty years later, on a winter day in 1957, a native of Sault Ste. Marie, in short-wave contact with his home town from his post in Little America, compared weather reports between the two places and announced that the members of Byrd's Antarctic expedition were enjoying milder temperatures than the citizens in the Sault. During the same winter, the car ferry *Vacationland,* second most powerful vessel on the Great Lakes, was wedged by a hurricane into an icefield twenty-five feet thick.

This winter, and all winters to come, shipmasters will drive their long carriers through the late autumnal storms to the desperate end of navigation because cargoes of wheat and iron ore and building stone would never be delivered if they waited upon the faint-hearted. It takes men to deliver the goods across the Lakes, the kind of men who brought the *W. E. Fitzgerald* out of a Superior storm some years ago and into port with twelve hundred tons of ice plastered over her as she rolled gallantly home under the northern lights.

Understandably enough, Lake Superior has never gone in much for the lower-Lake pastime of moonlight excursions, but the frosty breath of her *aurora borealis* has thrilled many a sight-seer on the deck of a luxury liner. A century ago the paddle-wheel steamboat *Planet,* for a round trip from Detroit or Cleveland at a fare of thirty-five or forty dollars respectively, offered the following inducements:

> New, 1,200 tons burden, low-pressure engine of 1,000 horse power; has an upper cabin 210 feet long, and splendid accommodations for 300 passengers, but on these trips, that they may be in fact, as well as in name, Pleasure Excursions, the number will be limited to 175. A good band will be in attendance to enliven the scene, and no expense will be spared to make these excursions the most agreeable that have been made to Lake Superior.

The most ill-fated passenger boat in the history of the big cold Lake was the *Algoma.* Her story involves two coincidences. One of the new liners operating in conjunction with the Canadian Pacific Railroad, she met her doom on the very day that the last spike was driven at Craigellachie

266

on Eagle Pass in the Rockies to join the eastern to the western rails of the road.

The second coincidence involving the *Algoma* is the fact that she was cut in two by her owners and later broken in two by Lake Superior. Built in Scotland, she crossed the western ocean and, in order to get through the locks in the St. Lawrence and the Welland canals, she was separated amidships at a Montreal shipyard. Then the two halves were towed through the system of locks in the St. Lawrence River, across Lake Ontario, and through the Welland cut around Niagara Falls into Lake Erie where another shipyard at Buffalo joined her together again, not an unusual procedure on the Seaway.

With her white cabins and her black hull, the propeller *Algoma* struck pride into the hearts of Canadians. Big and sleek and fast, she was put on the run between Owen Sound, Lake Huron, and Port Arthur, Lake Superior. Toward the end of her second season, on November 7, 1885, she ran into a storm on the upper Lake. Sleet froze her ropes and auxiliary sails, then snow squalls blotted out landmarks.

Captain John I. Moore displayed remarkable seamanship in handling his vessel under savage conditions, and he missed bringing her through the maze of rocks off the wild eastern tip of Isle Royale by a few feet, but a burst of the storm lifted up the *Algoma* and brought her down on a veritable pinnacle of doom one mile from Rock Harbor Light.

The floating palace that men had cut in two after painstaking hours of labor was broken in two by Lake Superior in as many minutes. There were thirty-seven persons who went to their deaths off the steep icy decks of the *Algoma* almost at once, many of them to be hauled up later in fishermen's nets that had been set before the storm.

A section of the cabin crashed down on Captain Moore, pinning him to the deck with serious injuries. As the forward end of the wreck broke loose with a vicious wrenching

267

of metal, he called the other thirteen survivors around him.

"Kneel down," he told them, "and follow me in prayer."

The thirteen knelt beside the fallen captain on a deck storm-swept with debris and drifted snow and sharp ice. Their prayers were answered hours later when the *Algoma's* sister ship, the *Athabasca,* came along to lower lifeboats and rescue them from the after half of the fatal breakup.

At the other end of rugged Isle Royale, on Rock of Ages Reef, the passenger liner *George M. Cox,* with 118 aboard, went hard aground in a dense fog, on May 27, 1933. Her stern settled and she filled quickly with water, but there was no panic. The well-drilled crew safely launched the lifeboats and removed all passengers to Rock of Ages Lighthouse, where they took turns standing inside throughout the chilly night. At dawn these lucky survivors of a shipwreck that cost not a single life were taken across the Lake by a Coast Guard cutter to Keweenaw Peninsula where the town of Houghton made them welcome, the town named in honor of someone who had not survived a Superior shipwreck.

Many a strange drama has been enacted under the northern lights of Lake Superior but none more weird than that mentioned in the shipping news of the 1887 season of navigation:

> *Thrilling End of the Arizona.* — The steamer *Arizona* left Marquette, November 17, for Portage Lake on her last trip. She was compelled to put back by a furious storm from the northeast. While laboring heavily in the high seas a carboy of acid was broken, filling the space between decks with dense and stifling fumes and setting fire to the steamer. The poisonous fumes made it impossible to fight the fire, and the engineers and firemen were soon driven from the engine room. The chief engineer was the last man to leave his post, and only when nearly suffocated. He turned on a full head of steam and joined the rest of the crew on the upper deck.

The navigation notice went on to record that there were nine hundred barrels of oil and acid in the *Arizona's* cargo.

Captain George Glaser stood with the man at the wheel. As the burning steamer drew near to port and swept around the breakwater, the fire blazed out from her sides, creating a general alarm, and the steamers at the docks began sounding their whistles. The *China* and the *Nyack* lowered boats to pick up the *Arizona's* crew. To continue verbatim with the contemporary account:

> Although the captain and crew had escaped death on the open Lake, they were in almost as great peril in the harbor, in charge of a burning ship, which was rushing on at full speed without a man at the engine. Sweeping around in a broad circle, Captain Glaser headed the burning steamer square toward the breakwater, determined to land the men there. She struck the pier just forward of the steamer *Nyack*, and the crew, twenty-three in number, leaped upon the breakwater. The burning steamer's engines still working held her nose up to the dock until the rudder swung her stern around, and the abandoned steamer shot along the pier into the slip by the water works. The crew, chased by the steamer, had to run for their lives along the breakwater to keep from being suffocated by the clouds of smoke and fumes of the burning acid. The *Arizona* finally buried her nose in the sand and found her last resting place.

Lake Superior, not to be outdone by Lake Michigan's story of a lunatic captain at the wheel of a doomed vessel, had her own wild tale of a berserk ship in hot pursuit of her pellmell crew under the spell of the northern lights.

7. Sailed Away on Superior

In the days of sail there were so many mysterious disappearances on the Lakes that schooner crews told stories of underground channels connecting Lake Erie with Lake Huron, and Whitefish Bay in Lake Superior with North Channel and Georgian Bay in Lake Huron. The old-time sailors had yarns to spin about big winds that blew ships from one Lake into another.

The Flying Dutchman of salt water soon found a way into the lore of the Great Lakes. Originally this spectral ship, seen in stormy weather off the Cape of Good Hope and considered an omen of bad luck, had been sighted by such English mariners as Sir Francis Drake. According to Sir Walter Scott, she had sailed from the Low Countries with a cargo of precious metal, but a horrible murder having been committed on board, the black plague broke out among the crew, and no port would allow the vessel to enter. To this day she wanders about like a ghost, doomed to be sea-tossed and nevermore to enjoy rest.

The first Flying Dutchman on Lake Superior dates back to June of 1847 when the schooner *Merchant* ran into a gale and was lost with all hands — seven crew members, seven passengers, and Captain Robert More.

Even before the Soo Canal was completed, the Great Lakes sailors had invented their own mythology to explain ships that vanished without trace: they had sailed through a crack in the Lake.

On November 21, 1902, the freighter *Bannockburn* cleared Duluth and was sighted by a passenger vessel the following evening. Unreported at the Soo Canal, through which all shipping must pass to the lower Lakes, she was given up for lost fifty-seven years ago, but many a sailor has claimed to see her since, through the frost of a pilothouse window in late October or through a porthole smoked with May fog. Her legend, perhaps because of some magic in the sound of her name — *Bannockburn* — is the most persistent of all the Flying Dutchmen stories on the Lakes. She has a captain and crew of twenty to man her across the timeless seas.

On the last day of August in the ill-fated year of 1905, the freighter *Iosco* went out of Duluth with a cargo of iron ore in her red belly and the schooner *Olive Jeanette* in tow. Two days later Captain Nelson Gonyaw's vessels were sighted by the *William A. Paine* going along in good shape off historic Stannard Rock Light near the Keweenaw Peninsula. A few hours later a violent northeaster hit that part of Lake Superior. At four o'clock the next afternoon the shattered hulk of the schooner washed up on the shore east of the Porcupine Mountains. No wreckage of the freighter ever appeared to indicate where the *Iosco* went down. She sailed off the chart with everybody aboard. None of the twenty-six men on the doomed tow outfit lived to return and tell their tale of what happened.

Captain John Eisenhardt of Milwaukee no doubt considered the month of April, 1914, the happiest of his life. It marked his first command, the steel freighter *Benjamin Noble*. She was bound up the Lakes with a cargo of steel rails for Duluth and Captain Eisenhardt took her through the Soo Canal in fine style early in the evening of April 25. The lock tenders watched her sail out of sight toward Whitefish Bay. That was the last of the *Benjamin Noble* for human eyes. Only minutes later the weather bureau notified all shipping to be prepared for dirty weather, but Captain Eisenhardt pursued his course, unwarned. The storm hit Duluth so hard that it blew out the south light on the entry pier, and the light tenders were unable to get out on the wave-lashed pier heads and fix the oil lamp. Sailors later speculated that Captain Eisenhardt, on the verge of bringing his ship into safe harbor, went off his course because of the unlighted lamp, and the *Benjamin Noble* sailed away somewhere off Minnesota Point with twenty men whose bodies have never been found because they are manning a ghost vessel under a master whose first command was his last.

During World War I a shipyard at Fort William on the Canadian shores of Lake Superior built two mine sweepers for the French navy. Completed in the last week of November, the *Cerisoler* and the *Inkaerman,* each with thirty-eight men aboard, hurried across the big cold Lake to get through the Soo Canal before winter locked up the Seaway. They are still unreported at the Soo, after forty years. Perhaps the pair of mine sweepers went down on the phantom island shown on charts of Lake Superior during the Revolutionary period, Isle Phelipeaux, which caused so much confusion when Benjamin Franklin tried to settle the boundary-line question with the British, because no such island existed. But there were so many rocks and dangerous reefs east of Isle Royale that the idea of a second large island in the vicinity had occurred to early mariners. From this phantom island the spectral mine sweepers *Cerisoler* and *Inkaerman* may have sailed away with a total crew list of seventy-six. No wreckage or bodies have ever been found.

In the winter of the big freeze, 1927, the Canadian tramp freighter *Kamloops* was plowing along through eighteen-below-zero weather in company with the steamer *Quedoc,* bound for Fort William. It was December and the men aboard both ships were in a hurry to get home for Christmas. Suddenly, with Isle Royale dead ahead, the crew of the *Quedoc* stared at the place on the Lake where the *Kamloops* had been. Without warning, perhaps weighted down with untold tons of ice, she had sailed away.

The *Kamloops* represents the last of the large Flying Dutchmen to sail through the fabled crack in Lake Superior, but there have been near misses in recent years. On May 11, 1953, the *Henry Steinbrenner* foundered in a gale off the Isle Royale light with a death toll of seventeen. Captain Albert Stiglin lost his license for alleged negligence. The reverse, and untarnished, side of this medal showed in September of the same year when the ore carrier *Maryland* ran aground near Marquette in a vicious storm. Superb seamanship by captain and crew along with gallant action by the Coast Guard brought all thirty-two men aboard safely ashore by breeches buoy and helicopter.

Another of the more recent gallantries of the Great Lakes showed again the breed of sailing masters the inland seas produce when, on May 1, 1940, the Canadian freighter *Arlington* sank during a blizzard-gale on Superior. The steamer *Collingwood* rescued the entire crew of sixteen, but Captain Fred Burke went down with his ship.

Navigation aids and modern rescue methods in the present generation have dwindled losses, but the phantom sails and the spectral smokestacks of the Flying Dutchmen are ever on the outlook for new additions to the eerie fleet that patrols the waters of Superior.

8. November, 1905

As long as there are survivors left alive to champion each cause, there will be fierce arguments as to which November storm was the worst, Lake Huron's of 1913, Lake Michigan's of 1940, or Lake Superior's of 1905. In loss of life and in complete loss of long steel ships, the Huron storm has no equal; in wind-gust velocity and in wave sharpness, the Michigan storm may take the palm; but in combined terms of snow, cold, wind, shipwreck, and heavy seas, the Superior storm is generally agreed to be the worst ever to strike the Great Lakes. In what seemed minutes the temperature dropped to twelve degrees below zero and a hurricane ripped the world of fresh water apart. During the last three days of November the wind went around the clock at seventy to eighty miles an hour. Mountainous seas rolled and thundered between Duluth and the Soo Canal.

Thirty vessels were wrecked on Superior. The storm drove fourteen steel carriers ashore. One of the long ships, the *Ira H. Owen,* went down with nineteen lives. The steamer *Western Star* was thrown so high and dry near Fourteen Mile Point along the Keweenaw that people were able to walk all the way around her. The Canadian steamer *Monkshaven* crashed on Angus Rock, north of Isle Royale, and sank.

The Pittsburgh Steamship Line, a division of U. S. Steel, the proud Silverstackers of the iron ore fleets, never before or since has paid such a toll to any storm. Captains of the steamship line, who had brought their own ships crippled into the harbor of Duluth during the blow, gathered in Lanigans, favorite restaurant among Lake men, and discussed with somber eyes and heavy hearts the latest reports of disaster.

A few miles from Duluth the Pittsburgh steamer *Crescent City* was blown ashore. Eight miles from Two Harbors the *Lafayette* was blown on the rocks and cut in two, her barge, the *Manila,* crashing into her, both crews, unbelievably, scrambling like spiders over the sides and to safety on the rocky shore. The *William Edenborn* was driven ashore on Split Rock and the barge she was towing, the *Madeira,* was broken in two. The flagship of the Silverstacker fleet, the *William E. Corey,* struck hard aground on Gull Island Reef. The *Cornelia* and her barge *Maia* crashed onto Point Isabelle. The steamer *German,* lost in the blizzard, went ashore at Glencoe.

But none of the reports of disaster that came into Lanigans could equal what happened outside at the height of the storm in full view of the city of Duluth. No disaster in Great Lakes history ever has come close to equaling the spectacular shipwreck of the 430-foot steel freighter *Mataafa.* Her story will be told in hushed tones as long as there are sailors on fresh water.

According to the Pittsburgh Steamship Line's own record of the chillingly dramatic tragedy, a steadily freshening wind was whipping snow in gusty flurries across Duluth Harbor in the late afternoon of November 27, 1905. Her lights dimly visible to those ashore, the 6900-ton *Mataafa,* with the 366-foot barge *Nasmyth* in tow, cleared the ship canal, moving past the lighthouse at the end of the pier.

In the pilothouse, Captain R. F. Humble gave the traditional farewell salute, three long and two short, as he put the *Mataafa* and her consort *Nasmyth,* both deep-laden with

274

iron ore for a Lake Erie port, out into the open Lake. Then he checked the time on the big moon-faced clock above him. It was just five o'clock, p.m. Starting out into the heaving slate-gray seas of Lake Superior, he spoke to the mate on watch.

"How's the glass look? Still falling?"

"Still falling, sir."

"It was too high yesterday," Captain Humble said, voicing sixteen years of Great Lakes sailing experience. "I don't like to see a barometer go that high. It's not good, not good at all. Once she starts down she's liable to just keep goin'."

The skipper glanced aft as his barge crashed past the dissolving light of the beacon. Twenty-four hours later, that lighthouse, washed from the pier, would be floating far out on Lake Superior.

While the lights on the steep streets of Duluth were still in view, Captain Humble realized that he was riding a violent northeast gale, but he had a young staunch ship under him and in her short six years of service she had ridden out her share of bad storms.

However, he kept a sharp watch as the seas began to break over his decks from both sides, and he rubbed his chin thoughtfully as the gusts of snow turned into a blizzard that cut visibility to a few yards. Now and then he and the mate exchanged glances but no words as they drove the ship onward through the howling night, her barge smashing along behind.

The fury of the wind and snow increased across the dark hours as the *Mataafa* and the *Nasmyth* plowed into roaring, thrashing seas. The angry water swept over the long spar deck covering the hatches with swirling foam. Inside the big steel carrier, men worked feverishly to secure every article as chairs slid crazily from wall to wall. Tools fell from their racks and men had to be human flies as they moved about, often walking on all fours to keep their balance.

In the galley a cupboard-door latch banged loose, discharging stacks of dishes that smashed to fragments on the pitching deck. Portholes were battered open by the wild sea, pouring streams of freezing water into the crew quarters.

Down in the engine room, a sweating chief engineer hung onto his levers, slowing the turn of the screw as the stern of the ship was lifted clear out of water, speeding it up as the ship fell back into the rolling sea. But even this strategy could not stop the pounding vibration that seemed about to shake the vessel to pieces. Firemen struggled to stay on their feet long enough to feed another shovelful of coal into the roaring boilers.

At four o'clock p.m., Captain Humble took another look at the moon-faced clock above him. It was a moment of life-and-death decision. He judged that the *Mataafa* and her tow would founder if he were to continue on his present course, so he gave his order in formal tones:

"Turn her about, mister."

"Yes, sir," replied the mate on watch.

The maneuver required an artisan at the wheel and magic down in the engine room. Captain Humble had gambled the seamanship of his crew against Lake Superior in a temper. The *Mataafa* settled into the trough of the waves for a moment, then swung her prow around into a giant swell, starting back for the shelter of Duluth.

Heading for that same harbor were two other battered ships, the R. W. *England* and the Pittsburgh Silverstacker *Ellwood.* Crowds gathered along the high Duluth shore to watch the race between four gallant vessels and their ancient adversary, the northeast wind.

With the violent breath of the gale on their after quarter, the *England* and the *Ellwood* drove onward, reaching the piers early in the afternoon. Hundreds of people in Duluth and Superior struggled through the blizzard that was burying stranded streetcars in huge drifts, to get down to the beach and build towering bonfires to guide the beleaguered mariners. They sighed their relief as the *England* made harbor safely in a brief lull of the lunatic wind with the *Ellwood,* bow dripping and cargo deck awash, close behind her.

Then, while they watched in horror-stricken silence from the shore, the spectators saw the *Ellwood* raised high on a giant sea and slammed against the pier. Bells clanged wildly in the wheelhouse on her bow and in her throbbing engine room. Wavering and staggering, with her black smoke streaming in the wind, she made the inner harbor. But frantic pumps could not keep up with the water pouring into her hold, and her battered hulk went settling on the shallow bottom. Her crew were all rescued but her plight foretold the tragedy about to unfold.

Out in the furious seaway a dark shape loomed through the blowing spray, the *Mataafa* with her consort. Captain Humble, struggling to bring his big steel carrier toward the entrance, made another vital decision. He judged it would be useless to attempt to ride the *Nasmyth* through the piers, and he gave the order that put life or death trembling in the balance for the crew of the barge, depending on whether his judgment proved right or wrong:

"Cut her loose, mister."

"Yes, sir," replied the mate on watch.

At a safe distance from shore the 366-foot *Nasmyth,* heavy with iron, was cast adrift to find her own destiny. Eighty-mile-an-hour winds swept the powerless vessel toward the rocky shore, but her two anchors finally caught and held. She rode out the storm safely, with seas crashing over her as though she were a tide rock, but the crew snug aboard.

It was another story for the *Mataafa.* With black smoke pouring from her silver stack, she kept struggling toward the entrance. At last she made a fair entry, about half her length inside the piers, when suddenly a backwater surged beneath her. For a moment, while thousands gasped ashore, she seemed to hesitate there, motionless. Then the wild sea drove her downward until her prow struck the muddy bottom, then swept her stern against the north pier. A hail of ice crashed down from her rigging, shattering on her steel deck. Giant waves washed over her with the spray flying higher than the tips of her masts.

As the *Mataafa* literally cried out in her anguish, Lake Superior swept her out to sea, spun her around bow forward into the open Lake, and then delivered the death blow. With a savage thrust the surf rose to smash the stricken ship's stern against the opposite pier. Her engines throbbed in vain — her rudder had been ripped loose like a piece of tin from a child's toy.

Out of control, black smoke still belching from her once proud but now battered and lopsided silver stack, the *Mataafa* was swept onto the rocks. In a matter of icy minutes the long ship cracked in two under the pounding seas, her stern settling slowly in the cold water.

Before the awe-struck eyes of snow-bound Duluth, while fingernails in warm houses on the steep streets scratched window views, three men made their way along the railing toward the forward cabin, icy seas breaking over them at every step. A fourth man started after them. Three times he was washed over the rail, nothing between him and eternity but the frozen wire railing clutched in his fists. He tried a fourth time and again he had to pull himself up from the water. He braced himself against the railing cables for a moment of decision, standing erect to let a great swell roll over him. Then, as Duluth held its breath before screaming "No!" into the wind, the man turned around and retraced his path over the broken deck. Inch by agonizing inch he made his way back to the after cabin, there to freeze to death with his mates during the night ahead.

As the stern settled, the fire under the *Mataafa's* boilers had been washed out. With the thermometer at thirteen degrees below zero, all hope for the nine men at the stern half of the vessel was given up.

Rescue squads stared helpless from the shore. No lifeboat could survive the berserk waves. The Coast Guard

278

shot rockets across the maelstrom and finally got a line aboard, but it froze and broke before they could haul out the heavy hawser and rig a breeches buoy.

Darkness settled on the rocky hills of Duluth and on the mountainous seas of Lake Superior. Bonfires blazed along the shore in the snowstorm. Forty thousand people gathered on piers and along the ice-swept beaches and on the heights of the city. They kept vigil with the awful knowledge that they had come to watch the *Mataafa's* crew freeze to death out there in the pitiless night on the big cold Lake.

At dawn the town itself had to dig out from under the blizzard. Milk wagons foundered in deep snow as their horses shied away from wreckage in the streets. Lumber and smashed buildings littered the shore. The harbor was a shambles of wrecked and stranded vessels, but the wind had died down and the seas were running smaller.

In this deceptive calm, the thermometer plunged to twenty below, but rescue crews were heartened by signs of life aboard the *Mataafa,* at the forward end of the broken ship. There, as it later developed, the men had huddled together in the captain's cabin, saved from freezing to death by close contact and the combined warmth of their bodies. As water by the barrel spurted through the broken portholes, they would rush to the other side of the cabin. There was no food. They broke off icicles and sucked on them.

Late in the morning the Coast Guard got a lifeboat alongside the *Mataafa* to bring off Captain Humble and the other survivors at the forward end. In the after end they found nine bodies with staring eyes and frost-gray faces. Some of the bodies had to be chopped free. An engineer was found completely encased in ice, an awesome northern mummy embalmed by Lake Superior.

For years this tragedy on the doorstep of Duluth was commemorated with the Mataafa cigar, bearing a picture of the wrecked freighter on its colorful band.

Clamped between the teeth of intrepid seamen, the lost *Mataafa* rode out many a storm on the greatest of all Lakes.

BOOK FIVE

SUNSET FIRES ON LAKE ONTARIO

Now all good wood scow sailor mans,
Take warning by dat storm,
An' go marry one nice French girl,
And live on one beeg farm.

Den de win' can blow lak hurricane,
An' s'pose she blow some more;
You can't get drown on Lac Ontair'
So long you stay on shore.

(French Canadian chantey, 1885)

This popular Lakeland ballad may have been original with the Canadian poet William Henry Drummond, or he may have adapted it from snatches of song that he heard along the St. Lawrence. His particular version of "The Wreck of the Julie Plante" places the disaster in Lac St. Pierre, one of the large backwater bays in the St. Lawrence River. Most versions set the locale on Lake St. Clair, the bulge of stormy shallow water in the St. Clair-Detroit river straits between Lake Huron and Lake Erie. No doubt sailors changed the location at will, along with other details, as above.

1. The Shirttail-Cousin Lake

Least of the Great Lakes, the magnitude of Lake Ontario still puts her above all but a scattered few of the crowned heads among the world's largest bodies of fresh water. She belongs to the true sisterhood of the majestic five daughters born to America's inland Neptune, but she always has been regarded as a poor relation, a sort of shirttail cousin, by her big sisters.

Upper Lakelanders generally pay lip service to Lake Ontario, but when they speak of the Lakes, their thinking and their intimate feeling stops — as the shipping used to stop — short of Niagara Falls. The foot of Lake Erie is the end of the line. Buffalo is the car barn where boats are swung around for the return trip.

This may not be fair, but it states the fact and, meanwhile, a day of reckoning is in store. The haughty upper Lakes are in for their comeuppance, and the long ore carriers that now show the broad of their backs to Lake Ontario as they wheel around at Cleveland and other Lake Erie ports will in due time go poking through the Welland Canal to pay their belated respects to the lower Lake.

The once called unlimited deposits of iron ore in the Lake Superior region are petering out like the sands in a giant's hourglass and the rediscovery of huge iron deposits in the Adirondacks of upper New York State together with other ranges along the St. Lawrence River will ultimately reverse the trend of the long steel carriers. Instead of going down the Lakes from Duluth and Two Harbors and Marquette, they will start coming up from the Adirondack shore, from Seven Islands down on the St. Lawrence, plowing across Lake Ontario toward the iron-hungry ports of Cleveland, Toledo, Wyandotte, Detroit, Gary, and South Chicago. In that era to come, the great upper Lakes will wait upon the great lower Lake.

The large grain freighters are already making regular passages from Fort William on Lake Superior to Toronto on Lake Ontario. For a few months the Canadian carrier *Lemoyne,* 633 feet in over-all length, home port Toronto, ruled the Lakes, but in the next season, 1927, the ill-fated *Carl D. Bradley* nosed out the *Lemoyne* with her over-all length of 638 feet, nine inches.

The Canadian ship set a record in 1929, hauling 17,173 tons of wheat in a single cargo representing 571,885 bushels. Since the *Lemoyne* first hit the 633 mark, freighters of the six-hundred-foot class have become common enough, and today four seven-hundred-footers are about ready for launching in Canadian shipyards, which means more traffic on Lake Ontario.

Undoubtedly her day is coming but, in a manner of speaking, Ontario, throughout her history, has been the Lake that "just missed the boat." There were naval engagements between the French and British on the lower Lake half a century before Commodore Perry went into action, but the famed victory on Lake Erie stole all the thunder of Ontario's cannonades.

It was Lake Ontario that, in 1816 and 1817, launched the first two steamboats on the Great Lakes, the *Frontenac* and the *Ontario,* but along came the colorful *Walk-in-the-Water* on Lake Erie in 1818 to catch the public fancy and grab most of the historical headlines.

Lake Ontario is just as much entitled to the fanfare and ballyhoo of Niagara Falls as is Lake Erie, but the lower Lake always has been left in the lurch while crowds came honeymooning and excursioning up from Buffalo and Cleveland and Detroit to sit in the Lake Erie grandstand and watch the spectaculars put on by Niagara landlords and publicity hunters, such as:

The steamboats and sailing schooners careening through

the rapids and over the cataract while the wild animals screamed from deck.

The famous aerialist Blondin tightroping across the Falls during the mid-years of the nineteenth century and, for an encore, carrying a ·man on his back over the gorge.

Sam Patch, building a wooden tower, ninety feet high, at the water's edge at the foot of the Biddle Stairway on Goat Island, and jumping from a platform atop into the Niagara River.

The parade of aerialists who came trooping after Blondin across the years at Niagara — Signor Farini, Steve Peere the Canadian who fell to his death, Signorina Maria Spelterina, the only woman who dared the high-wire crossing, Toronto's Samuel John Dixon, and others. They went across the gorge holding out hats as targets for pistol experts aboard the *Maid of the Mist* riding the rapids below; they dressed as monkeys and trundled wheelbarrows; they teetered across on stilts; they went over at night with colored lights on their balancing poles; they crossed with baskets on their feet and shackles around their bodies; they toted tables and chairs; they went across backwards and blindfolded; they walked with their ankles and wrists manacled; they went with their feet in a sack and they washed ladies' handkerchiefs out on the cables.

Then the scores of men and women who survived or were lost as they rode the Whirlpool Rapids in rubber suits, barrels, boats, balls, and even life preservers, only to have a forty-three-year-old woman schoolteacher come along in 1901 to make them look like sissies instead of daredevils by popping over the Horseshoe Falls in a barrel with a manhole cover.

In the successful wake of Mrs. Annie Taylor came pint-sized dapper Bobby Leach who spent ten years telling everyone he met that he intended to go over the Falls in a steel barrel of his own invention, finally talked himself into it during the month of July, 1911, convalesced for twenty-three weeks in the hospital, and lived to tell about his ride for years afterwards, until he slipped on a banana peel and was killed.

As late as 1928 the challenge of the wild tumbling waters was met by Jean Laussier, who went rolling over in a large rubber ball and poked his head out, smiling, but public opinion had begun to turn and outlaw this kind of showing off.

Lincoln Beechy flew a plane under the Falls Bridge the same year Bobby Leach went over the Falls in his barrel, after which this stunt was banned, too. But a nameless aviator flew under all Niagara's bridges the year of the Japanese attack on Pearl Harbor.

During all these circus shows, Lake Erie had the position of vantage, the bulge over Lake Ontario, but there was one exception that proved the rule and made a good story.

Until 1861 the lower Niagara River had been regarded as unnavigable between the Falls and Lewiston, Ontario, but the plucky little steamer *Maid of the Mist* was heavily mortgaged to Lake Erie creditors. Captain Robinson, faced with having his boat repossessed unless he got her out of the United States, took her full steam down the river through the roaring gorge. She lost her smokestack on the wild trip as the waves crashed over her decks, but she kept answering to her rudder and she must have broken all speed records for five miles until the rapids tossed her down into smooth water, and she rode free and clear out into the Lake below, having escaped shipwreck and bankruptcy in a single swoop.

For once in her life, Ontario had gotten the upper hand over Erie.

2. Middle of the Rainbow

The controversial St. Lawrence Seaway has long been visioned by its champions as symbolizing all the promises of the rainbow. Lake Ontario is in the geographical position of hoping that the mythical pot of gold may be found in the middle of the rainbow right where her wide waters beckon for trade.

Ontario is a commodious Lake, a broad boulevard that has accommodated shipping between the St. Lawrence River and the Upper Lakes for well over a century, although the worst disaster in modern annals of the inland seas must be charged against her. She would be navigable even in dead of winter because her extreme depth keeps her from freezing over, except around the shoreline.

Not being shallow and subject to sudden trouble in every puff of wind like her next-door neighbor Lake Erie, Ontario, with her other advantages, offers the mariner fewer problems than any of her sisters. Her shores are not dangerously rock-bound in Superior's frowning pattern. She has not the treacherous islands of Lake Huron until her mouth is reached, and there they are, the expected teeth in her smile. Her picturesque highway, paved deep-blue and bottle-green, throws open a clear road, a hundred and eighty miles long and fifty-three miles wide, from Hamilton in the west to the St. Lawrence River in the east, with hardly a shoal between, in water that goes 738 feet to the bottom in comparison with Lake Erie's maximum depth of 180 feet.

This Ontario expressway may now, with the lengthening of the locks and the deepening of the canals in the St. Lawrence, become the means of turning the poor relation of the Great Lakes sisterhood into a wealthy member of the family, but sending cargoes down to the sea in ships is an old story with Lake Ontario.

In 1844, four years before the completion of the Lachine and Beauharnois canals, a nine-foot channel with locks two hundred feet long and forty-five feet wide from Montreal to Lake Ontario, the Canadian brigantine *Pacific,* Captain George Todd, sailed from Toronto bound with wheat for Liverpool across the western ocean. This marked the first direct clearance for Europe from the Great Lakes.

The St. Lawrence Seaway was already open for business, at least in a small way. In 1859, forty-nine vessels left the Lakes on overseas trips. They kept going, year after year, quietly, with little fanfare, but lots of flour, pork, hides, hams, tobacco, kerosene lamps, oil, nails, copper, and gold hunters, among other items, bound for Liverpool, Glasgow, Scandinavia, South Africa, San Francisco, and points global. They came back freighted with salt, glass, herring, pig iron, paint, tea, anchovies, crockery, and immigrants from the Old Countries.

Following the American and Canadian trail blazers, the Europeans began fitting out ships for the Lakes. On August 2, 1862, the *Chicago Tribune* stood up and cheered the arrival of the Norwegian brigantine *Slepser* in prose that matched the hundred-gun salute given the sailing ship by the Lakeland city:

> The merchants of that stirring port, Bergen, Norway, with an enterprise unexpected, and a spirit of speculation keenly alive to the main chances, fitted out a staunch and neat little brig, loaded her with sturdy Norwegian farmers and their bouncing wives and daughters to seek new homes in the distant west, and put aboard a few fat Norwegian herrings to pay the expenses of the voyage, bidding the captain keep right on until he got to Chicago, fill up with wheat and corn and come right home again.

The feat was accomplished and the captain went back home with a tidy profit of ten thousand dollars for his seventy-one-day trip across. He had left Bergen on May 23, arrived at Quebec on July 6, passed the Welland Canal on July 21, arrived at Detroit and departed up the horseshoe July 25, and sailed into Chicago on August 2.

In the months and years to come along the modern St.

Lawrence Seaway, the ship's log of one of the old voyages may be of occasional interest. In 1857 the sailing vessel *Madeira Pit* went from Liverpool to Quebec in thirty-eight days, meeting dirty weather and even icebergs along the way, but it took her even longer — forty-four days — encountering adverse winds and calms and trouble along the Welland Canal, to get from Quebec up the St. Lawrence Seaway around to Chicago. According to the log:

June 1 — At noon came to at Quebec.

June 3 — Came to at Montreal — hauled ship alongside wall.

June 4 — Received orders to haul ship into the canal and proceed to Chicago.

June 5 — Aground — not able to haul ship through.

June 6 — At 6 p.m. sufficient water in canal, hauled through the bridge.

June 12 — Through the canals — enter channel of Thousand Islands. At noon came to at Kingston. Took on pilot to go to Chicago.

June 14 — Off Presque Isle (Lake Ontario). Light winds from W.N.W. to W.S.W.

June 15 — Arrived at entrance of Welland Canal.

June 19 — In canal, Schooner *Massilon* of Cleveland ran foul of us, and carried away two shrouds of the larboard main rigging.

June 20 — Getting ship ready for sea.

June 22 — At 10:00 a.m. proceeded on voyage. Winds westerly.

June 24 — Calm and clear weather. Tacked ship occasionally.

June 25 — Still calm — heavy fogs — employed in painting ship.

June 26 — at 6:00 p.m. Point au Pelee light, distant five miles. Light winds.

June 27 — At 7:00 p.m. came to at Detroit.

June 28 — Cook deserted the ship during the night, and no intelligence of him at 10 a.m. Weighed

— made sail — not sufficient wind to stem current.

June 29 — Light winds and calm — strong current making down.

June 30 — Weighed — made all possible sail — entered Lake St. Clair. At 2 p.m. came to in eleven feet of water, owing to wind getting high and inclining to the northward. At 3 p.m. weighed — strong winds from the westward. At 4 o'clock got into St. Clair River — all possible sail set. Winds bearing too light to stem current.

July 1 — Steam tug towed ship. Left at Newport [present-day Marine City] to tow other ships down over the flats.

July 2 — Proceeded in tow with the tug at 4:30 p.m. Left in Lake Huron — set sails in first reef, short sea, winds N.W.

July 3-6 — Weather hazy with repeated calms.

July 7 — Stiff breezes with thick haze — entered Straits of Mackinac.

July 8 — Light winds — calm — thick fogs. At midnight off Manitou Islands.

July 9-11 — Light breezes from E.S.E. Weather clear.

July 12 — Off Milwaukee — occasional winds from S.E.

July 13 — Light winds from S.E. to S. Latter port, stormy breezes, light rain, thunder and lightning. Plying to windward in the best advantage.

July 14 — at 8 a.m. off Chicago Harbor. Sailed up channel and came to at North Pier.

One of the key entries in the one-hundred-year-old log above and a foreshadowing of things to come along the modern St. Lawrence Seaway is the entry of June 19. Lake sailors claim such accidents will be repeated many times, always with the ocean crew at fault, of course, and inevitably with more serious results. Headlines in the *Detroit Free*

Press in the very week preceding dedication ceremonies of the Seaway might be offered in evidence:

CRASHES BLAMED ON OCEAN SHIP
FAULT OF CAPTAIN, LAKES MEN CLAIM

There were two collisions involving four large freighters in the eight-hundred-foot-wide channel of the Detroit River on Saturday, June 13, 1959. Captain Dermot of the 514-foot *Arcturus* later told a Coast Guard investigator that the ocean-going freighter *Wang Cavalier,* bound for Hamburg, Germany, passed the freighter *C. S. Robinson,* also southbound, near Windmill Point while breezing along at an estimated ten miles an hour in the narrow roadway. The German skipper just missed ramming the northbound Scottish freighter *Roonagh Head* before veering into the port bow of the *Arcturus,* also north bound.

After the collision the *Wang Cavalier* had proceeded toward her transatlantic destination while the *Arcturus* put into port at Ecorse for extensive repairs to her port plates and crew quarters. The fact that the German skipper would be interrogated by the Coast Guard on his next trip along the Seaway failed to mollify the captain of the American carrier and her outspoken first mate, Leon Debth, a veteran of thirty-five years of Great Lakes sailing.

Declaring that ships require experienced pilots when they move through the heavy traffic on our inland seas, he said: "A man who is not absolutely sure of what he is doing should never even attempt to bring a vessel up or down the waterway." His final remark summed up the Great Lakes attitude toward ocean captains who fail to treat fresh-water sailing with all due respect:

"Awful poor seamanship!"

3. Wonders of the Deep

The Great Lakes contain the largest surface of fresh water on our planet. There are 8,117 miles of shore line shared about half and half between Canada and the United States. During the twenty years between 1879 and 1899, some six thousand vessels were wrecked on these inland seas, and of this number more than one thousand were total losses: ships, cargoes, hands. Nowhere in the Atlantic or the Pacific is there an expanse of 90,000 square miles to muster such a record of death and destruction.

Lake Ontario is haunted here and there with her full quota of shipwrecks, none more poignant than the one noted in the shipping notice for the violent 1869 season of navigation:

> Among those lost was the bark *Naomi,* a fine vessel, Captain James Carpenter, which was wrecked under most distressing circumstances. Captain Carpenter had himself and wife lashed to the mizzen-gaff, and she breathed her last with her head resting on his shoulder. After saying to a member of the crew, "Mother is dead," he rolled off and disappeared in the waves.

In company with the other Lakes, Ontario has her story of a captain's wife and constant sailing companion who saved her life during a shipwreck by climbing as nimbly as any sailor to the top of a tall mast where she perched — a little above the water — while the schooner sank offshore.

Ontario also has her story of lone survival by a captain who lost his ship and crew, as attested in the shipping news of 1898:

> *Wreck of the St. Peter:* — The Canadian schooner *St. Peter,* bound from Oswego to Toledo with coal, sank about five miles northwest of Sodus, on Lake Ontario, on October 27. She had shown signs of distress, and the tug *Proctor* started to her assistance. When a mile away, the crew of

the tug saw the distressed vessel sink. The crew of nine all perished except Captain John Friffin, who was picked up in an unconscious condition.

Among the wonders of the deep encountered on Lake Ontario, none were dreaded more than the sea-going tornadoes known as waterspouts. In the prosperous navigation season of 1889, the two-masted schooner *George C. Finney,* with a cargo of wheat for Toledo, was struck by a waterspout on the open Lake off the Welland Canal in the late afternoon of October. She came into safe harbor barely afloat.

The crew of the *Finney* reported that they had escaped four waterspouts that day, but the fifth one came up under the stern and tossed her about like an egg shell. The propeller *Parnell* witnessed the near disaster, as the schooner's foremast was ripped off the deck, the mainmast broke in two, and the jib boom twisted off.

A deadly sight on the Lakes was the spectacle of two waterspouts, murderous black twins, traveling across Lake Michigan in close formation off the Beaver Islands in the Indian summer of 1955. They ripped hatch covers off freighters passing through the Straits of Mackinac and sent them spinning high in the air like giants playing tiddlywinks. Then with the sound of two hundred freight cars roaring overhead, they dipped across into Wisconsin and wrecked an airfield.

Each funnel cloud swirling aloft gave the impression of a coiled rattlesnake suspended upside down from the sky, its venemous head poised just above the water, fangs ready to strike.

Sudden visitations of waterspouts may explain many of the mysterious disappearances on the Great Lakes. No doubt cyclonic storms have created more than one Flying Dutchman, as well as countless shipwrecks. November weather has not been the only killer of the romantic names, the stately sails, the foamy paddle wheels that once graced Lake Ontario — the *Deer, Reindeer, Princess Charlotte,*

Farmer's Daughter, Rambler, Triumph, Mohawk, Appelona, Sachem, Blackbird, Jessie Drummond, T. J. Waffle, Homer Warren, and how many more only the bottom of the Lake can call the roll. They foundered, stranded, collided, went down somehow or other with all hands lost or, on fortunate and heroic occasions, with all hands saved as happened at Stony Point in Lake Ontario on November 12, 1832.

Captain William Vaughan took the side-wheel steamboat *Martha Ogden* out of Oswego in fair November weather bound for Sackets Harbor with a crew of six and twenty-two passengers. She sprang a leak, which put out her fires. Captain Vaughan spread sail but the wind turned sharp out of the north and kept the *Martha Ogden* from doubling Stony Point. The shipping news for the season carried a notice of what followed:

> Both anchors were thrown in eight and a half fathoms of water, and they held her fast from 4 p.m. to 11 p.m. when they successively parted, and she soon struck and bilged in ten feet of water. With much peril a man succeeded in reaching the shore, eight rods distant. He aroused the inhabitants and built fires. In the morning a line was passed to the shore, and the whole company on board was safely drawn ashore in a three-bushel basket rigged upon a line with a Dutch harness. Captain Vaughan was the last man to leave the vessel, which went to pieces soon afterwards.

Along with the other Lakes, Ontario had her towing disasters. In the unfortunate navigation season of 1889, the paddle-wheel steamboat *D. C. Calvin,* bound out of Kingston with the schooners *Norway, Valencia,* and *Bavaria* in tow, ran into a gale off Long Point on the last day of November. The towline parted, and the three schooners were left at the mercy of heavy seas.

The *Norway* and the *Valencia* managed to come to anchor after being waterlogged. Their crews clambered to the roofs of the cabins and perched there, without food, and drenched by freezing waves that washed over the wrecks, for twenty-four hours, until the vessels *Calvin* and *Armenia* arrived

SUNSET FIRES ON LAKE ONTARIO

at the scene and picked them up. Meanwhile, the schooner *Bavaria* went hard ashore on Galloo Island and her entire crew of eight perished. The captain of the schooner *Cavalier* reported on his arrival at Kingston that he had seen the skipper of the *Bavaria* clinging to the bottom of an upturned yawl and another man on floating timber, but could render them no assistance on account of the storm.

On September 26, 1892, Lake Ontario gave a demonstration of how assistance could be rendered in spite of how the storm raged. The three-masted schooner *John Burt,* bound from Chicago to Oswego, had almost reached her destination when her rudder head gave way in a fierce nor'wester and she was driven helpless past her port down the Lake.

Sighted from the Big Sandy lifesaving station by Keeper Fish, she wallowed under a reefed foresail and two headsails and was drifting toward shore, heavy rain squalls prevailing. Judging her powerless to contend with the storm, Keeper Fish launched the lifeboat with his men and took off to the rescue. He landed nearby just as the schooner came up in the wind and let go her anchors, which dragged until the cables parted when she stranded, the waves smashing completely over her, throwing spray into the mizzen rigging where the crew had climbed.

Keeper Fish and his lifesavers fired a line squarely through the main rigging, but the terrified schooner crew were reluctant to use the line. Two of them were so overcome with fright that they drowned themselves in very fear of dying, abandoning their places of refuge in the shrouds and leaping into the boiling sea.

The mizzenmast soon went by the board, followed by the mainmast a moment later, and the sailors who had refused to take the line shot to them were hurled into the Lake. Whereupon Keeper Fish and four surfmen, with lines attached to their bodies, went out and fetched every last man of the struggling crew to shore.

Old captains who sailed during the 80's and 90's, often have spoken about the way inexperienced sailors would

panic, often causing a shipwreck. They mention this factor
right along with the more obvious causes, such as the late
sailings to make one last profitable trip and the overloading
or sloppy freighting that resulted in cargoes shifting during
a storm.

Captains along the Lakes took whatever crews they
could get at the various ports. Fresh water had its crimps
and shanghai docks just as well as the ocean ports, but a
long sea voyage gave a salt-water captain and his bucko
mates a chance to whip a crew into shape. On the Lakes,
with their short hauls, lee shores, lack of sea room, and sudden storms, each skipper had to set sail in hopes that he
would be able to teach his crew to carry out orders before
an emergency arrived. But often, even when they understood the orders, the crew went into panic and contributed
to the shipwreck that cost their own lives:

> On wan dark night on Lac Ontair'
> De win' she blow, blow, blow;
> An' de crew of de wood scow Julie Plante
> Got scair an' run below.

Humorously phrased as it is, the ballad draws an accurate
picture and faithfully represents many a fresh-water tragedy.

> De Captinne walk on de fronte deck,
> An' walk de hin' deck, too —
> He call de crew from up de hold;
> He call de cook also.
> De Cook she's name was Rosie,
> She come from Montreal,
> Was chambre maid on lumber barge
> On de Grande Lachine Canal.

There was such a hurricane blowing by this time on Lake
Ontario that the wind went around the clock in every direction. The ballad states that the Julie Plante now had reached
a point "wan arpent from de shore," an arpent being an ob-
solete French measurement of land comprising about an

296

acre, its use in the song again showing the intimate relation between Lake and land, sailor and farmer. Rosie, frightened, cried: "Mon cher Captinne, mon cher, w'at I shall do?"

> Den de Captinne t'row de big ankerre,
> But still de scow she dreef,
> De crew he can't pass on de shore,
> Beco' he los' hees skeef.

The inexperienced and panicky crew no doubt had made a botch of things in their haste to launch the lifeboat.

> De night was dark, lak' one black cat,
> De wave run high an' fas',
> W'en de Captinne tak' de Rosie girl
> An' tie her to de mas'.
> Den he also tak' de life preserve,
> An' jump off on de lak',
> An' say, "Goodbye, ma Rosie, dear,
> I go drown for your sak'."

Next morning the captain, the scow, and Rosie were corpses on the shore, and there is many a truth spoken in jest in that old ballad.

In the sailing days, during another storm on Lake Ontario, a churchgoing captain scowled at the crew who had plunked down on their knees to pray for their lives. "I don't mean to be sacrilegious," he roared, "but while the weather continues boisterous, I'd recommend a little less praying and a lot more bailing!"

Although she "missed the boat" in certain respects, Lake Ontario has a number of "firsts" to her credit.

In 1804 the first lighthouse on the Lakes was erected at the point where the Niagara River enters Lake Ontario.

Earlier, in 1755, the British had built the first freshwater warships on Lake Ontario, but the most enduring memory of warships plying the lower Lake came from the way the armed schooners of our navy were hurried along during the war of 1812 by sweeps or extra long oars.

297

Named after the American commodore in the Ontario district, they were nicknamed "Chauncey's water spiders," as they crawled over the blue expanse. This marked an era when fresh-water sailors were at trigger cock to roar out innumerable verses of a ballad called "The Lakes — Land of the Free."

> Columbia's shores are wild and wide,
> Columbia's lakes are grand;
> The gale that curls her mountain pine
> Is full of grit and sand;
> And should a transatlantic host
> Pollute our waters fair,
> We'll meet them on the rocky coast,
> And gather laurels there;
> For O, Columbia's sons are brave,
> And free as ocean's wildest wave.

In 1831 the 142-foot side-wheeler *United States,* largest American passenger vessel on the Lakes, was launched at Ogdensburg, on the New York shores of Lake Ontario.

In 1840, in the steamer *Vandalia,* built at Oswego, New York, the lower Lake could boast the first commercial propeller not only on the Great Lakes but in the world, the first steamboat to have her engines located aft as well.

There were colorful captains on early Ontario. In one of the pioneer steamboats there was no engine room gong for signals from skipper to engineer, and orders shouted from the bridge were repeated by a crew member who stood outside the engine-room door.

The engineer's name was Ramsey and the captain's frequent use of the orders, "Give her a kick ahead, Mr. Ramsey," and "Give her a kick astern, Mr. Ramsey," came to be bywords on the Lake.

On one occasion when this captain was having considerable trouble bringing his boat alongside the dock, a spectator shouted: "Give her a kick sideways, Mr. Ramsey!"

Back in the days when the Redcoats and the Columbians were fighting for control of the Lakes, the British had por-

298

taged two hundred whaleboats from the Hudson River into Lake Ontario, and these sturdy thirty-five-foot double-enders with a large all-purpose sail may have had an influence on the development of the famed Mackinaw boat of the upper Lakes. But the whaleboats were not in a class as wonders of the deep with the picturesque whalebacks that came down into Lake Ontario from their spawning grounds at Alexander McDougall's shipyard in Lake Superior, starting in 1889.

At first glimpse of this Great-Lakes-born-and-bred vessel, fresh-water captains, sweeping the horizon with their glasses, were startled at what appeared to be the over-turned hull of a ship, with smoke funneling from the bottom. A longer and sharper look disclosed something low in the water, decks awash and rolling. The whaleback had arrived and it was no time at all before a sailing wag cried, "Thar she blows!"

Short on looks but long on seaworthiness and cargo-carrying ability, the whalebacks sailed down the upper Lakes and across Lake Ontario to wallow through the St. Lawrence toward ports around the world. No more than a hundred of them were built, because their rugged individuality did not fit in with new loading and unloading equipment, but their peculiar shape identified them far and wide as typical of the breed of Great Lakes ships.

On her maiden voyage from Duluth to Liverpool, the pioneer whaleback *Charles W. Wetmore* was laden with 95,000 bushels of wheat and, although she had a stormy trip, when her hatches were lifted at Liverpool the footprints of the trimmers at Montreal were still visible in the wheat.

An enthusiastic article in the *Chatauquan Monthly Magazine* of February, 1892, hailed the American innovation as the answer to all the world's shipping problems:

> The whaleback is a mastless steel craft with a flat-bottomed hull, cigar-shaped at both ends. The sides gracefully

299

tumble home above the water line, so that her visible hull is very like a whale indeed.

When a lofty wave strikes the incurving sides of a whaleback it rushes athwart the deck, over hermetically sealed hatches, and dissipates itself in harmless spray. When the same kind of wave hits the towering sides of a liner of today, the ship trembles under the stroke and is driven almost on her beam ends. The reactionary roll is frequently so great that passengers are dangerously hurt by being thrown from their berths or chairs. Heavy seas often leap over the tall steel sides of the biggest liners and break on board with fatal effect.

The success of the freight whaleback has naturally led her constructors to believe that the passenger whaleback is not wholly a nautical dream. It is the talk of skippers in every port.

Only one passenger whaleback was built, the 362-foot *Christopher Columbus* and her record puts to shame any other excursion boat in history. During the Chicago World Fair of 1893, she carried two million passengers without a casualty. She could clip-clip along at eighteen miles an hour and discharge her load of five thousand passengers in five minutes. After the Fair she went on the day run between Chicago and Milwaukee, and when she was finally dismantled after forty years of service — the wreckers having quite a job with her five steel turrets projecting from her promenade deck up through her hurricane deck in battleship style — she had carried more passengers than any vessel since Noah's Ark.

The year that saw the whaleback *Christopher Columbus* saw many a wonder of the deep sail across Lake Ontario, as a notice in the shipping news bears witness:

> *Curious World's Fair Visitors.* — An interesting event of 1893 was the arrival of three Spanish caravels, the *Santa Maria*, the *Pinta*, and the *Nina*, constructed in Spain in close imitation of the Spanish fleet in which Christopher Columbus, four centuries earlier, had made his first and successful voyage of discovery to America. These antique

models were manned in Spain and crossed the ocean in safety.

Another curious foreign arrival was the little *Viking,* a Scandinavian craft, of ancient build, which won unbounded admiration at the World's Fair, and then with the typical restlessness of the old Norse Kings left the strange waters of the Great Lakes and returned to the land of Eric the Red and Leif Ericson.

The year 1893 must have been a season of navigation for captains and crews and shore watchers to rub their eyes and stare. But Lakelanders have long been accustomed to strange sights and unusual phenomena such as the so-called Christmas trees created by the jagged line of the horizon on stormy days; the northern lights in a rare patriotic celebration of red, white, and blue; the ten thousand pillars of mist rising from the Lake on winter days before the ice has formed, ascending from the frost-bitten water like the smoky ghost of Algonquin campfires.

There are times when islands ride high above the horizon, times when ships navigate the sky, times when huge boxes appear to be sailing across the Lake, the latter a trick of the haze that frames and packages long freighters in their own smoke as if each one came two in a large crate.

Such wonders of the deep were noted in nineteenth-century travel books, the following extract being typical:

> The passage across Lake Ontario in calm weather is most agreeable. At times both shores are hidden from view, when nothing can be seen from the deck of the vessel but an abyss of waters. The refractions which sometimes take place in summer are exceedingly beautiful. Islands and trees appear turned upside down, and the white surf of the beach, translated aloft, seems like the smoke of artillery blazing away from a fort.

In August of 1856 a mirage of a familiar type but more splendid than usual was seen from the deck of the steamer *Bay State* on a trip across Lake Ontario. To quote the *Lockport Journal*:

It occurred just as the sun was setting, at which time some twelve vessels were seen reflected on the horizon, in an inverted position, with a distinctness and vividness truly surprising. The atmosphere was overcast with a thick haze such as precedes a storm, and of a color favorable to represent upon the darkened background, vividly, the full outlines of the rigging, sails, etc., as perfect as if the ships themselves were actually transformed to the aerial canvas. The unusual phenomenon lasted until darkness put an end to the scene.

Another wonder of the deep peculiar to the Lakes is the seiche, a German term, the literal definition being "running water." Our usage derives from the Swiss whose Lake Geneva kicks up in similar fashion to our Lakes. As a scientific experiment, take a half-filled soup bowl and tilt it until the soup rides high up one side, leaving the other side correspondingly dry. The same process, caused by wind, waves, current, air pressure, or whatever, is repeated on occasion to the enormous bowls of the Great Lakes. In recent years a seiche in Lake Michigan rolled up and snatched unsuspecting people on Chicago piers to carry them to their deaths.

The shipping news of the 1872 season of navigation gave notice of a seiche on the lower Lake:

A phenomenon of the most unusual kind occurred on Lake Ontario June 13, between 3:30 and 5 o'clock. There was but little wind, and that from the southeast, and the surface of the Lake was quite smooth. The water would rise with great rapidity by successive little swells for fifteen or twenty minutes, remain stationary for a short time, then fall with the same rapid, silent, imperceptible manner. This occurred five or six times, and then remained stationary at the lowest ebb until a gale in the afternoon came up, after which it found its normal condition.

This undulation of Lake water, similar to a tidal wave, may change the normal level five or six feet in a few hours and leave large expanses of Lake bottom exposed. The most graphic illustration of a seiche is the experience of

Fritz Riebenach, a Michigan lumberman, who was in the market to buy a boat, took a trip to see the steamer *Arabia,* and contracted to buy her just as he had seen her, "afloat in Buffalo Harbor." Then he took the night boat to Cleveland to raise the rest of the money. But when he returned to Buffalo the *Arabia* was no longer afloat. A seiche had picked up the steamer and deposited her high and dry on the dock. Back to Cleveland rushed Mr. Riebenach to fetch his lawyer and start legal proceedings for the refund of his deposit on the grounds of breach of contract. On his arrival in Buffalo again he discovered that the grounds no longer existed. Another seiche had lifted the *Arabia* off the dock and put her right back in the harbor where she belonged.

On November 1, 1915, the tug *Frank E. Barnes* sailed away on Lake Ontario with all hands to join the fleet of the Flying Dutchmen, but, considering the wonders of the deep, it is the greatest wonder of all that there are not more Flying Dutchmen in the haunted lanes of sail and steam.

4. Red Skies and Glowing Water

Of all the Great Lakes, the lower Lake has the most ominous history of conflagration and holocaust — disastrous fires touched off aboard ship by accident or by design. Her first steamboat cast a blood-red shadow of coming events on Ontario's blue waters. In 1827, the *Frontenac,* forerunner of all Lake steamers, was set on fire by incendiaries and burned to the waterline at the head of Lake Ontario, with an unknown toll of lives.

A veritable trail of flaming brands and torches has burned across Ontario through the years. The avenging fury that seemed to pursue Canada's three sister passenger liners — *Hamonic, Noronic,* and *Quebec* — had to chase the palatial

Quebec out into the St. Lawrence River where she was making one of her popular Saguenay side trips in the year 1950 before the maenad with blazing hair caught up with her victim.

The *Quebec,* with 350 passengers and a crew of 150 aboard, was cruising along the scenic Saguenay late on a pleasant August afternoon when the fire alarm sounded. With five hundred lives depending on his decision, Captain C. H. Burch judged that the best chance lay in trying to reach the dock at Tadoussac, where the Saguenay flows into the broad St. Lawrence. It was twenty-five miles away, and every mile a race with death as the deck crew fought a losing battle with the flames and the engine-room gang piled on the steam, but Captain Burch brought the *Quebec* into dock with all but three lives saved, thanks to cool and gallant action by officers and men who inspired the passengers with courage and who even managed to run some of the automobiles off the deck onto the dock before the flames forced them ashore.

A torch illuminating the night of August 14, 1950, the *Quebec* burned to a total loss while fire engines by land and fire tugs by sea poured fountains of water onto her blazing hulk. A court of inquiry later found that the fire, believed to have started in that deadly sleeping demon aboard ship, the linen closet, was due to sabotage by a person or persons unknown.

The trail of the firebug led from the *Frontenac* at the head of Lake Ontario in 1827 to the *Quebec* at the foot of the Lake in 1850, a lurid path of glowing water across 180 miles and 123 years.

Were we to charge against Ontario's account all the burnings, scaldings, and explosions that have occurred along the St. Lawrence River, her record would include two, instead of one, of the holocausts deserving rank among the thirteen worst disasters in the annals of the inland seas. But should we do so, we would also have to chalk against her score other major shipwrecks, such as the collision in

which the ocean liner *Empress of Ireland* lost 1,024 lives on the St. Lawrence, shipwrecks that have no relation to the Great Lakes proper, and therefore we have drawn an arbitrary line of division at the tiptoe of Lake Ontario, except for the story of the *Quebec* which is related to the similar tragic stories of her two sisters. Passing notice, however, is here made of an item in the shipping news for the navigation year of 1857:

> *Holocaust Aboard the Steamer Montreal.* — The most deplorable disaster of the season was the destruction of the steamer *Montreal* by fire on the St. Lawrence River and the loss of 264 lives.

The fire occurred only a few miles below the lower Lake, but enough flaming disaster is listed against her without including the *Montreal*.

On April 30, 1853, the combination passenger-and-cargo steamboat *Ocean Wave*, freshly painted for the new season, sailed out of Kingston bound for the other end of the Lake. Her decks were piled high with inflammable freight, including fat pine cordwood to feed her engine. Only a couple of hours from port, twenty-three miles from Kingston and two miles off the Duck Islands, fire broke out shortly after midnight. Inside twenty minutes the ship was a blazing furnace. People ashore on the Duck Islands could read newspapers by the glow in the sky.

Almost immediately the fire blocked the only exit from the ship's lounge, and a courageous purser seized an axe to chop an escape hole for the passengers trapped in the cabin. Captain Wright could not get lifeboats launched because they were set above the flaming upper cabins. Fire buckets could not be reached because the flames were consuming the very walls where they had been hung for such an emergency.

Two schooners saw the red glow in the sky and hoisted all sail toward the scene. Gallant rescues of twenty-one survivors were made by the *Emblem* and the *Georgina* but twenty-eight people were lost as the *Ocean Wave* went down in thirty minutes from the time fire had been discovered aboard.

The years kept taking regular toll. In 1856 the steamer *Welland* burned at Port Dalhousie in Lake Ontario and the steamboat *Inkerman* exploded in Toronto Harbor with all hands lost. In 1873 the steamer *Bavarian* caught fire at a cost of fourteen lives.

Late in the afternoon of October 23, 1889, the popular wooden excursion boat *Quinte* was steaming along out of Deseronto, Ontario, bound for Picton, on another ill-omened last trip of the season. Among the passengers aboard were Captain Duncan B. Christie's mother and twelve-year-old brother.

Three miles out on the chilly Lake, while tea was being served in the dining hall, a deck hand burst into the engine room, yelling, "Fire!" Chief Engineer Thoias Short started the pumps, and bent to his engine.

Captain Christie ordered full speed ahead and ordered the wheelsman to steer for shore. "Grassy Point's only a few minutes away," he said. "Stand by your post and we'll bring her in safe." Whereupon the Ballad of John Maynard, which had not run its course on Lake Erie, came true, with cruel exceptions, on Lake Ontario. The wheelsman aboard the *Quinte* fulfilled the final heroic stanzas:

> *Through flames and smoke that dauntless heart*
> *Responded firmly, still*
> *Unawed, though face to face with death,*
> *"With God's good help, I will."*
> *The flames approach with giant strides,*
> *They scorch his hands and brow;*
> *One arm disabled seeks his side,*
> *Ah, he is conquered now!*
>
> *But no, his teeth are firmly set,*
> *He crushes down the pain;*
> *His knee upon the stanchion pressed,*
> *He guides the ship again.*

306

One moment yet! One moment yet!
Brave heart, thy task is o'er!
The pebbles grate beneath the keel,
The steamer reaches shore.

With the flames surrounding him, the wheelsman stayed at his post in the pilothouse until he felt the keel of the *Quinte* strike the beach at Grassy Point. Then, badly burned, he made his escape from the blazing top shed, a hero in true ballad tradition, and more fortunate than John Maynard in that he lived to hear his praises sung.

Meanwhile, Captain Christie had been all over the steamboat, giving encouragement, saving passengers trapped by flames, setting an example to the crew. He landed all but four of those who had come aboard entrusted in his care. Despite frantic attempts, resulting in burns that made him a cripple for life, he could not rescue the cook's helper and her little son, nor his own mother and twelve-year-old brother. But until the day of his own death, the scar tissue on his face and hands offered mute testimony of how Captain Christie had tried to live up to the trust that all traditional sailing masters take to heart.

The years continued to collect their toll. In 1897 the Canadian car ferry *Southeastern* burned; in 1917, the steamers *Lloyd S. Porter* and *Conger Coal* went up in smoke. Then the citizens of Toronto, bordering on the lower Lake that always has been cheated of her proper share by Lake Erie in the circus shows at Niagara Falls, decided to stage a spectacle right on their own water front, never dreaming that it might come true with disastrous reality sixteen years later.

In August of 1933, Toronto treated herself to a rare sight indeed, setting torch to the *Lyman M. Davis* and watching the stately old schooner die in the flames. One of the last of the commercial sailing vessels on the Lakes, the Muskegon-built *Davis* had served well for sixty years, outlasting several generations of Lake sailors, and there were some who said she deserved a better fate.

Sixteen years and one month later, the flagship *Noronic* of the Canada Steamship Lines started out on a regular post-season cruise down into Lake Ontario and the Thousand Islands, a leisurely jaunt very popular with the passenger trade during what is generally the most delightful time of the year on the Great Lakes. It was the *Noronic's* custom to loaf from port to port, taking in all the sights. On this occasion the cruise started out from Detroit where passengers swarmed across the gangplanks and proceeded to Cleveland where more throngs came aboard.

Built in the ominous year 1913, the *Noronic* was constructed in the large and luxurious tradition of Great Lakes passenger liners. In accommodations and general size, she compared with the late *North American* and her sister ship, the *South American,* often called the ocean-going liners of the Lakes, which carried, until recently, about five hundred passengers on week-long cruises. The *North American,* en route to Piney Point, Maryland, under tow, became a shipwreck herself September 13, 1967, when gales from the fringe of Hurricane Dora sank her in 250 feet of water off Nantucket Island in the Atlantic without loss of life. The *South American* celebrated her last season of navigation shuttling between Detroit and Expo 67 at Montreal, then proceeded under tow to Piney Point where her new owners, the Seafarers International Union, conduct a school for officers and unlicensed men.

Fresh-water passenger vessels are a proud breed. The present-day *Aquarama* that plies between Cleveland and Detroit has a cruising speed of twenty-two miles an hour, nine decks that offer a constitutional stroll of two miles around, two decks for automobiles, accommodations for 2,500 day passengers, cafeteria, soft-drink stands, lunchrooms, bar, nursery, amusement center, TV room and movie theater, gift shop, shuffleboard courts, two dance floors, escalators, elevators, stairways, picture windows, among other navigational items such as radar, gyropilot, ratio direction finder, and ship-to-shore telephone.

But the luxury car ferry came upon sad days, a decade ago. Slated to succeed the famed *Milwaukee Clipper* on the run across Lake Michigan, she went into forced retirement when a conflict arose as to who would pay to dredge Milwaukee harbor to the necessary 24-foot depth to accommodate her ample proportions. The 1968 season of navigation found her still nodding and napping on the Muskegon waterfront, like a lady old before her time, while the effervescent *Clipper* frisked back and forth across the Lake, docking in the very shadow of the once haughty dame who had steamed proudly up from Lake Erie and around the Michigan mitten to replace her.

The *Aquarama* stems from a giant clan. The old excursion boat *Put-in-Bay* used to be able to bundle 2,800 day passengers aboard for a jaunt into Lake Erie. The *Greater Detroit* and the *Greater Buffalo* each measured sixteen feet longer than the 520-foot *Aquarama*, carried a crew of 275, accommodated 2,127 passengers with sleeping quarters in 625 staterooms, and had a dining-room capacity of 375. The *City of Detroit III*, the *City of Cleveland III* and the *Eastern States* were slightly smaller, but they came from a family large enough to serve as naval training ships and go down to the sea as aircraft carriers in wartime.

The five-hundred-foot *Seeandbee*, built in the *Noronic's* ill-starred birth year of 1913, had been the largest side-wheel steamboat in the world until the *Greaters* came along.

The *Seeandbee's* four decks were overshadowed by the six decks of the 385-foot *Noronic*. In fact, the Canadian liner looked a bit top-heavy on the water, but in an attractive way, like a handsome lady wearing a lofty new bonnet creation. Her white cabins contrasted with her glistening black hull and her huge single smokestack bore the line's familiar red and white design with a black smoke band at the top.

On this last trip of a long and honorable career during which she had safely carried tens of thousands of passengers, the *Noronic* cleared Cleveland with a crew of 171 and a passenger list of 524. With a total of 695 lives aboard, she crossed Lake Erie in broad daylight while vacation crowds enjoyed meals in the dining room on the top deck or looked out the picture windows in the observation salon or used other conveniences such as the writing room, music room, buffet bar, smoking salon, barber shop, beauty parlor.

This floating palace bulged high on the land horizon as she moved her stately way through the Welland Canal from Lake Erie around the roar of Niagara Falls into Lake Ontario. After a short jaunt across the Lake she reached Toronto where Captain William Taylor brought her to berth alongside Pier 9 with her bow toward the land and her starboard side to the dock, at six o'clock Friday evening, September 16, 1949.

Passengers knew from their cruise programs that the *Noronic* would be in harbor until the next evening. They could look forward to a full day of sight-seeing and shopping in Canada's ultra-British metropolis, Ontario's largest city. Meanwhile, numbers of them went ashore for a quick look to get their bearings for the long outing on the morrow. Many of the crew also went ashore. Captain Taylor himself went off to visit friends.

It was a pleasant Indian-summer night, a friendly breeze prevailing. People passed casually to and from the boat. They clustered in little groups on deck or on the dock, cigarettes glowing like fireflies in the darkness. The older folks exchanged politics or told party jokes or bragged about their grandchildren. The younger set talked baseball and argued about the World Series or flirted toward shipboard romances that promised such wonderful hours during the long cruise ahead. Newlyweds yawned their way to staterooms early. Many of the passengers, unfamiliar with the large ship, had to ask directions or be guided to retirement.

At midnight the *Noronic* lay quiet in her berth. A skeleton crew of fifteen men took over duty for the small dark hours. At 1:15 a passenger, strolling along a corridor, noticed a wisp of smoke curling up from under the door of a linen closet. He called a steward and the two of them forced the door open. Flames leaped out at them. They cried, "Fire!" and the panic was on. A woman screamed in the night. Pandemonium followed.

A dock watchman telephoned the Toronto Fire Department, and the trucks roared promptly to the scene, but the *Noronic* had gone up in flames like an old-time steamboat chunk of cordwood dipped in turpentine. By this time Captain Taylor had returned to his ship but he and the small crew were inadequate to handle the situation. In a last futile attempt to fight the blaze, he manned a fire hose, then fled before the flames.

In the roaring inferno of the *Noronic,* passengers died smothered in their sleep, they died beating their fists against the doors of trapped cabins, they died in flaming nightgowns and pajamas as they lost their way in the maze of passages on the six decks, they died locked in one another's arms in last embrace.

The entire crew, familiar with the four gangways, escaped to the dock. They had helped 406 passengers get safe ashore, but 118 were left behind, with the *Noronic* for their funeral pyre.

Far and wide on Lake Ontario, there were men in homes ashore and pilothouses at sea who stared at the red glow in the heavens, men who said a prayer for the unknown who lay dying beneath that unmistakable portent of fiery doom.

BOOK SIX

THE WRECK OF THE EDMUND FITZGERALD

In a musty old hall in Detroit they prayed
in the maritime sailors' cathedral
the church bell chimed 'til it rang 29 times
for each man on the Edmund Fitzgerald.

The legend lives on from the Chippewa on down
of the big lake they call Gitche Gumee
Superior they said never gives up her dead
when the winds of November come early.

(1976 ballad, *Gordon Lightfoot*)

© 1976, Moose Music Limited

1. Queen of the Inland Seas

In the same year — 1958 — that the *Bradley* died on raging Lake Michigan off the Beaver Islands in a darkling November storm, the *Edmund Fitzgerald,* namesake of a Milwaukee banker, was christened under sunny June skies, slipping slaunchways Great Lakes style into the Detroit River, the biggest object ever dropped into fresh water in recorded history. With no more than a discreet splash, she slid gracefully into her River Rouge basin that was hardly large enough to hold her, and launched a new era of transportation on the inland seas.

From the start the *Fitz,* as her crew called her affectionately, was a charmed ship, indeed a banker's dream and a seaman's pride, all 729 majestic feet — seventy-five feet wide, thirty-nine feet deep — and 8,686 net tons of her. The men took such pride in their bonny ship that they could not bear the sight of a seagull desecrating her spotless decks and hatch covers or even daring to land near the sanctuary where the captain walked or kept vigil — an insult not to be tolerated. One observer tells of a shocked deckhand rushing forward to shoo away an alighted seagull and immediately cleaning up after the sacrilegious fowl.

The undisputed queen of the freshwater seas, carrying a banker's name on her bow and stern and a king's ransom in ore between — that was the *Fitzgerald* in her days of youth and glory. Even after she had weathered the blows of almost eighteen full seasons of navigation, many still considered her to be among the best afloat, one of the finest examples of the shipbuilder's art. She normally carried a crew of twenty-eight but could bunk thirty-five persons, including guests, in two luxury staterooms.

The ship always had close ties with Detroit, and one of her constant observers and greatest admirers was Charles Thei-

315

sen, the *Detroit News* marine writer who kept his readers informed of her progress. She was the largest ore carrier of her day as soon as she took her shakedown cruise. She set record after record — most tons of iron ore carried during a season, most tons carried in one trip, most tons carried through the Soo Locks — for season after season. And the freighter carried her cargo with a rakish silhouette that endeared her to shorebound boat buffs.

The Columbia Transportation Company, which operated the *Fitzgerald,* has newer vessels, such as the *William R. Roesch,* the *Paul Thayer,* and the *Wolverine.* But the newer ships were built on more Spartan designs, with straight lines and boxlike superstructures, in the uncertain 1970s, a time when costs prohibit spending for the luxury features sported by the swinging *Fitz.*

The styling of the Queen (some sailors called her the "King of the Lakes") was such that reporters flocked to marvel at the vessel as finishing touches were being applied to tiled baths and deep pile carpeting was installed to set off leather-grained vinyl wall coverings. The prestigious J. L. Hudson Company was responsible for designing decorations and furniture, which included leather swivel chairs in front of panoramic windows at the bow and porthole draperies in the guest quarters. The *Fitzgerald* was the first ship to be constructed of prefabricated steel subassemblies, which were welded together to form the hull. From the time her keel was laid in 1957, she was one of a kind, a standout on the water.

Also unique about the Fitzgerald was her ownership, the Northwestern Mutual Life Insurance Company of Milwaukee — first American life insurance company to invest in a Great Lakes ship. Oglebay Norton leased the ore carrier for twenty-five years under a charter scheduled to expire in 1983.

Naturally the Queen became the flagship of the Columbia fleet of twenty Great Lakes vessels and thus rated salutes from all her sister ships of both older and newer vintage when they met on the shipping lanes. She took the homage modestly, but her enamored crew guaranteed that she was kept up in the style to which she was built.

In due time the *Fitzgerald* was eclipsed by newer Great Lakes vessels, larger and stronger boats with advanced technology and instrumentation. Still a giant of the Lakes, however, she could look back to the summer of 1958, the August when her cabins were completed, her smokestack installed, and her paint job ready to bear the flag of the Columbia Transportation Division of Oglebay Norton Company. She remembered how tenderly her first skipper, Captain Bert Lambert, took her on trial runs in Lake Huron before guiding her gently through the Soo Locks, bound for her first cargo at Silver Bay, Minnesota, and then how she returned through the MacArthur Lock with 25,000 tons of iron ore on a glorious September day.

Although a few lake carriers haul cargoes undreamed of when she entered service, the *Fitzgerald,* because of her grace and design, always aroused an admiration denied her younger competitors.

She reigned as Queen to the very end.

2. Last Trip of the Season

The *Griffin,* first ship ever to sail the upper Great Lakes, failed to return from its maiden voyage in 1679, and sailors on the Lakes have courted tragedy ever since. The Great Lakes carry a herculean share of the world's supply of fresh water and, during a November storm, the whole bulk of it seems aimed personally against any ship that has dared to defy it by venturing out of safe harbor.

On Lake Superior, and the lower Lakes as well, the gales of November, caused by the cold air of the Arctic meeting the lingering warm autumn air, can raise a riot of weather and bring instant havoc to navigation. Cyclonic blows, often with winds of extraordinary force, spring up unexpectedly and toss giant freighters around like pieces of driftwood.

There are sailors who prefer Lake Superior to the lower Lakes in foul weather, largely because its wide reaches allow room for maneuvering in a storm; but there are seamen who would rather be almost anywhere else because of the dangers inherent in Superior's extreme depth of 1,333 feet and average depth of 500 feet. When high winds whip the length of Lake Superior, monstrous waves can build up across almost 400 miles of maverick water.

An ancient legend of the Chippewa tribe also warns the modern mariner that Superior "never gives up its dead." The legend has some basis in fact. The largest, most treacherous, and most relentless of all the Great Lakes, it is also the coldest, forty degrees in summer or winter — deadly not only to man but also to the organisms that infest drowned bodies in milder waters and bring them to the surface.

The veteran captain and seasoned crew of the *Fitzgerald* were well aware of the legend and the uncertain temper of Lake Superior as their ship took its cargo of 26,013 tons of iron ore pellets called taconite. The men were weather-wise and realistic about the risks of November, but they were also restless to leave the Duluth-Superior area at the top of the lake and head for home. This was the last trip of the season, and they were anxious to see their loved ones down below.

Captain McSorley, with his forty-four years of honorable service at sea, was looking toward retirement, and a majority of the crew had earned seniority status. They were sentimentally sorry to leave their first cook behind as they made their merry way to home and holidays. The cook had been treated ashore for bleeding ulcers but had wanted to report for duty on Sunday, November 9, the day of departure. After a final examination, however, the doctor forbade him to go aboard. A relief cook was pleased to continue on the job as his replacement. He had sent a postcard to his wife a few days before: "I may be home by Nov. 8," the card said, but added, with a sailor's typical fatalism: "However, nothing is ever sure."

318

Even with that undertone of foreboding, already proven true because that date had passed, the twenty-nine seamen aboard the *Fitz* were in high spirits as the ore carrier moved out of harbor into the waiting lake. Finally they were underway on the last trip of the season, with faith in the Old Man, faith in the Old Lady, faith in God above, and with elegant weather for November.

When the seven- to eight-million-dollar vessel steamed from port at Superior, Wisconsin, it was 1:15 on a sunny Sunday afternoon, November 9, 1975. As the long length of her danced and sparkled in the reflection of sun and water, she had the proud bearing of a ship that has weathered many storms and is prepared to cope with the worst. The *Edmund Fitzgerald* seemed the very model of an unsinkable boat. They were bound for Detroit, more than 700 miles away. They were due there about five o'clock Tuesday afternoon. Waiting for them were five bags of laundry and a bag full of mail on the Detroit mailboat *J. W. Wescott*.

3. A Day Like the BRADLEY Went Down

The weather changed from Dr. Jekyll into Mr. Hyde during that night — a screaming Hyde at his most murderous and schizophrenic. All day long high winds and driving rain battered northern Michigan, smashing small boats against their docks, blowing out windows and toppling building projects, forcing schools to close and felling trees like Paul Bunyan's axe working overtime. Winds up to seventy miles per hour whipped out of the west and across the country, leaving power failures in their wake. Three youths were caught in a giant wave and washed off a Lake Michigan pier. One was rescued by nearby surfers, but police began searching for the bodies of the others.

319

The Mackinac Bridge, spanning more than five miles of frenzied water between Michigan's upper and lower peninsulas, seemed to sway in the roaring elements. A truck driver with his Boy Scout son had doubts about making the crossing: "We were hitting bad winds all the way from Escanaba, so when I got to the bridge I asked the guy in the booth if it was safe to cross, and he said yes. We were leaning all the way, about forty-five degrees, it seemed, and when we got three-quarters of the way across, I was shaking like a leaf." At that point a heavy gust hit the empty trailer rig and it "seemed to go over pretty slow. We landed on the trunk of a man's car and that may have cushioned the whole thing. I saw all these people milling around outside but it looked like nobody was going to rescue us. So I rescued us myself by kicking out the front windshield and crawling out with my son. We were a little hysterical by then. It seemed like the wind was going to blow the two of us right off the bridge. But the bridge people finally came and gave us a ride."

The "bridge people" also closed the bridge to further traffic until the weather eased. As the truck driver said: "I've been driving trucks for ten years, but I never saw a storm like that one before."

But there were people along the northern shores of Lake Michigan who were reminded of another storm on a November day much like this one. Then, instead of rain there had been snow, hard pelting snow that rattled against picture windows like buckshot from a shotgun. Instead of the tenth of the month, it had been the eighteenth, but the watchers along the waterfront and the Lake Michigan bluffs could look back across seventeen years and recognize the similarities to the storm that took the *Bradley*.

The seascapes were the same: wild, beautiful, terrifying, and hypnotic in the size of their waves thundering into the beach and exploding against the piers like nuclear weapons. The winds were unrelenting, and there were observers who knew the incredible fact that in a hurricane-force storm energy is released at the rate of four atomic bombs per second.

All day Monday, while the *Fitzgerald* drove down Lake Superior toward Whitefish Bay and Sault Ste. Marie, old Mother Nature kept reminding mankind both afloat and ashore that she was still the boss, in the driver's seat, that man for all his science and advanced technology — his Coast Guard radio setup, satellite weather warnings, air-sea rescue teams, and the engineering know-how to make ships larger and stronger — is no match for her awesome forces.

Landlubbers along the shore have their own way of identifying a great storm from an ordinary November blow. If they can see "Christmas trees" — jagged outlines of waves on the horizon — then the storm would be the expected intensity for this turbulent season of the year. But if no orderly ranks of "Christmas trees" were in sight, it signaled a major storm with gale and hurricane winds blowing the tops off the waves on the horizon, flattening them out in mass confusion.

An old Great Lakes prayer — "God help the sailors on a night like this" — automatically occurred to the former national network newsman who had reported the wreck of the *Bradley* and interviewed the survivors in their hospital room. Now, as he parked his car at a lookout point above Lake Michigan, he marveled at how two men had clung to a raft for fourteen hours in roaring darkness and icy seas, much like the seas below as they smashed the shoreline, their tops blown into spray by following winds.

The afternoon had gone past four o'clock. Skies were getting darker, and night was almost ready to lock up the lakes and swallow the long ships until dawn. The newsman felt uneasy as his car shook under the buffeting of the gale winds. He took a last look at the horizon. There were no "Christmas trees" in sight. His thoughts echoed the foreboding of others who had compared the identical-twin storms that had lashed the Upper Lakes in Novembers seventeen years apart. He turned away in awe and anxiety, shaking his head:

"A day like the *Bradley* went down!"

4. Brink of Eternity

Up on Lake Superior, the long carriers went plowing through the storm into the evening. They were weathering thirty-foot waves and fighting hurricane-force winds. The *Fitzgerald* seemed about ready "to make the turn" into the comparative safety of Whitefish Bay, which offers some shelter against the lake's high winds and seas.

Captain J. B. Cooper, master of the *Arthur M. Anderson*, a U. S. Steel ore carrier that was trailing the *Fitzgerald* by about ten miles, had been in radar and radio contact with the *Fitzgerald* most of the day. About 3:30 that afternoon Captain Cooper heard Captain McSorley come on the radio. He wanted to report that his ship was taking on water through two broken ventilator covers and operating at a list but that there was no immediate danger. He gave no indication of worry. He mentioned that the fence wire around the deck was gone. Finally, he asked the *Anderson* to shadow the *Fitzgerald*, just in case. But he said all this in a calm and easy voice that carried the meaning: "Here's the problem, and I have it under control." Because it was snowing, Captain Cooper never saw the *Fitzgerald* again, but he continued to follow it on his radar screen.

Another skipper in the area, Captain Woodard, Great Lakes pilot of the Swedish freighter *Avafors* bound up the lake for Duluth, made contact with the *Fitzgerald* later in the day when Captain McSorley sent out a call for "any vessel near Whitefish Point" to ask if the light at the point and the radio beacon from there were functioning. Captain Woodard responded by radio that there was no light but between snow squalls he could see the tower. He said the radio beacon was not operating, or at least the *Avafors* could not raise it. McSorley mentioned that he was taking on some water and had developed a list. He gave Woodard the impression that he was not in much difficulty, but he sounded worried to the *Avafors* pilot, and the voice did not sound like McSorley's at all. In fact, it was so difficult to recognize that Woodard asked to speak with the captain but was told the captain was speaking.

Later, after the *Anderson* reported that she was gaining on the *Fitzgerald*, Woodard called McSorley for information. The *Avafors* was getting set to leave the lee of Whitefish Point and inquired about "conditions out there." He explained that he was making the inquiry because a ship on the other side of the Soo Locks had reported winds at seventy knots, gusting up to eighty-two, about ninety-six miles per hour.

McSorley reported winds of sixty to seventy miles per hour and thirty-foot waves. When the *Avafors* reached open water, Woodard found out that the estimates were accurate, but he never forgot McSorley's last words: "Big sea — I've never seen anything like it in my life."

Further signs of possible trouble had been noticed during the day. The master of a freighter in the *Fitzgerald's* vicinity reckoned that she was making only two miles per hour in the face of raging winds and towering waves, a far cry from her average speed of sixteen and full cargo speed of ten miles per hour.

Captain Cooper, now about nine miles behind the *Fitzgerald*, thought that when she passed Caribou Island, where relatively shallow water posed a possible danger, the ship was closer to the island than he himself would like to have been. But there were no calls for aid, no signals of distress, no cries of "Mayday."

From his own experience as a merchant mariner in World War II, Jim Doherty, dean of northern Michigan newspaper editors, described for readers of his column in the *Petoskey News Review* the probable scene aboard ship under normal storm conditions:

> If the *Fitz* crew were standing watches as we did, at 7:10 p.m., the Captain would have the Bridge on such a night, along with the third mate, a wheelsman, and probably another seaman. They would be operating their radar, sonar, and radio.

323

With an oiler and an engineer type, the third engineer would be running the engine room with 50 minutes to go to be relieved by the second officer.

The cook's helpers would be finishing dishes from dinner. As for the rest of the crew, who stand four hours *on* and eight hours *off* watches, no doubt some would be in the sack. That's the most comfortable spot on a wild night. A few might be writing letters to mail at the Locks — perhaps the young cadet would be getting off a letter to his parents, a pal or girl friend, or even an instructor at Northwestern Michigan College where he was a maritime student.

But most of the men off duty were probably sitting around talking of other storms,. other adventures. The old timers would be telling of past November gales which would be somewhat embellished by many times of retelling, and the passing years which make waves higher, winds stronger, and the peril of ships even greater.

Old freshwater salts are great story tellers and the young men listen and question them with keen interest, never sure they're hearing it like it was or being put on. But on such a night everyone is keyed up, the senses are more acute, the usual noises of the ship and sea are louder and more intense. The younger men are more comfortable with others and they want to know how this night compares with past storms that the old timers and their ships weathered.

Whatever the exact scene aboard the *Fitzgerald,* the captain and crew knew they were off Copper Mine Point, nearing Whitefish Point and the last leg of their long run to the Soo Locks. They had a nor'wester on their tail, but the *Fitzgerald* was built to take the pounding, engineered to be flexible, giving in slightly to the pressures of wind and waves in a manner that characterizes skyscrapers such as Detroit's Penobscot Building, and bridges such as the Mackinac. Her hull twists and vibrates in the confused seas like a sea monster of legend, a tortured creature longer than the Penobscot is tall.

At about 7:10 p.m., Captain Cooper was again in the *Anderson's* wheelhouse, and the mate reported contact several minutes before with the *Fitzgerald*, now nine miles or less ahead. The sea return (interference) was tremendous because of high waves and the *Fitzgerald* kept disappearing in and out of it. A watchman on duty reported "seas running thirty feet and a couple were higher than that." Minutes later the radar picked up two salt-water ships about seventeen or eighteen miles away. The *Fitzgerald*, which should have been in the middle, was nowhere to be seen. Everyone in the wheelhouse started looking, but there were no running lights ahead — no lights anywhere. Both the *Anderson* and the salt-water ships were unable to raise it on the radio.

Lights out, radar gone, radio contact lost — three strikes and out.

Convinced that the *Fitzgerald* was gone, Captain Cooper notified the Coast Guard. They were as stunned as he had been, unable to believe a ship could go down so fast. "But I know she's gone," he said grimly. "You'd better start the alerts." In one heartbeat of fate, a great ship had disappeared from the chart of Lake Superior, vanished with her captain and all hands. The water temperature in the area at the time was forty-nine degrees and the air temperature forty-one degrees. A healthy person would go into shock within thirty minutes in the water.

According to Lieutenant Commander Roger Roznoski, Commander of the CGC *Sundew*, the *Fitzgerald* carried two fifty-man lifeboats aft, one port, one starboard, and two twenty-five-man rafts, one forward and one aft. Lifeboats take at least ten minutes to launch. They are the weakest part of the survival system in a major storm, especially where time is all-important. Difficult to launch, they tend to break up in rough seas and wash ashore empty. Experts agree that no sailor in recent history has succeeded in escaping a sinking Great Lakes vessel by lifeboat in a storm.

The only survivors of major storms in modern times on the Great Lakes have "lucked onto" rafts. This includes the solitary survivor of the freighter *Daniel J. Morrell* on Lake Huron in November of 1966. The *Fitzgerald* carried only the two self-inflating rafts, and they were far apart. If by some

325

miracle any survivors were to be found, rafts seemed the only possibility. But it takes up to four minutes to launch a raft. Did anyone aboard the *Fitzgerald* have that precious amount of time when there wasn't even a chance to call "Mayday"? The rafts could take care of their own launching, but could any sailor reach one of the rafts?

Rescue operations wasted no time in begging the question. The Coast Guard set up a rescue central at the Soo and started contacting ships in the general area, requesting them either to turn around or proceed in the direction where contact was lost. Vessels talked back and forth in a wilderness of darkness and waves reportedly ranging from twenty to thirty-two feet high. There were periods of long silence on the radio ship frequencies. It would be hours before some of the ships reached the scene, but captains risked their crews, their carriers, and their own lives to hasten to the area where the *Fitzgerald* had literally dropped from sight, and where the *Anderson* kept dangerous vigil.

There were exceptions. Two Great Lakes pilots of Liberian freighters in the vicinity of the catastrophe explained why the Coast Guard request for the assistance of the ocean-going vessel was declined. The pilot of the *Benfri* was dumbfounded at the request because he did not think his captain would want to try to turn around for fear of rolling over in the twenty-five-foot waves and wind speed of seventy-five knots. The captain refused to turn around but agreed to alter course. The *Benfri* pilot added that he doubted they could have helped save anyone in any event, because of the difficulty of lowering boats in such a storm.

The pilot of the *Nanfri* estimated the winds at over seventy knots and the seas at up to thirty feet. He pointed out that there had been no flares, no distress calls, no nothing: "I didn't attempt to turn the vessel. I wouldn't have turned it, no way. You couldn't have turned it. You couldn't turn that stern up into the wind no how."

326

5. Desperate Search for Survivors

An armada of ships and aircraft, some flown from as far as North Carolina, joined the search operations at dawn. Other vessels spent all night crisscrossing the area, firing flares to illuminate the darkness in hopes of locating survivors in lifeboats or on rafts or floating wreckage. The first wreckage was sighted just before dawn about thirteen miles north of Whitefish Point and eight miles west of Copper Mine Point, Ontario, near the area where the *Fitzgerald* vanished. No survivors were found — just debris and a 1,000-yard-long oil slick, about fifty miles northwest of Sault Ste. Marie. (The ship would normally carry about 72,000 gallons of oil, and approximately 48,000 gallons would still have been aboard.) At first there were fears of oil pollution, but they died down.

Coast Guard helicopters swept low over the scene of the wreckage. They dropped smoke bombs whenever they spotted any flotsam or driftage, including objects as small as a bottle, in hopes that these would provide some clue to what had caused instant disaster. "Whatever happened to the *Fitzgerald*, it came so fast that we still can hardly believe it," said Captain Charles Millradt, commanding officer of the U.S. Coast Guard group at Sault Ste. Marie and director of the dogged search efforts. "Maybe that's because we still don't want to believe it happened."

Later in the day, the Coast Guard reported the recovery of lifeboats, one capsized just off Copper Mine Point on the Canadian coast, damaged rafts, life jackets and rust-colored life rings bearing the *Fitzgerald's* name.

At midweek fresh gales accompanied by snow squalls assaulted Lake Superior and hampered the continuing search for survivors, now a desperate quest with fading hopes since the finding of the battered wooden lifeboats and the orange

327

rubber rafts that had inflated automatically but carried no men to safe haven.

Regardless of the apparent hopelessness, the search went on. The weather forced the grounding of a C130 cargo plane circling the disaster area, but two ships kept up their diehard efforts. A Coast Guard officer expressed the sentiment of those who searched and those who prayed that their loved ones might somehow — against all evidence — have survived and would be found in good time: "There's always a miracle."

But when twenty-four hours had gone by, and another twenty-four, in an environment where survival time is three and one-half hours, miracles were despaired of. Reluctantly and unofficially, the Coast Guard conceded on Wednesday, November 12, that all twenty-nine men aboard the *Edmund Fitzgerald* went down with their ship in 530-foot waters in Lake Superior, the worst shipping disaster on the Great Lakes in seventeen years. Toward the close of the week, the seamen were officially declared dead.

Memorial services were scheduled to be held in Toledo, Ohio, the ore boat's home port. Sault Ste. Marie, Michigan and Sault Ste. Marie, Ontario drew up plans for a joint memorial during which Coast Guard vessels from each city would drop a wreath near the wreck of the *Fitzgerald*. Ironically, high winds similar to those of the night the ship sank developed just as the vessels assigned to the service departed, forcing the participants to hold the observance near the Soo Locks instead.

Newsweek Magazine's November 24, 1975 write-up of the tragedy was headed "GREAT LAKES: The Cruelest Month," and its wrap-up of the shipwreck read:

> The aftermath was all too familiar. Relatives of the missing men gathered in Sault Ste. Marie, Michigan, to wait forlornly. Sailors banded in small groups and spoke quietly of previous November shipwrecks on Lake Superior. And in the stone, 126-year-old Mariners Church in downtown Detroit, a minister offered prayers for the lost seamen and tolled the

church bell 29 times in grim tribute to the unslaked furies
of Lake Superior.

The State of Texas has a proud but bitter boast: Thermopylae had its messenger of woe; the Alamo had none. The *Bradley*
had two messengers of woe and the *Morrell* had one; the *Fitzgerald* had none. No seamen returned to tell the tale, to explain the death throes of his ship and his shipmates, to be
haunted the rest of his life by nightmare memories, to cringe
from the bitterness, the scorn, even the hatred in the eyes
of the bereaved, eyes that say, "Why you and not *my* sailorman?"

As has been noted in other sections of this chronicle of
Great Lakes shipwrecks, a survivor's lot is not a happy one.
Psychology is in tune with "Many Brave Hearts Lie Asleep
in the Deep." And now twenty-nine of them were 530 feet
deep in Lake Superior, entombed with their ship.

When the *Fitzgerald* rounded Whitefish Point shortly after
seven o'clock on Monday evening, November 10, 1975, she
ran into what some officials have called the worst storm on
the Great Lakes in thirty-five years. In the grandest tradition
of the seas, she fought to the finish and went down with all
hands, no "Mayday," no survivors — the ultimate loss. Just exactly what caused the death of the *Fitzgerald* and her seamen
may never be known for certain, but her story will be told
as long as there are sailors to brave the elements and wager
their very lives on the outcome.

6. No Winter Layover

The *Fitzgerald* carried a sea-
soned crew. In age they ranged from sixty-two to twenty:
Captain McSorley and four other seamen were in the sixty-
year-old category; ten men were fifty or over; six were in their
forties; two in their thirties; and six in their twenties. All but
three hailed from Great Lakes states: Ohio (14), Wisconsin

(8), Minnesota (2), Michigan (1), Pennsylvania (1), and then Florida (2) and California (1).

Duties aboard ship included captain; chief engineer; first, second, and third assistant engineers, plus an extra engineer; first, second, and third mates; three wheelsmen; A. B. maintenance; three watchmen; three deckhands and a deck cadet; a steward and second cook; two porters; two oilers; special maintenance and wiper.

At Toledo, the home port of the *Fitzgerald,* where in former years friends and relatives had gathered to celebrate the winter layover, waving and shouting as the ship would come to dock, they now came together in solemn ceremony to mourn their dead. This Monday afternoon, one week after the tragedy that united them here in sorrow at the riverfront Naval Armory, the wind was bright and warm, skipping down the Maumee River to Lake Erie under a pleasant sun. There were 500 people — the families, the union officials, the ship owners, military men, and friends — assembled in the cavernous hall, awaiting some kind of explanation from a man of God.

Father Armstrong called for a hymn: "To our men taken by God in the duty of their land." The words of the hymn were dry — "Oh, God, our help in ages past, our hope for years to come" — and the song failed to touch the bereaved. Nor were they touched by his homily: "God who made the sea, made the storm, took the lives of our friends. . . ." The priest tried to explain, but he could not fit the tragedy into a plan any better than marine experts have explained the sinking: how this great ship, in close company with others, sank suddenly in a northwest gale while the others survived. In the end, Father Armstrong spoke of hope that comes from knowing that this land can produce fine, strong men.

Then a Navy petty officer tolled a bronze ship's bell as each crewman's name was read, and the sound of the bell touched the mourners where words had not. As each name was tolled, another person wept. The group stood to sing again, this time the mariner's hymn, with its poignant last line: "O hear us when we cry to Thee for those in peril on

330

the sea." A single wreath of roses and palm fronds was lifted by two seamen and carried to the door, while the crowd slowly followed to the dockside.

There Father Armstrong stood with a Protestant minister and a rabbi: "Oh, God, be well disposed to our prayers," he prayed. "Bless this wreath. May it bring tranquillity to the departed and to ourselves in a sea of sorrow." He explained that the wreath would be cast overboard in Lake Erie, far enough from shore so that no one would see it again. The two seamen reverently placed the ring of roses and palm fronds aboard the Coast Guard patrol boat waiting at pierside.

Among the watching crowd of people, gathered into knots of grief and concern, one man stood alone, holding a tiny mistletoe wreath bound with a black ribbon. He hesitated a moment, then stepped forward and handed it to a crewman on the boat. As the boat pulled away bearing the two wreaths, someone at pierside blew taps, and the man wept. He identified himself to James Harper of the *Detroit Free Press* as Gene Burchell. The wreath was not for a kinsman. "Not exactly, but he was just like a brother to me — Gene O'Brien. It was just something from me to him."

Eugene W. O'Brien, fifty, Toledo, Ohio, Wheelsman, *Edmund Fitzgerald;* deckhand at sixteen. A tiny wreath of mistletoe afloat with a black ribbon to remind him of his "brother" ashore.

7. Nothing Is Ever Sure

As noted above, only a week before he went down with the *Fitzgerald,* a skeptical crewman had mailed a postcard from Duluth to his wife in Toledo. He had said that he might be home by November 8 but added that nothing is ever sure. His doubts were well founded. He could not have reached home by November 8 because the

Fitzgerald did not steam away from Superior, Wisconsin until the day after that date. By a quirk of fate he saved the regular cook's life and lost his own by signing on the *Fitzgerald* as a relief cook and chief steward to replace the ailing cook about three weeks before the ship began her last voyage.

Even up to the final morning the regular cook had wanted to come aboard and resume his duties, but last-minute doctor's orders forbade him to do so, and the skeptical steward gladly accepted extended duty. On the list of crewmen lost on the *Fitzgerald* the name of first cook is missing by a whim of fortune, but the name of his replacement, the seaman who believed nothing is ever sure, fills the space: Robert C. Rafferty, sixty-two, Toledo, Ohio, Steward.

In all, seven members of the *Fitzgerald*'s crew were from the Toledo area. Toledo has always been a sailors' town, a port where many of the Great Lakes ships lay up for the winter. Seamen are attracted there because it is a center of their job market, a congenial place to live among people like themselves; and they have their favorite sailors' hangouts along the Maumee riverfront.

Robert Rafferty was born in Toledo. He first shipped out right after his high school graduation. Until last season, he had been a regular crewman on various ships since 1931. He even signed up for three tours of ocean duty in hopes of visiting his son in Vietnam after the latter had joined the Air Force. The senior Rafferty had also served on liberty ships during World War II. This year, his wife explained, he had signed up through the Seafarers' Union as a relief crewman so that he could have more time at home with the family. He was eagerly awaiting the birth of a fourth grandchild.

Well respected as a chief steward, he was an accomplished cook, especially known for his baking. When the chance came to board the *Fitzgerald* for the last three weeks, he seized the opportunity. His family said he was "giddy as a fuzzy-cheeked cabin boy" about serving again on the famous freighter that had long been his favorite. According to his sister, he had always said that the *Fitzgerald* was the King of the Lakes. "It had the biggest kitchen he had ever seen, and the ship was so big they'd never have any trouble." Other members of his family said he had been a sailor too long to worry about bad weather.

Forty-four years of sailing freshwater and saltwater seas in times of war and peace and memorable storms. "Isn't it strange that he should go through all that safely," his wife said, "and then have this happen to him."

Russell Haskell, forty, Millbury, Ohio, Second Assistant Engineer, was born in Wisconsin to a family of sailors. He had been on the Lakes for twenty-three years, beginning as a wiper. In August a teenage stepdaughter had been killed by a car while crossing a Toledo street. Haskell had just finished a funeral leave for her when he rejoined the *Fitzgerald*.

He had been on the Lakes since the age of eighteen and aboard the ore carrier for three years. The ships he worked on had gone through some bad storms, but, said Mrs. Haskell, her husband's ship would always seek shelter from a storm behind an island, where the crew would ride out the winds for as long as five days. She could not understand why the *Fitzgerald* did not do the same during the fatal storm.

Like many of the freighter's men, Haskell had taken his family on Great Lakes cruises aboard the luxurious boat. "I don't know if I could ever go on another ship now," Mrs. Haskell said, her eyes red from weeping. It had taken her four years of marriage to adjust to the lonely life of a sailor's wife. Her husband would come home for only three or four days every two weeks, and for two months during the winter layover. Like many sailors, he was a quiet man who liked to play pool and cards, and hoped to someday become a chief engineer. His job was in the bowels of the huge ship, among the giant, shining machines of the engine room.

"He never worried about the weather," his wife said, "but I used to worry about it a lot. I watched the weather and looked for the storms on the map. I used to worry myself sick. Then it just growed on me that he was a sailor, and I didn't worry about it. . . . Maybe I should have."

333

In her worry and despair, her gradual acceptance of her husband's role in life, her lashing out at why the ship had not sought safe haven to ride out the storm, and her final resignation to fate, Mrs. Haskell epitomized the true wife of a sailor.

Captain Ernest R. McSorley, sixty-two, Master of the *Fitzgerald,* was born in Ontario and started as a deckhand aboard ocean-going freighters when he was eighteen. Transferring to Great Lakes freighters, he skipped his way up the chain of command, from wheelsman to third mate, and from second mate to captain, the youngest on the Lakes.

McSorley's life centered around the Lakes and the boats he commanded. His favorite, of course, was the *Fitzgerald,* his pride and joy. His stepdaughter said, "He loved this boat. He didn't even come home when he was sick."

A friend who had recently helped repair the propellers on the ore carrier called him "a super guy." "He was one of the best boat handlers on the Great Lakes, and the *Fitzgerald* was one of the better boats. They would give the better boats to the better captains. With these guys, the Lakes was their life. McSorley didn't gamble and he didn't drink. Many times these guys are real characters, but not McSorley. He was one of the finest people I ever met. He spent nine to ten months a year on the *Fitzgerald,* and every time he brought the ship home — about once a month — he would see his wife, who is very ill in a rest home here in Toledo. He was such a good man — always had everything under control."

McSorley's stepdaughter said that he had talked about retiring this year.

A few days after the wreck of the *Edmund Fitzgerald,* a Coast Guard Board of Inquiry convened in Cleveland in an attempt to determine the cause of the disaster. The role of the board in such an investigation is similar to that assumed by the Federal Aviation Administration after a plane crash. Investigators planned to conduct interviews, to inspect the debris and flotsam already collected on Lake Superior from the sunken freighter, and to study the sonar scans taken by the specially equipped *CGC Woodrush* out of Duluth. These scans had determined that the ship was in three pieces in about 530 feet of water in Whitefish Bay. Proceedings continued into the following summer.

The inquiry turned up nothing but the highest praise for McSorley's seamanship and personal character. The fact that he had been honored with the command of the flagship of the fleet spoke for itself. Another facet of the skipper's attitude toward the *Fitzgerald* was revealed by seaman Richard Orgel, now a tug captain on the Atlantic Coast, who had served from mid-October to mid-November 1972 as third mate aboard the ship. He testified that the *Fitzgerald* had a worrisome tendency to bend and spring during storms, specifically during one of Lake Superior's November storms when he had been aboard. Captain McSorley had ordered him to change the ship's course if the motion became too pronounced.

"On one occasion he told me the action of the hull sometimes scared him," Orgel said. "Looking aft, there was quite a bit of action there; she bends and springs considerably." Asked to describe the motion, he said, "Well, it's like a diving board after somebody has just jumped off."

McSorley clearly feared for his boat. The great skippers love their ships for their strengths and their idiosyncrasies, the special traits that set them apart from others and make them come to life. But they never cease to worry about them. They coddle them the way they would a sweetheart. They look after them, love them, feel for them, fear for them — every living moment.

Captain Peter Pulcer, retired former master of the *Fitzgerald*, appeared before the board of inquiry and spoke of the ship as if he were talking about a favorite pet. He said he had run into some "pretty good storms" on Lake Superior and the vessel "always handled like a good little girl." He said that she never seemed to take on much water in storms, but heavy weather made her roll to such a degree that "I've seen it where I could walk on the walls already, I'll tell you that!"

The appearance of "swinging" Captain Pulcer reminded observers of the heyday of the *Fitzgerald,* as recounted in a special report to the *Detroit News* from Sault Ste. Marie on November 17, 1969.

Ship ends record year with carols.

Most lake freighter captains observe the holidays quietly by decorating the topsides of their ships with lights and evergreens.

Not Capt. Peter Pulcer, master of the 729-foot *Edmund Fitzgerald,* holder of a number of cargo records and a self-styled sea-going disc jockey.

Pulcer came into the Soo Locks yesterday on the *Fitzgerald's* 47th and last trip this year, with the season's cargo record tucked in his record book.

As the "Big Fitz" eased into the lock, Capt. Pulcer had the ship's public address system going full-blast playing Christmas carol recordings which could be heard for blocks away in the stillness of the quiet morning.

His ship carried a cargo of 26,076 tons of taconite pellets, making the season total 1,349,404 tons — the most any ship has carried through the locks since they were put into operation in 1855.

This is the sixth time Pulcer's boat has broken the record.

The "Big Fitz" carried more than 30,000 tons of cargo at least five times this past season, and was the first boat on the Great Lakes ever to carry a cargo exceeding 30,000 tons.

The *Fitzgerald* led a magic life. On the day of her launching she became the biggest and the best on the Lakes. She set records, collected trophies, enjoyed triumphs galore. Admiring eyes followed her stately appearance wherever she went. She had the look of a champion, and they nicknamed her "Big Fitz" because there was nothing that could beat her on the Inland Seas. She was a winner all her life, until her final battle with the elements; and, even in defeat, she could claim honor. The meteorologist in charge of the National Weather Service in Chicago read her epitaph: "There has probably never been as severe a storm on the Lakes as the night the *Fitz* went down."

8. In the Wake of the Wreck

During the Coast Guard Board of Inquiry proceedings it was revealed that Captain Cooper, whose ore boat *Anderson* had trailed the *Fitzgerald* down the lake from Duluth, had sent out a message by radio at about the time the doomed vessel met her fate: "I am very concerned with the welfare of the steamer *Edmund Fitzgerald*. He was right in front of us, experiencing a little difficulty. He was taking on a small amount of water, and now the upbound ships have passed him and I see no lights as before, and don't have him on radar. I just hope he didn't take a nose-dive."

This is the shortest, most dramatic, and authoritative description of what may have happened to the *Fitzgerald,* made by the captain who had been in closest touch with the ship all day — *she took a nose-dive!*

People all around the Lakes were asking incredulously: "How could a steamer, bigger than a good city block, vanish without a trace in the night, disappear with all her crew, while other lesser vessels survived the storm in the same vicinity and proceeded on their way toward the Soo Locks or, up-bound, toward Duluth?"

There were no other severe accidents in the storm, and many limestone carriers, ore boats, grain freighters, and others continued to go about their business — running essential errands for the nation and earning a fair profit for their ship-owners — with no major difficulties through the turbulent Upper Lakes.

Then what about the *Fitzgerald?* Survivor of many storms in her eighteen years on the freshwater seas, she was still in her prime, in fact, in Great Lakes shipping terms, one of the newer freighters. Still one of the largest ships on the St. Lawrence Seaway, she was given a clean bill of health on her safety tests and properly loaded with the same weight of taconite pellets she had carried hundreds of times out of west Lake Superior ports like Silver Bay, Minnesota and Superior, Wisconsin. Labeled "the most stable and our best" in Oglebay Norton's fleet of twenty ships, she was skippered by the top captain in that fleet, the captain who had the most time in as master and rated A-1. With all this going for her, why did the boat go down? How could she? It was unbelievable that a ship like the *Fitzgerald* should be killed by a storm that spared all other shipping.

C. G. Captain Millradt described the weather that Monday night as "one of those typical big November storms. They have this tremendous northwester every so many years, and then you have a disaster." Asked why the *Fitz* did not tie up and seek shelter when the big storm hit, the C. G. group commander explained: "There's no place to hide once you get halfway across Lake Superior."

Several other boats on the lake had tied up, however, and sharp criticism of Captain McSorley's failure to do so came from retired Coastguardsman Lieutenant Joseph Etienne, who had directed the search and rescue efforts for the *Bradley* as commander of the Charlevoix group.

Interviewed by professional writer Tom Dammann, Etienne said: "They had no business being out there. This was a massive storm, and the skipper of the *Fitzgerald* had plenty of warning in time to go into Keweenaw Bay and anchor until it had passed. What kind of men are these skippers who are more concerned about getting that iron ore delivered than the safety of their ship and the men on board?"

Twenty-nine years of service with the Coast Guard in the South Pacific (during World War II), the North Atlantic, and the Great Lakes had earned Lieutenant Etienne the right to express his outspoken opinion.

However, another retired Coastguardsman, Commander Frank Sperry of St. Ignace, emphatically disagreed: "The captain and the crew were unlucky in the fact that they were casualties of the sea," he said. "It's the hazard of the sea, of the profession. It's a challenge and those who engage in it do so with pride. We have never mastered the sea, learned

338

to control it; sailors are betting their lives against it. But it always happens to the other guy, not to you."

There is a point to the above psychology. However, the basic factor would appear to be that Great Lakes cargo carriers are not manned by "summer sailors" but by workers and administrators who are hired to deliver goods which the national economy depends on, and it demands delivery on time. If ship captains waited in port until ideal weather conditions prevailed, there would be precious little business through the Soo Locks or around the Straits of Mackinac. Putting too much trust in weather reports is folly on the Upper Lakes, where the whole climate is subject to instant change without notice. Despite the weather satellite system, the standard meteorological advice from Chicago and Detroit to Duluth still is: "Look out the window and if you don't like what you see, wait a minute, it'll change."

Advance reports of both fair and foul weather are often inaccurate regarding regions bordering the Great Lakes, where the temperature is likely to dip to winter or skyrocket to spring in an hour and yoyo back again. The Great Lakes states are lands for all seasons — often in one day.

So, no matter what weather predictions Captain McSorley had received, he made his own hard decision to steam out of harbor while the weather was fair and deliver another cargo of iron ore to the waiting steel mills down below. He was paid to make the decision and do the job, but he would never have ventured forth if he had dreamed that he was taking his ship and his crew into mortal danger. As it turned out, he drove the *Fitzgerald* to within an estimated fifteen miles of the comfortable lee of Whitefish Bay and safety from the storm, when they broke up suddenly and catastrophically, alone in the raging blackness, with no time even to send out "Mayday," no messenger to bring back tidings of woe to Toledo and the other towns where the seamen had made their homes. Not even a floating bottle with a note explaining the wreck.

Baseball celebrity Leo Durocher provides an unlikely but appropriate source for an old answer to post-disaster questioning.

There is one question sure to be asked after any disaster: "Knowing what you know now, would you do it differently?" Durocher's answer was: "Well, sure. If everybody on the *Titanic* had known that it was going to hit an iceberg, the ship would have left England with three passengers, all of whom would have just taken out a double-indemnity policy with Lloyd's of London."

9. Theories About the FITZGERALD Shipwreck

When news broke about the *Fitzgerald,* veteran sailors immediately speculated that she had shared the fate of the *Bradley* and the *Morrell,* who were victims of fierce November storms in 1958 on Lake Michigan and in 1966 on Lake Huron respectively. The *Bradley* barely managed to send out a "Mayday" before she went down, and the *Morrell* went down so rapidly that she had no time to radio her plight. The cause of both these wrecks was diagnosed as structural failure due to brittle steel. But these were much older ships than the *Fitzgerald,* and the kind of steel with which they were built had been outmoded years before her keel was laid.

The theory that the ship was probably riding two gigantic waves at once — one at the bow and one at the stern — and that the unsupported weight of her taconite cargo cracked her in half and drove her own gross tonnage of 13,632 plus her iron ore load of more than 26,000 tons to the bottom in a plunge that took only seconds, was popular, just as it had been in the days of the *Bradley.* But the limestone carrier *Bradley* was returning home empty, except for some water ballast, and it seems generally agreed that laden freighters, riding low, are more comfortable in heavy seas than unladen ones riding high and skittery. In other words, the tons of iron ore she carried would have been helpful rather than hazardous to the *Fitz*. A freighter would be in higher stress if unloaded or in a ballasted condition, rather than loaded.

The head of a well-known commercial fishing family on the Lakes had another theory about the iron ore. He believed that when the boat began to take on water and developed a list, the cargo shifted and the pellets of taconite started to roll around like mad marbles, until the *Fitz* lost balance in the waves and rolled over to the bottom. In answer to this theory, a merchant marine safety expert said that he had never heard of taconite shifting. The reaction to that is obvious: there is always a first time.

A theory of the *Bradley* days — the "Pinnacle of Doom" theory — was not revived to haunt the *Fitz*, but at that time there was avid speculation about the possibility of a sharp steeple of rock under the surface out in Lake Michigan in the area where the *Bradley* went down. She was supposed to have ripped herself in two on this uncharted "Pinnacle of Doom," a legend later attributed to the early fishermen or Indians.

Another theory was that the *Fitzgerald* might not have gone down if she had been built with separate watertight cargo compartments. "That's a pet peeve of mine," an executive in the Coast Guard's Merchant Marine Safety in Washington frankly admitted. "Bulkheads would make it possible to limit flooding to the extent that you could save a vessel for several hours."

One theory was pinned to testimony by the *Anderson*'s skipper and mate that the *Fitz* passed close to the shallows north of Caribou Island about two hours before she sank. The ship was at least partially blind because her radars were inoperative, and the *Anderson*'s mate had been giving Captain McSorley navigation fixes. This combined information raised questions about the possibility that the already somewhat crippled vessel might have touched bottom and sprung a leak that would ultimately have caused her to founder in the heavy following sea.

Another theory, related to others, postulated that the ship-

341

wreck was caused by metal fatigue. This is a problem that occurs in planes as well as ships, an unknown factor that puzzles most marine experts, largely because it is difficult to determine in safety inspections. In fact, it is rarely detected until it betrays its presence in a sinking ship or a crashing plane. However, Raymond Yagle, professor of naval engineering at the University of Michigan, said that material fatigue was unlikely: "The *Fitzgerald* was much too young for its metal to be fatigued under the kind of conditions Great Lakes vessels operate," he told Charles W. Theisen, *Detroit News* marine writer. "There are so many factors working when a ship is underway that, at this point, it's impossible to say what might have caused the sinking. Obviously, there was a combination of conditions which it had never encountered in its seventeen years of sailing."

Professor Yagle went on to note that there was severe wave action and severe winds, and that he had read about the captain reporting that his ship had taken on water. "If there was free water in the hull, and a list," he told Theisen, "you have a whole new set of conditions. The *Fitzgerald* may well have been subjected to more severe stresses in the past, but never that precise combination of stresses."

Another theory advanced the idea that structural weakness and ultimate failure could be traced to the outmoded methods of loading and unloading that older ships had been forced to practice before improved techniques were designed, such as the conversion of "straight deckers" (the *Fitzgerald* type) to self-unloaders, the very popular change in profile of increasing numbers of cargo carriers.

Captain Jacobsen, Oglebay Norton's marine superintendent, had a theory about reports of the *Fitzgerald* taking on water through vents. "I assume they're talking about the ballast tank vents," he said, adding that he could only imagine that some object, perhaps a floating log, may have sheared off the vents at the deck. He said that if the eight-inch diameter vent pipes were broken off flush with the deck, the ship would have taken on "a lot of water," but the ballast pumps should have been more than able to keep up with it. "I don't have any idea what happened, but it must have happened fast," he said.

All theories agreed that death must have come with merciful swiftness to the seamen, whether the ship plunged off one of those gigantic waves and nose-dived into the next without recovering, whether the twisting, yawing, sheering action split the hull, or whatever combination of factors brought her down so suddenly.

One other theory suggested that the wheelhouse glass could have been shattered with tons of water pouring in, knocking out all communication as well as the wheelsmen and the officers. If the ship had split, the resulting total power blackout would have paralyzed the *Fitz* and tobogganed her to the bottom. In any case the men indoors were probably trapped without a chance of getting outside and were sealed in their own vessel, perhaps for all time — if the legend of Lake Superior holds true.

There was a theory that when the *Fitz* took on water and began to list, she had started her slow turn into Whitefish Bay and thus exposed herself vulnerably to the broadside onslaught of cannonading waves that bowled her over into the deep.

The theory to end all theories hypothesized that the *Fitz* was overwhelmed in a sudden and murderous squall within the storm, a squall that hit and ran, that diminished and dissolved as quickly as it had appeared, leaving the *Fitz* its solitary victim. This would have been a squall of confused, tumbling, bursting seas, a squall of rogue waves and cyclonic winds, a squall with a maelstrom at its center, a colossus of a whirlpool that could have broken the *Fitz* into the three parts that now lie at rest on the bed of Lake Superior.

No amount of theorizing can bring the dead to life, but some theories might help save the lives of other sailors and their ships.

10. Board of Inquiry

Witness after witness appeared before the four-man USCG Board of Inquiry, but few of them spoke of how or why the shipwreck might have happened. They spoke of why the *Fitz* should not have sunk. Like the general public, none of the marine authorities could believe initially that the tragedy had occurred.

In a move toward prevention of future ship disasters, Local 5000 of the U.S. Steelworkers of America, which represented twenty of the twenty-nine men aboard, and District Two of the Marine Engineers Beneficial Association, which represented eight of the nine officers, jointly asked the Coast Guard:

To issue "large craft warnings" in severe weather which would forbid ships of any size to sail.

To document "near misses" between Great Lakes vessels.

To require all lake freighters to have watertight bulkheads (wells) between cargo compartments.

They also said that November sailing should be regulated with particular care because of historic bad weather during the month; and that sophisticated lifesaving equipment should be installed on "all vessels plying the Great Lakes."

Also in Cleveland, the president of the shipping company said: "The *Fitzgerald* was one of the finest vessels on the Great Lakes and her captain and crew among the most experienced. In the interest of all who sail the Great Lakes, we must do everything possible to determine the cause of the sinking of the *Fitzgerald*."

According to USCG Rear Admiral Winford Barrow, head of the Board of Inquiry, a visual survey of the sunken freighter would provide the "last word" on what caused the shipwreck. Barrow made the statement as he recessed the investigation pending the results of an underwater visual survey of the ship scheduled to take place in spring of 1976.

"So far as the Board of Inquiry is aware, we have talked

with all those witnesses who are apparent to us and whose testimony would be productive for determination of the cause of the casualty," said Barrow. He revealed that the underwater survey would be conducted on April 15, 1976 by CURV III, an unmanned television and camera-equipped submersible vehicle owned by the U.S. Navy. He noted that CURV III has a claw which can be used to bring small objects to the surface.

"The ultimate witness is going to be the vessel itself," Barrow declared. He said that cameras would check for any indications of what caused damage to the ship's structure and what happened to its life-saving equipment. Typical winter weather and ice conditions on the lake were cited as reasons for putting off the underwater survey until a better weather season.

Barrow said accumulated evidence and testimony would be reviewed by the board between the investigation and April. And he said that one board member would ride on a Great Lakes ore carrier before the end of the shipping season and the other three would ride ore carriers in the spring when the season reopened.

The admiral estimated that it would likely be as late as the summer of 1976 before the board could complete its final report and submit it to the Coast Guard's commandant.

11. Farewell, EDMUND FITZERGALD

One week after the *Fitzgerald* went down, a 1.5 million-dollar lawsuit was filed against both the owner (Northwestern Mutual) and the operator (Oglebay Norton) by two new widows in behalf of their husbands. They claimed that the *Fitzgerald* was unseaworthy, not adequately equipped, negligently operated, and should not have been permitted to travel at that time of year in dangerous waters.

345

In due course Northwestern Mutual and Oglebay Norton routinely filed a motion to limit liability to $817,920 in connection with other suits filed by families of crew members. President John Dwyer said: "Oglebay Norton is in close touch with every family involved to make sure that none lacks the immediate financial support it needs."

A maritime lawyer for two of the victims said he planned to challenge the Board of Inquiry on possible negligence in the Coast Guard's handling of rescue efforts. He said it took too long for the Coast Guard to respond to the disaster, and that the Coast Guard's Board of Inquiry should not be able to judge its own conduct in regard to the shipwreck.

Another suit for $2.1 million was filed in behalf of another dead seaman, and no doubt there would be others to come, and in due time the court would decide on appropriate compensation for all families.

But the *Fitzgerald* and her crew were beyond such matters; they belonged with the immortals of the freshwater seas, the great ships that had fought the greatest November storms of the century. Between November 9 and 11, 1913, ten ships went down and 235 sailors were lost. During a similar period in 1940, the so-called Armistice Day storm sank five ships with sixty-seven seamen drowned.

Farewell, *Edmund Fitzgerald*. You will inherit the honor of having your shipwreck anniversary observed in company with theirs. And you will be remembered, all alone, among the giants of your day, because you were "Big Fitz," one of a kind, and there will never be another like you. Future shipwrecks will be measured by the date November 10, 1975.

*   *   *   *   *

The Long Ships Growing Longer

In the bicentennial year of 1976, there were two notable continuing trends in Great Lakes shipping: the long cargo carriers getting longer, and the season of navigation extending into a full calendar year.

In 1958, when Mrs. Edmund Fitzgerald, wife of the chairman of Northwestern Mutual Life Insurance Company, cracked the traditional champagne bottle over the big ship named for her husband, there were people who said that the *Fitzgerald* was the ultimate — the largest vessel that would ever sail the Inland Seas. "Big Fitz" was a solid fit for the largest lock at the Soo, the MacArthur, one foot shy of the 730-foot limit set by the Army Corps of Engineers for ships using locks along the St. Lawrence Seaway.

No sooner had the superfreighter been christened than the construction of comparable cargo carriers was ordered by shipowners: another 729-footer for the Bethlehem Steel Corporation, and a 690-footer for the Interlake Steamship Company.

Before "Big Fitz" set the new standard, the largest boats on the Lakes had been the 715-foot Canadian *T. R. McLagan,* the *Joseph H. Thompson* of the M. S. Hanna fleet (714 feet), and the 710-foot *George M. Humphrey,* operated by Hanna for the National Steel Corporation. But the winter before the *Fitzgerald* was launched, the 620-foot *Cliffs Victory,* of the Cleveland-Cliffs fleet, was lengthened to 716, a procedure that would become increasingly familiar in the new era, particularly when the new Poe Lock was opened on the site of the original Soo Lock of 1855.

Formal dedication of the $40-million facility took place in June of 1969, though it had been opened the year before by the *Philip R. Clarke* as she locked through downbound with a cargo of iron ore. The 647-foot *Clarke* was dwarfed in the huge dimensions of the Poe, the largest of any lock in the 2,342

347

miles between the Atlantic Ocean and the west end of Lake Superior. It was expected to be the model for expansion of other seaway lock systems, such as the Welland Canal.

Great Lakes shipbuilders and designers were quick to take advantage of the opportunities the Poe offered. They embraced the chance to increase their cargo loads by adding to their present ships' lengths, and that process continues today. For instance, U.S. Steel's Str. *John G. Munson* was scheduled for lengthening during the winter of 1975-76. The 666-foot self-unloading vessel would get a 120-foot addition in midbody, increasing her length to 768 feet and her productivity by 23.5 percent. The first boat to lock through the Poe Lock, the *Philip R. Clarke,* received a similar addition and so did the *Arthur M. Anderson,* the winter before that ore carrier shepherded the *Fitzgerald* across storm-bound Lake Superior.

Since 1968, dozens of lakers have been increased in size to carry larger cargoes through the Poe Lock. But there is a limit to making smaller ships bigger. Owners and builders began to think in terms of fresh starts with innovative ideas, brand new boats, and different designs.

In 1975, American Steamship Company launched the 770-foot self-unloader *St. Clair* at Sturgeon Bay, Wisconsin. The future coal carrier became the largest vessel ever side-launched in the Great Lakes, breaking the *Fitzgerald's* oldest record.

A giant step forward in the size of the Great Lakes ships came in the early seventies when the 1000-foot ore carrier *Stewart J. Cort* was put into service in May 1972 to carry taconite pellets from the Lake Superior mines to mills on lower Lake Michigan. During sea trials in 1971 she went from full speed ahead to a crash stop in about 3200 feet and five and one-half minutes, less distance and time than some smaller vessels required.

The *Cort* ruled supreme on the Lakes until late November of 1973, when a real departure in traditional designing appeared in the unfamiliar shape of the *Presque Isle,* named for a Lake Erie peninsula instead of a company executive, the more standard practice. The $35-million *Presque Isle* consists of a 975-foot barge powered by a 153-foot pusher-type tug attached to a "V" notch in the rear of the barge. This combination self-unloading bulk freighter is essentially 1000 feet in length, with most of the tug portion nested and riding on the stern of the barge except for about twenty-five feet, which extrudes and completes the given length. So unusual in concept and appearance was this newcomer to the Lakes that an executive of the shipowners, Litton Great Lakes Corporation, promised to make an effort to bring the vessel through the Detroit River on her first voyage during daylight hours, at a time announced in advance, to enable shipping buffs to witness her passage, just as they had the *Fitzgerald* on her first outing.

The incredible tug-barge is capable of carrying 50,000 tons of iron ore pellets — enough to manufacture 15,000 cars — at a speed of 16 miles an hour. And both of the 1000-foot vessels on the Lakes — the *Cort* and the *Isle* — were outfitted with sophisticated equipment. They are "instrumented," as are other "mod" vessels in regular service.

Professor Yagle also pointed out in the Theisen interview that designers "can anticipate most things" — but not all. However, he said, a continuing research effort attempts to amass ever more information on which to base design; and instrumentation is a vital part of that on-going effort. It means, for example, that for several minutes of every hour in which the ships are in operation, stresses are automatically recorded at a number of crucial parts of the vessels. Also measured are the height and force of waves against the hull.

"During unusual conditions, such as storms," the naval engineering professor explained, "instruments make constant recordings, providing an immense amount of data to be analyzed by designers." This instrument data has become even more important in recent years, with the jump to 1000-foot carriers and the lengthening of existing freighters in practically wholesale lots, to over 750 feet, then over 800, with no end in sight.

Monarchs of the Lakes for a few brief years, the *Cort* and the *Isle* were destined to be challenged by other 1000-foot boats, and there were boats either on the drawing boards or in the shipyards of even greater dimensions. The tug-barge *Presque Isle's* tonnage capacity of 50,000 was the greatest on the Lakes until well into 1976. But a vessel known simply as *Hull 905* was scheduled for launching in October 1976 from the Lorain, Ohio yard of the American Shipbuilding Company, a self-unloading iron ore carrier with a capacity for 59,000 tons. And there were more of the same kind in the making, along with others even more advanced in design and overall bulk.

A significant event in Great Lakes history occurred on March 1, 1975. After the Poe Lock was closed for repairs, the 767-foot Str. *Cason J. Callaway* was permitted to pass through the 800-foot MacArthur Lock, to be followed by other 767-foot vessels. This marked the first transit of the lock by a ship over 730 feet. As Vice Admiral Paul E. Trimble, President of the Lake Carriers' Association, pointed out in his annual report to members:

> [This] should ease the way for transit of 1000-foot vessels through the 1200-foot Poe Lock, pending enlargement of a second lock. . . . Again, this will facilitate design of future vessels.

Another memorable aspect of the unprecedented parade of the 767-foot vessels through the MacArthur was that one of the longest and most powerful ore carriers on the Lakes could not take part in the event. In June 1971 the U.S. Steel ore carrier *Roger Blough* lay ninety-eight percent completed in the American Shipbuilding Company's yard in Lorain, Ohio, when an explosion and fire killed four workmen and ravaged the huge boat. In December 1975 the families of the victims were awarded a settlement of more than $1 million, almost half of that award ticketed for a widowed mother and her six children.

Meanwhile, *Roger Blough* rose like the proverbial phoenix from glowing ashes to earn the image of a powerhouse on the Lakes. At 858 feet and 14,000 horsepower, *Blough* could smash through the ice fields of the extended season of navigation with comparative ease, but her very size and power were what de-

350

feated her at the MacArthur. When the Poe shut down, there was no way *Blough* could squeeze her 858 feet into the Mac-Arthur's 800 feet. It was another version of an old problem on the Lakes, where the motto has always been, "Gangway for Tomorrow!" This problem was exemplified by the building of the original Soo Canal — tiny in retrospect — to allow passage into the mineral resources of Lake Superior.

Iron ore is by far the most important cargo tonnage handled on the Great Lakes, with coal, limestone, and grain following it in that order. Powerful steel interests supplied the push that finally prompted Congress to join hands across the St. Lawrence River in the nick of time, just when Canada seemed ready to build the seaway alone on its own property. American steel companies have long had their eyes on the iron ore of Labrador available down the St. Lawrence River. The same pressure of economics which dictated that the U.S. join in building the seaway is expected to dictate larger locks all along the way in due time.

In the meantime, the Welland Canal's present size keeps supercarriers such as the *Cort* and the *Presque Isle* from access to Lake Ontario and the St. Lawrence River. But this has not disturbed the steel corporations who ordered those giants. They are intended, for the time being, as special purpose tools to carry iron ore from Lake Superior to ports on Lake Erie and Lake Michigan.

Steel corporation planners look far ahead. The *Edmund Fitzgerald,* for example, was equipped with a water conversion system that would allow it to operate in salt water and thus be ready to travel the St. Lawrence Seaway route to Seven Islands, Quebec to pick up loads of Labrador ore.

When the *Fitzgerald* broke up in Lake Superior, there were cries that Great Lakes shipbuilders were turning out boats much too long for safety. However, traffic safety on the Lakes can stand up against any safety records on land or in the air: three cargo carriers shipwrecked in three major storms scattered across seventeen years. To meet the challenge of foreign competition

351

in delivering more of the goods the nation needs, and to deliver them faster, it seems clear that the Great Lakes long ships are going to become longer — and still longer.

They will probably not become as long as the 214,000-ton British supertanker *Ardshiel,* a ship as wide as a football field, almost a quarter-mile long, and capable of carrying enough crude oil in her tanks to supply the total energy needs of a city of 40,000 for an entire year (as described by Noel Mosert in *Supership*). Probably not — and almost certainly not as long as the 484,000-ton *Globtik Tokyo,* the world's longest to date. At least not until they lengthen the locks to suit.

"Operation Taconite": Full Calendar Navigation

Ever since Captain Jack Wilson — who later died a hero aboard the *Lady Elgin* — took the first boat, the sidewheel steamer *Illinois,* through the Soo Canal in 1855, the traditional season of navigation on the upper Great Lakes measured from April breakup to December freezeup. Sailors looked forward to the winter layover with its many pleasant opportunities to relax in a different job, have fun with the family, chum around with pals, go hunting and fishing, and so forth. It was a song: Oh, for the life of a sailor!

Ambitious masters and shipowners, not as complacent about the long layovers each winter, tested the limits every season, trying to make that one last trip to boost the national economy and their own profits, a last trip that occasionally — rarely but inevitably — became the final voyage, with captain and crew sacrificed on the thirty-below-zero altar of squaw winter in Mackinaw country.

So it was risky to challenge the boreal elements on the Straits of Mackinac, the St. Mary's River, Whitefish Bay, and Lake Superior proper. But as the crewman of the *Edmund*

Fitzgerald wrote his wife: "Nothing is ever sure." The Great Lakes have thrived on risks, because the motto of the men who sail them in all kinds of weather is "nothing ventured, nothing gained."

The first concerted effort to initiate year-round navigation on the Lakes originated during World War II. Success or failure in that war depended on the steel production of the United States, and the ships that carried iron ore from the mines of Lake Superior down to the steel mills of Lake Erie and Lake Michigan became indispensable to our war effort. Longer and bulkier ships were hurried to completion, and the MacArthur Lock was constructed to accommodate more of their kind. The building of the ten-million-dollar *Mackinaw*, most powerful icecutter in the world at the time she was launched, was authorized by the government, and a fleet of smaller icebreakers were pressed into action on both the upper and lower Lakes. These opened up ice-locked channels and ports and cleared the way for the ore boats, grain freighters, limestone vessels, coal carriers, and Great Lakes cargo ships of all kinds that would ultimately lead the way to victory around the world.

For example, the single-season record for transporting iron ore prior to 1940 was sixty-five million gross tons. With the war effort's resolve to unlock the Lakes earlier and keep them open later, the figure rose to eighty million in 1941, and shot up to niney-two million tons in 1942, an all-time record in that era. Totaling all bulk commodities, the record prior to 1940 was 138 million net tons. In 1941 that record reached 169 million, and in 1942, 178 million net tons.

In 1943, bad weather shortened the season of navigation and dropped the tonnage of iron ore to less than eighty-five million; but in 1944 the government set a goal of ninety million minimum, and the Great Lakes backed it up by launching twenty-five cargo carriers, fifteen of them ore boats.

That year the season of navigation was opened at least two weeks ahead of the regular season. In early March icebreakers cleared the St. Clair River above Detroit and plowed past Port

Huron into open Lake Huron on March 23. On March 28, a limestone carrier steamed out of Indiana City bound for Port Inland. On April 4, two freighters from South Chicago entered Escanaba Harbor, while a fleet of icebreakers struggled to reopen the Straits of Mackinac, where shifting ice floes had trapped at least twenty-eight ships.

Above the Straits, in both the St. Mary's River and beyond the Soo Canal complex in Whitefish Bay, the ice was so thick that it seemed like it might be anchored to the bottom. Led by the powerful package freighter *Hamonic,* along with *William G. Mather* and *William H. Downer,* other ships trailed through the frozen river, making seven miles in twenty-four hours. They squeezed through into the Soo Locks and then into Whitefish Bay. Here they were jammed up again, their smokestacks puffing for second wind, while dozens of vessels crowded impatiently behind them, tooting shrilly for passage to open water in Lake Superior.

On April 10, 1944, the late Milo M. Quaife, distinguished historian and author of the Great Lakes classic *Lake Michigan,* received a letter which was written on April 8 by an observer at Sault Ste. Marie, Michigan:

> There are about 30 vessels above the Sault and some 40 below, all battling ice, some of which is yet 20 inches thick near Whitefish Point, trying to reach Duluth and other upper Lake Superior ports. A steady stream of vessels passed upbound within a hundred feet of this hotel yesterday. . . .

The same observer telegraphed Dr. Quaife with the victorious news that, by noon of April 11, 122 ships had passed through the Locks into Lake Superior, while the *Youngstown* had already raced back from Marquette with the first ore cargo of the season for the Lower Lakes, seventeen days earlier than the first ship locked down in 1943.

The memorable extended season of 1944 was further distinguished by the March launching at Toledo of the 292-foot *CGC Mackinaw,* destined to be known all over the Lakes by her nickname, "Mighty Mac." She was also seen as the Great

354

White Whale, the Moby Dick of the Inland Seas, and further imagined by some as Super Polar Bear padding between the frozen reaches of the Straits of Mackinac and Lake Superior, smashing icebergs with her paws. One look at the *Mackinaw* conjures up visions of infinite power, instant impact, irresistible force against the most immovable object of winter's thickest ice. James P. Barry, author of *Ships on the Great Lakes*, tells a story in point about the *Mackinaw* during the spring of 1956, when prolonged cold weather kept the ice at the eastern end of Lake Superior from softening.

On April 2, the *Mackinaw,* bound from her home port of Cheboygan, Michigan, passed through the Soo Canal into frozen Lake Superior, quickly meeting ice thirty inches thick; but she pushed straight ahead at a steady eight miles per hour. Occasionally she met pressure ridges, thicker bands of compressed ice; but only one of these, a band fifteen feet deep, stopped her. She backed up half a mile, thrust forward again, and chopped into the ice so hard that huge chunks flew into the air on either side. Gordon MacCaulay, a newsman who was on board with the crew of 176, reported:

> The worst ice was found in the area between Gros Cap and Parisienne, and for the first day the *Mackinaw* made several parallel cuts in this area over a course of five to seven miles. Almost playfully at times she would cut visible figure eights with all the grace of a figure skater across the parallel cuts she had previously made. At other times she would get into one of the cuts and run the length of it at full speed, her wake smashing ice for some distance on either side, and doing considerably more damage than her original passage. With darkness the ship wedged herself into the ice and quietly lay until morning.

Mackinaw didn't arrive on the scene in time to help significantly in the World War II extended season of navigation, but she was very much on deck to join in the thrust toward a year-round season. This began in 1967-68, the year the Poe Lock became operable, paving the way for longer, wider, deeper

355

ships with more cargo room and more power to carry the increasing loads.

The mere list of closing dates serves to record the progress of each extended season from year to year: 1967-68, Jan. 2; 1968-69, Jan. 8; 1969-70, Jan. 15; 1970-71, Feb. 2; 1971-72, Feb. 4; 1972-73, Feb. 8; 1973-74, Feb. 7. Meanwhile, cargo tonnage more than kept pace, doubling, trebling, even quadrupling as the extended seasons stretched longer. The number of participating cargo carriers increased from forty-seven in the December 15, 1971 to February 1972 Winter Run, to ninety-one ships the following season, and then to 122 vessels during the December 1973 to February 1974 period. Actual tonnage transported during the above Winter Runs of 1971-1974 was, respectively, 1,976,407 gross tons, 3,363,974 gross tons, and 4,780,000 gross tons. This was quite an increase from the first two years of the extended season program, when only 399,000 gross tons and 472,000 gross tons were carried down the Lakes.

As far back as the fall of 1971, the *Bulletin* of the Lake Carriers' Association, a priceless maritime news source, was saying that many Great Lakes boats had plans to sail into the extended season, and for good reasons: technological advances in transportation and processing materials were making the world much smaller and more competitive, and outside industry and foreign shipping were out to grab the markets that used to be served exclusively by and within the Lakes. Therefore, freshwater seamen decided that the best way to cope and compensate was to work overtime. In shipping, idle days are losses for ships, ports, and the national economy in general, so it behooved the Lakers to skip winter layovers and stay on the job, hustling cargoes.

Even the mild success of the early extended season operations indicated that the Winter Run would become a winner. In addition, seamen were encouraged by the recognition of the Great Lakes as America's fourth seacoast in the new maritime program which Congress enacted into law in the early seventies. This focused such attention and interest on inland waterborne commerce that it resulted in the federal funding of a three-year study and demonstration program of extended-season navigation for both domestic and ocean-going shipping. The study was later extended two more years, up to December 31, 1976, with renewals expected.

On a balmy summer day out on the sparkling blue waters of the Great Lakes, it may be difficult for holiday yachtsmen to recall the weather reports of the past December's cold spells, January's blowing snow, and February's ice partially blocking the Great Lakes and their connecting channels. But sailors who had manned vessels moving iron ore and other products during the Winter Navigation season of the banner year 1974 remembered. Among them were some 400 crewmen who sailed fourteen boats of U.S. Steel's fleet through that arctic weather and who, seven years past, pioneered the successful approach toward an extended shipping season on the Lakes.

To give recognition to this special breed of men and their unique contribution, U. S. Steel officials presented each person who sailed aboard its ships after January 1, 1974, a navy blue jacket decorated with the Great Lakes-Saint Lawrence Seaway blue and white emblem, proud symbol of the seamen's accomplishment, the Winter Run's record year.

But records are made to be broken. The extended season of December 15, 1974 to April 1, 1975 broke all records, with 152 cargo carriers participating and hauling 9,134,539 gross tons, almost doubling the tonnage of the previous year's record Winter Run. This carried the season of navigation all the way around the calendar, a famous first of uninterrupted shipping on the Great Lakes.

True, only a few of the original 152 ships that started the run were in at the April finish; but the first part of February saw about fifty ships still operating, and by March the U. S. Steel's Great Lakes fleet of *Callaway, Clarke, Munson, Olds, Ferbert, Fraser, Voorhees,* and *Fairless* were still on the move. Only *Roger Blough* was out of business during the time the Poe Lock was being refurbished. Then, on the eve of April, seven stalwarts of the original extended season completed the

357

full winter run, U. S. Steelers every one, the first to make twelve months of full calendar navigation a reality, and to prove it profitable by hauling record tons of iron ore in "Operation Taconite."

Steel is the backbone of the Winter Run. "Operation Taconite" is the heart of the extended navigation system, with a team of blockers, led by "Mighty Mac" clearing the way. But there are other U. S. icebreaking operations on the Great Lakes: "Operation Oilcan," the oil tanker traffic in Green Bay and Grand Traverse Bay in Lake Michigan, which has an extended season all its own; "Operation Coalshovel," the nearest approach to year-round navigation until "Taconite" went into high gear. With icecutter help, freighters such as Ford Motor's *Robert S. McNamara* and American Steamship's *Ben W. Calvin* would, in a typical season, restore waterborne coal service to the Ford River Rouge plant and Great Lakes steel mills toward the end of February after spending most of the month in annual maintenance and needed repairs. There is also "Operation Open Buffalo" every spring, whose name speaks for itself.

In his annual report to the Lake Carriers' Association in early 1975, Vice Admiral Paul E. Trimble, LCA President, hailed the first year-round shipping "season" on the Lakes as truly an historic event, giving freshwater commerce a new dimension. But he was quick to point out problems ahead. Among them were the need for equipment and manning for round-the-clock icebreaking in troublesome areas, and the sociological transition for vessel crews from curtailed to lengthened seasons. Trimble also spoke of spurring activity toward modernization of the Soo Canal with another lock but said that the present timetable for such a development "looks like about ten years," making it extremely difficult to design the optimum vessel for the long-range bulk trade on the Lakes.

Some forward-looking think tanks in the shipping industry point toward a new lock that will accommodate 150-foot-wide vessels that are up to 1500 feet in length. Options under consideration by the Corps of Engineers are to modernize the Sabin Lock or the Davis Lock, or to make one lock of the

Sabin and Davis, now the longest locks in the world but too shallow and narrow for the larger lake boats. It will be remembered that the skipper of the *Edmund Fitzgerald* took her through the fourth lock upbound on her maiden voyage, but, laden with iron ore downbound, she had to make her return passage via the MacArthur.

Vice Admiral Trimble mentioned environmental problems, including erosion in the St. Mary's River, further easing of bends, deepening channels, and ice control in the Soo Locks. Ice control in all the locks along the St. Lawrence Seaway has been researched. Heating seaway locks to keep them ice-free is now in the experimental stage. Scientists have planned consultations with Russia and eight Baltic nations to study ice-clearing techniques.

Trimble urged that a current look should be given to the old proposal for a canal across the Upper Peninsula, from Au Train Bay through Hiawatha National Forest, Whitefish River, and Little Bay De Noc. Benefits would include a shorter trip to Lake Michigan, more trips, reduced fuel consumption, less navigational hazards, less problems for islanders, reduced navigational aid maintenance, and less navigational delays during periods of low visibility, such as fog, snow, or "lake steam," as "sea smoke" is called on the Lakes.

Preventive icebreaking and ice reconnaissance are vital to the success of the Winter Run. In addition, all-weather precision navigation aid is needed.

Vice Admiral Trimble's report to the Lake Carriers' Association in the spring of 1975 focused proudly on the year-round achievement just completed, a twelve-month *season* of navigation. He never used the words "safety" or "safekeeping," but they were evident in his discussion of problems and remedies, of research and experiments, of his genuine concern to improve facilities and navigational aids for the ships and men for whom he judged himself and all the Coast Guard responsible. He could have had no intimation that the *Edmund Fitzgerald*, which was busy on its taconite run, was spending out its last season, every trip to Lake Superior bringing her closer to the stormbound night of November 10, that she was fated to perish with all the lives she carried, on the Whitefish Bay they had crossed so often.

Involved in a continuing study of winter navigation for the Maritime Administration, Harry Benford, University of Michigan professor of naval architecture and marine engineering, said in effect that winter navigation is here to stay. He pointed to April 1, 1975 as a milestone of progress in Great Lakes shipping: "On that day the locks at Sault Ste. Marie were open for business as usual and had remained so for the previous 365 days, thus quashing the widely held opinion that winter navigation on the Lakes was a far-fetched dream."

Benford maintained that year-round service through the Seaway should help capture a reasonable share of the international traffic in manufactured products that now flows from the Midwest to the East Coast by rail or truck. He said:

> The Midwest is the nation's leading originator and receiver of foreign trade in manufactured goods, with some eighty-five percent of that commerce, in terms of dollars, going overland to the East Coast. This surely presents a tempting target for maritime entrepreneurs.

The major disadvantage of winter navigation is the public cost of keeping the shipping lanes open, Benford observed. He noted that other "peripheral" problems might be of potential damage to some shore structures, inconveniencing certain island communities by breaking up ice crossings to the mainland, and increasing the risk of environmental damage from ice punctures of hull tanks (which will remind readers of the early fear of oil pollution after the *Fitzgerald* sank with 48,000 gallons of oil in her tank). "Ships would need at least modest degrees of structural reinforcement," Benford said, "and alternatives to buoys, such as aids in navigation, would have to be developed."

John D. Hazard, a Michigan State University authority on marketing and transportation, figured that year-round shipping on the Great Lakes and St. Lawrence Seaway would produce a $1.5 billion annual bonanza for surrounding states, with Michigan, Illinois, and Ohio becoming the primary beneficiaries. Hazard said that the economic benefits of year-round navigation would fall to steel shipping and manufacturing companies which rely on low-cost water transportation to ship raw materials to their plants and to ship their finished products to market.

There was one catch: providing the winter shipping would cost at least $500 million over the next ten years. "But on a 50-year lifespan," Hazard said, "with U.S. and Canadian funding, the project would be an outstanding investment for our future prosperity." Of the $1.5 billion increase in the economic output of the region, Hazard said that some $600 million would go for wages, and that the extended calendar would create 35,000 to 42,000 jobs.

But oldtimers, who never saw a university but who learned all the hard knocks in the school of experience, warn that the picture of year-round navigation is not all wine, roses, and rubles. Recent winters, including 1975, have been relatively mild. There could be savage winters ahead that would raise Holy Old Mackinaw with the Winter Run, stop every ship cold in its tracks until spring thaw, perhaps squeeze some of them to death in the ice.

Even the commanding officer of "Mighty Mac," Lawrence A. White, Captain, U.S. Coast Guard, had certain reservations: "In a severe winter the Lakes freeze almost completely, and navigation on Lake Superior in particular, but on all the Lakes, would require continuous escort. This would slow turn-arounds of ships to a perhaps unacceptable level."

In other words, the cost in manpower and money might not be worth the effort. "The question of whether the public costs of keeping the shipping lanes open will be outweighed by the benefits is currently being examined," Professor Benford has said. "Our tentative overall assessment is that year-round navigation on the Great Lakes will prove to be of considerable net benefit to the public." Captain White has said: "The economic benefits of running year-round are apparently clear to

U. S. Steel. . . . Since 1967, [its] Great Lakes Fleet has been pushing back the closing date of navigation."

Captain White's remarks on the advantages and disadvantages of year-round shipping are contained in an unpublished paper entitled "The Winter Run — A Fully Extended Shipping Season on the Great Lakes," parts of which will be quoted below. His preface states:

> This is simply about winter operations on the Great Lakes, especially the ore trade from Head of the Lakes (Duluth, Two Harbors, Lake Superior) through Whitefish Bay, the St. Mary's River and into Lake Michigan via the Straits of Mackinac or into Lake Huron, to lower Lake ports. Others will write about economic benefits of the trade, or in detail about various experiments being undertaken to support these operations. This is simply about ice breaking operations, especially those of the Coast Guard icebreaker *Mackinaw* in the early months of 1975.

"The Winter Run" notes that although running all through the winter was done for the first time in 1974-75, winter navigation on the Great Lakes is not new. The ideas and techniques developed here have been the basis for much of the modern development in winter navigation elsewhere in the world. Even foreign ship design has been influenced by experiments on the Lakes.

Captain White went on to explain that taconite plays a vital role in the achievement of a fully extended season. He said a technical development which was the result of the less-rich taconite (iron ore), as richer ore played out in Minnesota, led into all-winter navigation. The lesser ore meant more bulk for an equivalent yield. So the ore was reduced — ground, crushed, magnetically separated, and melted into a richer concentrate. This in turn is reduced to pellet form, small marbles. Since there is no water in them, these taconite (processed iron ore) pellets do not freeze the way ore did; so now year-round shipping makes more sense. Cargoes do not freeze fast in the holds and, so far, most of the deep winter shipping is iron ore.

362

COMPLIMENTS, CAPTAIN WHITE, ICEBREAKER *MACKINAW*

As commanding officer of the *Mackinaw,* Captain White gave his views of the element he wars against all winter and explained why some ships were able to cope with it better than others.

He said that one-year ice is a maximum of three feet thick, but that rafting and ridging in open stretches can produce a thickness of thirty feet. Snow cover and repeated icebreaking in narrow channels creates a mush, somewhat like ice cream, which can pack to the bottom. This causes great resistance, and ships with low horsepower-to-length ratios just slow down and stop, even when closely escorted.

Three factors seem to have a major effect on the ability of a ship to navigate in ice, Captain White said. Trim in ballast is important because the bow-high trim suitable for sheet ice will be very troublesome in brash or mush-filled narrow channels. Here an even trim, with the bow immersed, will give a cleaner entry by parting the ice, and reduce the chances of sea chest icing. Radius-bowed ships push an extensive volume of ice ahead of themselves in a narrow cut channel, while those with a sharp entry part the ice and reduce the work they must do.

Horsepower-to-length ratio, White said, gives a good indication of a ship's potential for navigating in ice. The *Mackinaw*'s horsepower/length is about 34.5; our 110-foot icebreaking tugs, who do extensive ice work, rate at 9.1; U. S. Steel's major new ore carrier *Roger Blough* rates 16.3. But many successful Winter Run ships rate as low as 7.5. Ships rating below about 6.5 or 6.0 are virtually certain to have too low a horsepower/length ratio to navigate in ice, even with extremely close and constant escort.

One such ship could only be moved a few lengths at a time with the *Mackinaw* ahead and a tug on each bow cutting relief tracks. For the mixed and unclassified ships showing up in late March, the horsepower/length ratio is a useful tool by which to quickly classify the potential performance of ships and arrange convoys, predicting with some accuracy those who would have trouble with navigation. White said that they could place escorts quite well within each convoy.

Westwind, near sister to *Mackinaw,* had to be called up in early 1975 from her Straits of Mackinac duties to help handle the shipping congestion in the Soo bottleneck and White-fish Bay area. This jam-up was caused by unseasonable ice even for mid-March and the fact that ships had been lured into earlier than usual spring sailings because of talk of an easy winter. Perhaps the weather was relatively moderate in certain other areas of the Lakes, but in the St. Mary's River and Whitefish Bay the ice was hanging on later than usual. About 200 new-season vessels were greeted by more than they bargained for, but they enjoyed safe escort by *Westwind* and *Mackinaw* and their smaller but able helpers.

However, Captain White rated determination as perhaps the major factor in carrying out the Winter Run, especially the determination of a ship's master to get her through, provided she were graced with attendant professional skill. He and his men consistently found that certain ships, even though their horsepower was low, would get through. Captain White then discussed the kinds of icebreakers used during the extended season program. The Operation Taconite task group normally included *Mackinaw,* a *Wind* class icebreaker (such as *Westwind* in 1974-75), one or more 180-foot icebreaking buoy tenders (such as *Sundew, Mariposa, Woodrush, Mesquite, Bramble*), and at least two 110-foot icebreaking tugs (such as *Naugatuck, Arundel, Kaw, Raritan*). The tenders and tugs were very useful either singly, in pairs, or with a larger icebreaker in preventive operations or during actual escort.

Except on straight courses, direct escort in unbroken ice is quite inefficient. Preventive operations — with the icebreaker preparing the track before a ship's passage — moves more ships in less time. Once a track is established in the ice, it is readily discernible and the helmsman can be ordered to "follow the black line." At night or in reduced visibility, this is especially helpful, Captain White pointed out. "Just so it's cold enough so that the track doesn't shift."

About a third of the time we worked at night. Ice lights are fitted on Winter Run ships, and *Mackinaw* had one astern as well, since a lot of work was done backing down. While this would be dangerous in the thicker polar ice, in rivers and channels the packed brash can be readily worked going astern. The singular stern shape of *Mackinaw* does part the ice and partially protect the rudder, which is kept amidships. . . .

Some days it was so cold it was freezing faster than we could break it. Loosening up the Johnson Point turn downbound, for example, we would go on down Sailor's Encampment range past the Winter Point turn and on to the Mud Lake junction buoy. Coming about and running upbound with a small convoy only two hours later, we would find the Johnson Point turn very nearly as hard as it had been before we broke it out on the way down.

At about 15 below zero, the hair freezes in your nose. At 20 below, your nose freezes.

The voice of the "Taconite" Task Group Commander is Soo Control. Through this operation center, active command and control can be exercised to keep shipping moving safely. Several times during the Winter Run the Straits were closed due to weather and ice conditions: ships were advised to seek shelter. The St. Mary's River was similarly shut down because of weather, usually low visibility. There were two conscious objectives on the Winter Run: to move ice and to move traffic.

In deep winter our day would start during morning twilight. Underway from the Soo about 0630, perhaps in lake steam, we ease downbound past the Sugar Island ferry, then enter the deep brash in lower Little Rapids Cut with all six main engines on the line. Working up power as the engines warm and the exhausts clear, we will work the several miles to Nine Mile Point and back to the ferry route, cutting each side to the buoy line and running the center at as high a speed as we can without creating wake damage. Sometimes, at full power, our wake white beneath us, we nearly stop.

Naugatuck and *Arundel* may work with us for awhile. The ice line in the cut moves several hundred yards downstream. It's working.

By 1100, satisfied that the ice flow is sufficient to keep the ferry route clear and manageable for *Arundel,* who has duty with the ferry that day, we are downbound with *Naugatuck* on our quarter to prepare the track for a small upbound convoy consisting of *A. H. Ferbert, Philip R. Clarke,* and *Roger Blough.* Captain Neil Rolfson in *Blough* and Captain Ben Sime of *Clarke* seldom need any help if we can just loosen the turns wide enough for them. These are powerful ships with skillful masters.

The smaller and less powerful *Ferbert* does not have the muscle of the larger ships, but Captain Art Smoger will push her hard. If she can stay with *Clarke* and *Blough,* she can get to the locks without help. We would hope that *Blough* would go first, with *Ferbert* next and *Clarke* last. If *Ferbert* gets stuck, *Clarke* can run past her to provide a relief cut. If we prepare the track well before their passage, we will assist no ships directly, but three will make the passage without incident, helping each other to get through. . . .

When you're as big as *Blough,* you go where you want.

Captain White told how the passage of the three large ships, especially *Blough* and *Clarke,* would help flush a lot of ice downstream. They would plow ahead, fishtailing their huge bulk carriers with an easy grace that belied the real mastery of their ship-handling. The commanding officer of *Mackinaw* described the scene:

We make our deep cut and heave to, deep in the Winter Point turn. The three lakers come by on one whistle. Neil and Ben exchange salutes with us. Art may later when he knows us better. The Great Lakes salute is rather like exchanging toasts at a formal dinner; you don't presume.

Captain White checked traffic. *John G. Munson* and *Leon Fraser* were due upbound day after tomorrow. Four downbounders were due off Whitefish Point about eight o'clock tomorrow morning: *Cason J. Callaway, Irving S. Olds, Enders M. Voorhees,* and *Benjamin F. Fairless.* White decided that the three carriers that he had been involved with would easily lock through the Poe before it closed at eleven P.M. He was unsure whether his duties would keep him from locking the *Mackinaw* through in time or whether he would have to wait for the morning reopening at seven o'clock. The MAFOR (weather forecast) was for clear and cold, no wind for a couple of days, the kind of weather that makes ice. The *Mackinaw* locked through at about ten P.M., with *Blough, Clarke* and *Ferbert* ahead and going well.

By morning twilight *Roger Blough* reported being slowed by the heavy ice pack in Whitefish Bay, which was unusual because, in the clear, *Blough* does not normally have problems. White asked *Clarke* to let *Ferbert* pass before the going got too tough for them, and he poured on the steam with all six engines of "Mighty Mac" going full blast. Running fast enough to keep up momentum through the thickening ice, Captain White raced ahead of *Blough* and outdistanced his convoy of three. He went back four times to stir up the ice pack and shake the ore carriers loose. He had a dilemma: he had to keep going fast or he would slow and stop. But he worried about getting beset ahead of Neil Rolfson's *Blough* who, if he were moving well, might not be able to stop. In White's language: "We do not relish being drop-kicked by a 45,000 ton toe."

By the time the *Mackinaw* cleared its convoy, and the three ore carriers were enroute to Two Harbors to load (probably to return in less than three days), Captain White had to turn his attention to the downbounders already mentioned. The *Voorhees, Olds,* and *Fairless* were bunched close near White-fish Point, while the *Callaway* was caught in some heavy rafting toward Ile Parisienne.

But the *Mackinaw* helped the *Callaway* free and then shepherded her new convoy toward the Soo Canal with the immediate objective of getting everyone through the locks before the eleven P.M. closing. They made it!

And so it goes — the Winter Run.

FOLLOW-UP: WINTER RUN II

More than one Doubting Thomas declared that the first year-round season of navigation was all due to an easy winter; they were going to wait until a hard one came along. The extended season of 1975-76 promptly filled the bill. Bad weather came early, but the dedicated seamen who drove their cargo carriers and Coast Guard cutters into Winter Run II were unaware that more powerful forces than sub-zero blizzards and frozen miles of manic-sculptured waters lay ahead.

In the generally "mild" month of December, the weather gave early notice that boisterous times were in store. Downbound from a Wisconsin port, the S. S. *Frank R. Denton* survived a fierce Lake Superior storm and came in weighted down with a glazing of ice (some crew members called it a "shellacking") whose thickness ran from twelve inches on the deck to twenty-four inches on the portside rails.

Barely halfway through January the so-called Banana Belt of Michigan, including its Miami (Detroit), was struck with record-breaking readings from eighteen to twenty-five degrees below zero. This caused huge ice jams in the St. Clair and Detroit Rivers, the vital passages connecting Lake Erie and Lake Huron. The Coast Guard closed the St. Clair to navigation when American and Canadian Coast Guard cutters failed to break through eight-foot-thick ice to free ships carrying cargoes which required immediate delivery or higher utility bills for consumers. From up above the deep-freeze Straits of Mackinac, Captain White and "Mighty Mac" came pounding to the rescue, while *Sundew* moved up from Lake Michigan to patrol the St. Mary's River and Whitefish Bay, the most critical arena in the winter navigation program.

In about the third week of January, there were some twelve ships in the Sault area, including nine familiar stalwarts from the U. S. Steel's Great Lakes fleet which had participated in the first Winter Run: *Roger Blough, Philip R. Clarke, Cason J. Callaway, Arthur M. Anderson, Leon Fraser, A. H. Ferbert, Benjamin Fairless, Irving S. Olds, Enders M. Voorhees,* as well as the chartered *Presque Isle*. Others operating in the vicinity at that time were Algoma Steel's *Yankcanuck* and CSL's *Frontenac*, both fresh from adventures with ice jams along the Detroit River. The *Presque Isle* had learned a lesson from getting stuck in the St. Mary's ice; instead of laying up in Erie, Pennsylvania at the end of the season, she would go down broad Lake Michigan to Milwaukee rather than chance the ice problems in the narrow St. Clair River.

In the closing days of January the largest boats, such as *Presque Isle* and *Roger Blough,* found it difficult to squeeze into the Poe Lock because of the heavy ice buildups on its walls and approaches. No matter how hard the lock crews worked to steam the ice away and use the lock water outlets to flush out the ice, the fact remained that both *Blough* and *Isle* are 105 feet wide, and the Poe Lock is only 110 feet wide, which leaves only a squeaky clearance of two and a half feet between walls and vessel during a normal passage.

Under the prevailing frigid conditions, with ice steadily building on the walls and floor of the largest lock in the Soo Canal complex, it took the U. S. Steel chartered tug-barge *Presque Isle* about twelve hours to wedge her thousand-foot length through a downbound passage. The powerhouse *Blough,* thwarted on an attempted passage, had to be towed from the lock entrance and moored to await another try.

Despite such wintry tidings, U. S. Steel presently announced letting a contract for another superfreighter as long as the *Isle,* with an option to build it 100 feet longer if the Army Corps of Engineers would allow that extra length in passage through the Poe. Also in line with the trend of long ships growing longer, marine editor E. J. Sundstrom of *The Evening News,* whose closely followed column "3 Long, 2 Short" is the *first* word about the world parade of navigation passing through the Soo Canal locks, reported that the 730-foot M.V. *Walter A. Sterling* of the Cleveland Cliffs fleet would soon be "jumboized" by getting a new 96-foot midsection that would make the freighter 826 feet long, fourth largest vessel on the Lakes.

On Monday, February 2, United Press International tele-typed Michigan and its surrounding waters:

> You can forget Ground Hog Day. He froze to death Sun-day night.
>
> The creature traditionally expected to look for his shadow didn't have a chance. A vicious cold front with tree-bending winds and drifting snows rolled across Michigan in one of this winter's worst onslaughts. (He did see his shadow, assur-ing six more weeks of winter.)

Dramatic temperature drops occurred from the Banana Belt to the Upper Peninsula. Detroit's thermometer fell ten degrees in less than an hour; Sault Ste. Marie lost thirty degrees in less than six hours, and the heart of Winter Run II survived at 19 below. There were near blizzard conditions on Lake Su-perior, and gale warnings also were up in Lakes Michigan, Huron, and St. Clair, with waves reaching twelve feet.

Heavy ice, up to twelve feet thick, halted shipping in the Soo area. The *Mackinaw* labored to free several U. S. Steel boats caught in Whitefish Bay; others were moored below the locks waiting for better conditions. The Coast Guard tugs *Naugatuck* and *Arundel* helped canal crews clear an entrance for ship passage. Later the gallant little *Naugatuck* lost her wheel battling Little Rapids ice and the Coast Guard cutter *Mesquite* towed her to Sturgeon Bay, Wisconsin for a new propeller.

Navigation limped along in the wake of the storm, and by mid-February only the hard core of "Operation Taconite" was still on the move: *Blough, Callaway, Anderson* and *Clarke*. *Presque Isle* had just made her final run and headed to Mil-waukee, where *Ferbert, Voorhees,* and *Fairless* already had gone for their winter layup. The remaining two of the original nine cargo carriers in the U. S. Steel taconite fleet — *Olds* and *Fraser* — had made recent downbound passages, and even ma-rine editor Sundstrom said it was not certain whether they would continue much longer. He predicted that only three boats would be operating after the end of the month: *Ander-son, Callaway,* and *Clarke*.

Sundstrom's prediction came true ahead of time. The 1,200-foot-long Poe Lock had to be closed for March maintenance three days earlier than planned. Her fender boom had suffered a damaging blow when struck by the stern of downbound Str. *Cason J. Callaway*. This put *Roger Blough* into layup several days sooner than in the first Winter Run, because its size prevents passage through the MacArthur Lock, which the other members of the U. S. Steel team can use. So then there were three. And they took off on their U. S. Steel errands as soon as the MacArthur Lock could be flooded and placed in operation.

March blew in with its usual huff-puff-blow-the-man-down, but winter navigation on the upper Great Lakes went smoothly along — for the first two weeks or so. Str. *Benjamin Fairless* returned from a brief layup to rejoin the three musketeers of "Operation Taconite." With the situation apparently under control, the icebreaker *Woodrush* had returned to duties at Duluth for spring breakup operations, and *Westwind* had left the Straits of Mackinac to patrol the Milwaukee vicinity. By the third week of March things were generally quiet, with the *Mackinaw* and her helpers doing small chores and standing by at the Soo.

Then with victory just around the bend, trouble struck on Whitefish Bay, where workhorse "Mighty Mac" was involved in icebreaking a passage for *Philip R. Clarke*. In one of the intricate maneuvers, the *Clarke* could not stop in time and sideswiped the *Mackinaw*, scraping her more than a hundred feet in length. The collision put an eight-foot crease on *Clarke's* port bow, damage that later required a temporary patch at the Soo. But both ships made it to mooring under their own power, and the crews suffered no injuries. Next morning the *Mackinaw* licked her wounds and set out to break more ice to open more shipping lanes.

Despite extensive damage and the chilling awareness of what might have happened out in the wasteland of petrified waves, the near-tragedy turned out to be the last gasp of a harsher than ordinary winter.

At midnight on March 31, 1976, Winter Run II completed the second consecutive year of full-calendar navigation on the upper Great Lakes. Rear Admiral James S. Gracey, Commander of the Coast Guard's Ninth District, led the congratulations:

> The men of the Coast Guard ships and the lakers involved in winter navigation are pioneers. We've still got a long way to go to make year-round navigation a solid tradition. And we have to work out a way to keep the seaway open so the 'salties' can trade all year. But we have two years of success under our belts and I'm proud of that.

But pride cometh before a fall, and every March 31st is followed by April Fool's Day. While the icebreakers and the taconite carriers were fighting their way through Winter Run II, military officers, company executives, and officials of the commercial navigation demonstration program were making observations and inspections. Public meetings were held by islanders, shoreline owners, and concerned citizens. Some felt that the ecology and environment were threatened by the all-winter turmoil and commotion of icebreakers and superfreighters; others claimed that the cost was prohibitive and that the price should not be taken out of the public's purse. A northern Michigan congressman charged that the Coast Guard lacked the equipment to handle icebreaking duties on the Lakes. In short, seamen had proved that they could solve the rigors of the winter weather — but perhaps not the climate of public opinion.

The blow fell within days of the longest continuous navigation season — 731 days of it — in the annals of the Soo Locks. Hardly had the ink dried on the record books than word was released that the Winter Navigation Board would recommend that Congress provide funds to conduct a shipping season only through the end of January in years to come. A secondary alternative was that operation should continue through the end of February.

However, at the Soo, marine editor Sundstrom noted that although winter navigation might possibly be cut short a season or so, western coal-shipping facilities were under construction in Superior, Wisconsin to handle the low-sulphur western fuel from Montana and other states, which was needed to supply energy for massive coal-powered electric generating plants in the Lower Lakes area. Within a few short years, hundreds of millions of tons of this priceless material would be needed to power the national economy with its most vital and abundant source of energy. In order to supply the necessary raw materials, fleets of special coal-carrying vessels were also underway, soon to appear on the horizon.

*   *   *   *   *

Meanwhile, in late spring of 1976, Coast Guard teams anchored above the wreckage site of the *Edmund Fitzgerald.* Using sophisticated television search devices, including movie and still cameras lowered on an unmanned Navy cable-controlled underwater research vessel (CURV), lowered from the Coast Guard cutter *Woodrush,* they probed the depths of Whitefish Bay with two major objectives, stated by Rear Admiral W. W. Barrow: "to positively identify the wrecked ship and to determine and document by photography the condition of the wreck in enough detail to assist in determining the cause of her sinking." Coast Guard officials soon reported that the words "Edmund Fitzgerald, Milwaukee" were clearly visible off the vessel's stern, which is upside down in the water, with the bow upright and taconite pellets spilled all around the disintegrated middle section.

The second objective of the admiral, the determination of the cause of the *Edmund Fitzgerald* shipwreck, may never be fully resolved. Informal observers who have studied the shipwreck patterns of *Bradley, Morrell,* and *Fitzgerald* might agree on a blanket consensus: *structural failure due to metal fatigue under extreme stress.* But a number of lakelanders have their own suspicions, or superstitions: "They're building the boats too long. That's why they crack in the middle."

As happens in the wake of catastrophe, investigating groups called for improvements that might have saved lives: newer, safer freighters, better techniques in cold weather life-saving, improved navigational aids, a fleet of modern Coast Guard vessels. There was much interest in all-weather survival capsules that would float free when a vessel sank. These would be non-capsizable, protected from wind and water, equipped with radio and all other necessities. They would each hold several sailors and would be placed where crew members had ready access.

Much interest also was focused on monster-man, all-weather survival suits, built in one size to fit anyone up to six feet eight inches tall, with a donning time of twenty to sixty seconds and a U.S. Navy survival time of thirteen hours and more in water temperatures of thirty-five degrees. In fact, their ultimate limit has yet to be tested, although they have been used for safety by Antarctic explorers and North Sea oil riggers.

If the multi-man capsules and the survival suits described above had been available when the *Bradley* and *Morrell* went down, many a good sailor would still be alive today, because some members of both crews were able to don lifejackets or "luck onto" rafts. But only three men were able to survive without them.

What would have been the chances of the *Fitzgerald*'s crew? Reluctantly, this shipwreck chronicler must agree with the observation of a veteran, Captain J. B. "Jessie" Cooper, master of the Str. *Arthur M. Anderson,* who visited the Sault in late June 1976 to receive the VFW heroism award for the gallantry he and his crew showed in their search for the *Fitzgerald*'s men. "You don't think of a ship that size going under. I assumed she had a blackout and was without lights. . . . In my opinion, it was structural failure of some kind. He [Captain E. J. McSorley] knew his ship was damaged. He told us so. . . . Of course, you don't bandy that about on the radio and scare the crew."

After Cooper turned his ship around in a masterly feat of seamanship and returned to the scene, they searched the area for more than twelve hours. Deckhands manned the searchlights and everyone not on duty elsewhere was on deck in the storm, a classic demonstration of maritime bravery. From almost forty years of sailing, *Anderson*'s skipper realized the awesome responsibility, the daring risk he was taking with his ship and his crew. He had been on Lake Michigan during the Armistice Day storm that sank Strs. *Davoc, Minch,* and *Novadoc.* He had been nearby when the *Bradley* went down. He said: "The *Bradley* storm was in the same kind of sea as the *Fitzgerald.* She broke up just like the *Fitz.*"

Cooper said the storm that sank *Fitzgerald* was comparable to a tropical storm: it kicked up quickly, and more or less unforecasted winds gusted up to eighty miles per hour. Conditions were just right for such a storm. It had been his experience that when the Lakes undergo an unusually warm fall, they are not quick to cool off. Then when a low pressure system crosses the warm water it creates the violent weather. "Whatever happened to the *Fitz,*" Cooper said, "happened so suddenly, in fact, that pockets of air were probably trapped inside when the ship sank. It is conceivable that the men lived for some time after she went down."

He expressed his hope that the investigations would be fruitful. "I would hate for those twenty-nine men to have died for nothing. Perhaps they will learn something that can be put into future ships to make them safer." But then he expressed the seaman's fatalistic philosophy: "No matter what they come up with, this will happen again. No matter how big they make them, as long as there are ships that sail, and they are in the right place at the right time, this will happen again."

Despite the usual rash of hearings and investigations, including the official marine board at Coast Guard headquarters in Cleveland, not to mention the airings of expert opinion, educated guesses, street-corner gossip, and shipboard scuttlebutt, the real fate of the *Edmund Fitzgerald* remained one of the great mysteries of the Lakes. However, certain "insiders," who had paid close attention to Captain Cooper's observations on the scene during the catastrophic day and night of November 10, were inclined to believe that the doomed ship might have "bottomed out" unbeknown to captain and crew in the clamoring storm, scraping on a reef near Caribou Island, before she foundered fifty miles later, so near to safe haven.

More cheerful tidings, contagious as shipboard scuttlebutt, hummed along the seaway when Admiral Paul Trimble, chief of the Lake Carriers' Association, predicted that increased demands for iron ore, western coal, and other basic materials should assure continuous year-round shipping on the Great Lakes. He urgently called for construction of a new lock at the Sault bottleneck, a super lock to accommodate vessels in the plus-1100-foot size, capable of hauling 60,000 tons of cargo and built for operation in ice (as others of more traditional size are now being built).

In midsummer 1976, U.S. Representative Philip E. Ruppe of the Upper Peninsula, an outspoken but constructive critic of the Coast Guard and Great Lakes shipping in general, announced that he had introduced a bill in Congress to provide a two-year extension for the winter shipping season. And in the waning days of the bicentennial year, the Great Lakes, all dressed up in patriotic regalia, witnessed the proud sight of the tall-masted, sail-billowing, picture-book "Clipper" ships of a bygone era saluting and being saluted by the long ships of the future.

The newly christened, self-unloading coal carrier M.V. (Motor Vessel) *St. Clair*, first birth of a new era in Great Lakes navigation, a husky 770-footer, was built to play a leading role in transporting low-sulphur fuel from the western states to eastern electric generating plants, to pioneer in delivering from Superior, Wisconsin the "black diamond" resources that would last a thousand years, outlive atomic energy, make way for solar power, and give life to Middle America for a long time to come. And the even newer M.V. *James R. Barker*, flagship of Pickands Mather Interlake fleet, largest of the super-freighters because of her fifty-foot depth, latest of the 1000-foot club, made her maiden voyage to Taconite Harbor, Minnesota. She has a six-story-high stern cabin containing all integral services from living quarters to operations, and her various decks are served by elevator. She is capable of carrying 59,000 gross tons of iron pellets or 52,000 tons of coal; she is another self-unloader designed to discharge 10,000 tons of pellets per hour, coal at 6,000 tons, and she can travel at sixteen miles per hour.

They all were a sight for sore eyes on the Lakes: the long ships, getting still longer, pushing toward the 1100-foot mark in the Poe Lock and demanding more and bigger locks to come. In a way they were saying what young Charles Harvey said when doubters told him he might as well try to dig a canal on the moon as build one at Sault Ste. Marie: "Gangway for Tomorrow!"

While the deathless saga of the *Edmund Fitzgerald* resounded over the listening Lakes, there were ominous rumblings of things to come — the crash of relentless ice fields massing against Winter Run III. As early as December 10, 1976, sixty long ships, with more arriving every hour, were backed up in the St. Mary's bottleneck to the Locks when heavy ice forced the 716-foot *Cliffs Victory* into the role of corkplug. Reportedly the worst Great Lakes traffic jam since the 1926 "City on Ice" (see pages 264-265), it was only the start of a foredoomed winter run beset by the worst cold spell in nearly a century. On the Upper Lakes even the newest and most powerful boats ran into weather that could freeze a ship in its "tracks." Mid-January found Lake Erie almost completely icebound, and Lake Michigan was expected to freeze over for only the fourth time in seventy-five years.

Finally, after herculean duty by Coast Guard and merchant seamen alike, the Winter Navigation Board bowed to the elements and suspended commercial shipping to and from Lake Superior. So came to a close an historic effort of uninterrupted operation through the Soo Canal — thirty-four months of continuous shipping, since April 1, 1974.

But the taconite fleets, as well as the western coal carriers and the grain carriers, will return and with them the promise of future Winter Runs by gallant seamen in their ever larger boats.

INDEX

Note: Names of vessels are indented and italicized.

Algoma Steel, 369
American Shipbuilding Company, 350
American Steamship Company, 348, 358
Armstrong, Father, 330, 331
  Acacia, 149
  Acadian, 244
  Adelaide, 186
  Alabama, 207
  Algoma, 266-268
  Alpena, 68
  Amazon, 74
  Amelia, 216
  American, 200
  Anderson, Arthur M., 322-326, 337, 341, 348, 368, 370, 374, 375
  Andrews, Matthew, 131
  Antelope, 236
  Appalonia, 76
  Appelona, 293, 294
  Aquarama, 208, 308
  Arabia, 303
  Arcturus, 291
  Ardshiel, 351
  Argus, 131
  Ariel, 171
  Arizona, 268, 269
  Arlington, 272
  Armenia, 201, 294
  Armstrong, Frank, 113
  Arundel, 364, 366, 370
  Ashcroft, 224, 225
  Asia, 68, 103
  Athabasca, 268
  Atlantic, 68, 212-214
  Augusta, 44, 45, 48
  Avafors, 322, 323

Barclay, Commodore, 173, 177, 181
Barrow, Adm. Winford, 344, 345, 373

Beaver Island Transit Company, 40
Beechy, Lincoln, 286
Benford, Harry, 360, 361
Bethlehem Steel Corporation, 145, 150, 151, 160, 163, 347
Blondin, 285
Bradley Transportation Line, 17, 19, 22
  Bannockburn, 270
  Barker, James R., 376
  Barnes, Frank E., 303
  Bavaria, 294, 295
  Bavarian, 306
  Bay State, 301
  Belle, Clayton, 108
  Benfri, 326
  Bessemer & Marquette No. 2, 232
  Blackbird, 293
  Black Haw, 42
  Billings, Frank R., 219
  Blough, Roger, 350, 351, 357, 363, 366-371
  Boyd, J. Oswald, 39, 40
  Bradley, Carl D., 13, 16-33, 41, 58, 67, 68, 75, 76, 77, 81, 84, 85, 86, 117, 118, 123, 147, 162, 176, 284, 315, 319-321, 329, 338, 340, 341, 373-375
  Bramble, 161, 364
  Brewster, 113
  Bruce, Kate L., 144
  Buffalo, 187, 207
  Bully Kate, 74
  Burt, John, 295
  Butters, Marshall F., 218, 219

Cambria Steamship Company, 145
Champlain, Samuel de, 14, 167
Cleveland-Cliffs Iron Company Fleet, 113, 347, 369
Clinton, De Witt, 182
Columbia Transportation Division, 316, 317